The Scope of Philosophy

An introductory study book

F. W. Garforth

Department of Educational Studies,
University of Hull

Longman

LONGMAN GROUP LIMITED
London
*Associated companies, branches and representatives
throughout the world*

© Longman Group Limited 1971

First published 1971

ISBN 0 582 48018·3 Cased
      0 582 48019·1 Paper

Printed in Great Britain by
Butler & Tanner Ltd, Frome and London

For Anne, Christopher, Michael and Bernard

And though a philosopher may live remote from business, the genius of philosophy, if carefully cultivated by several, must gradually diffuse itself throughout the whole society, and bestow a similar correctness on every art and calling.

David Hume, *An Enquiry concerning Human Understanding*, I, 5

Contents

Acknowledgements

We are grateful to the following for permission to reproduce copyright material:

Basil Blackwell & Mott Ltd, for extracts from *Wittgenstein: Philosophical Investigations* translated by G. E. M. Anscombe; J. M. Dent & Sons Ltd and E. P. Dutton & Co. Inc., for extracts from *Aristotle: Metaphysics* translated and edited by J. Warrington, and *Kant: Critique of Pure Reason* translated and edited by J. M. D. Meiklejohn; Victor Gollancz Ltd and Dover Publications Inc., for extracts from *Language, Truth and Logic* by A. J. Ayer; Hutchinson Publishing Group Ltd and Barnes & Noble Inc., for extracts from *Kant: Groundwork of the Metaphysic of Morals* by H. J. Paton; Oxford University Press for extracts from *St Thomas Aquinas: Philosophical Texts* translated by Thomas Gilby; Penguin Books Ltd, for extracts from *Descartes: Discourse on Method* translated and edited by Arthur Wollaston.

Preface

The impulse to write this book came initially from discussions in educational philosophy which I have enjoyed with students—mostly teachers seconded for study—attending diploma courses in the Institute of Education of the University of Hull. Increasingly it has seemed to me that to understand (and still more to practise) educational philosophy requires some insight into philosophical problems of a more general kind; without this there is a sense of disengagement, of isolation from a mainstream of activity, and hence an impoverishment of thought.

Students can be introduced to philosophy through problems, through persons, or through both together; it is the last of these methods that I have attempted—by posing a problem in general terms and then examining it in the work of a particular philosopher. For I have been anxious to show that, while philosophical problems have a generality which transcends time and place, they nevertheless arise from and are discussed within a context which is historical, social, personal.

Despite its origin the book has no special bias towards educational philosophy; it is written as an introduction to philosophy for students of any discipline as well as for the general reader. And although the philosophers appear in chronological sequence, it is not in any sense a history of philosophy. It is an attempt to indicate the range of philosophical problems and to illuminate their nature.

I am well aware that to study philosophy is not the same as to practise it, and that students may easily indulge in the former as an excuse for neglecting the latter. Yet an acquaintance with what philosophers have thought and written, with the problems that have exercised and still are exercising them, can lead both to a clearer understanding of philosophy and to a more effective practice of it; at the same time it can stimulate thought and imagination by the inspiration of greatness.

I am greatly indebted for advice and correction to Alan White, Professor of Philosophy, University of Hull, and to Ernest Bowcott, Lecturer in

Preface

Education, University of Durham. Their help has enabled me to eliminate many of the faults which would otherwise have appeared in the book; for those that remain they are, of course, in no way responsible. My grateful thanks are also due, once again, to my wife for her help in reading the proofs and making the index.

November 1970   F. W. G.

1   Philosophy

Philosophy has a long and honoured history in the civilisation of western Europe. It first clearly showed itself in ancient Greece about the start of the sixth century B.C.; but its roots go deeper than this. They lie in preceding centuries, in questionings and perplexities which either went unrecorded or can be seen only dimly in the earliest literature. As a distinct and recognisable activity, however, European philosophy may be said to have begun in Greece about 600 B.C. With some fluctuations it has flourished ever since. In the twentieth century philosophy is still very much alive; its practitioners argue with no less force and urgency, though on different themes, than did their predecessors of two and a half millennia ago. Nor is its pursuit confined to professional philosophers and their students: it is a regular subject of study in adult classes and has found its way into radio and television programmes.

But despite its long history, coterminous almost with European civilisation itself, and the enormous labour of thought and writing which has been devoted to it, there are few, if any, philosophers who would state with confidence, or at least without fear of contradiction, what philosophy is. Indeed, it must be said at once that the present enquiry will not reveal any single, definitive account of the nature of philosophy. Instead there will emerge from it two broadly different views, each bearing some common ground of affinity with the other, yet fundamentally opposed in their account of what philosophy can, cannot, and ought to do.

The Greek word *philosophia*, said to have been invented by Pythagoras, means 'love of wisdom'. But 'wisdom' is a word hedged around with ambiguities. It can mean 'knowledge', 'experience of life', 'a discriminating sense of values', or all three together; but what knowledge is and whether some forms of it (and if so, which) are preferable to others, what sort of experience qualifies as wisdom, and by what criteria one chooses between competing values—all this is left obscure and provides material for unending controversy. If philosophy is defined as 'love of wisdom', its nature must

I

remain in doubt until the meaning of wisdom itself is clarified. In fact, this is such an unsatisfactory definition that it is best avoided; the derivation of the word, though interesting historically, gives little clue to its meaning.

There are numerous accounts, both ancient and modern, of the nature and function of philosophy, some couched in very general terms, others more specific. Plato in the *Republic* describes the philosopher as 'the man who is ready to taste every form of knowledge, is glad to learn and never satisfied . . . whose passion is to see the truth . . . whose heart is fixed on Reality itself'.[1] Aristotle echoes him when he states that 'philosophy is rightly called the knowledge of the truth'.[2] Epicurus regarded philosophy as 'an activity which secures the happy life by means of discussion and argument'.[3] In the Middle Ages philosophy became the handmaid of theology; its purpose was to combat heresy, to elucidate the revealed truths of the Christian faith and to demonstrate such doctrines of natural religion as the existence and unity of God.

Up to this point in its history philosophy had never been far distant from religion; sometimes, as in Stoicism and Epicureanism, it had been a substitute for it, offering comfort and security in a perplexing and dangerous world. Nor was it far removed from problems of conduct; men looked to it for moral guidance, asking of the philosopher, 'What ought we to do?' It was characterised, too, by the search for 'reality', by a concern for 'ultimate' problems, by the attempt to secure comprehensiveness and logical coherence, to provide a complete, systematic account of the whole of human experience. This may be called the traditional view of philosophy, which associates it with the great perennial problems of human experience and human conduct.

In the transition from the medieval to the modern world the links with religion became less binding; the moral element, though it remained strong, was often obscured by preoccupation with problems of knowledge and the methods of scientific enquiry. An element of scepticism appeared, not new by any means, but increasingly insistent. John Locke set limits to the mind's capacity for knowledge: 'The comprehension of our understandings comes exceeding short of the vast extent of things.'[4] David Hume denounced as 'sophistry and illusion' whatever does not fall within the spheres of mathematics and natural science.[5]

[1] *Republic* 475c–e, 480, trans. and ed. H. D. P. Lee (Penguin, 1955), pp. 237–8, 244.

[2] *Metaphysics* 993b 19, trans. and ed. J. Warrington (Dent, 1956), p. 362.

[3] Sextus Empiricus, *Adversus Mathematicos*, XI, 169.

[4] *Essay concerning Human Understanding*, ed. A. S. Pringle-Pattison (Oxford, Clarendon Press, 1924), p. 12.

[5] *Enquiries*, ed. L. A. Selby-Bigge (Oxford, Clarendon Press, 2nd edn, 1902), p. 165.

In twentieth-century England the note of scepticism is even stronger, the field of philosophy more restricted. Here and there traces of the traditional view remain. Professor Jessop describes philosophy as 'the obstinate scrutiny of the whole spectacle of experience';[6] Dr Curtis calls it 'the search for ultimate truths and principles conducted through the light of human reason'.[7] But the tendency at the present time is to describe philosophy in far less ambitious terms. For instance, R. G. Collingwood has written: 'Philosophy is the free activity of critical thought, and is applicable to any problem which thought can raise.'[8] For Professor D. J. O'Connor it is 'a laborious, piecemeal effort to criticise and clarify the foundations of our beliefs'.[9] Such statements can be paralleled in American philosophers: 'Philosophy in the full sense', wrote William James, 'is only *man thinking*, thinking about generalities rather than particulars';[10] John Dewey called it 'thinking which has become conscious of itself'.[11] Moral guidance and the solution of 'ultimate' problems are no longer widely accepted as within the scope of philosophy: 'Ethics', writes Bertrand Russell, 'is traditionally a department of philosophy. . . . I hardly think myself that it ought to be included in the domain of philosophy.'[12] Elsewhere he asserts: 'What philosophy should dissipate is *certainty*.'[13] (It is an apt illustration of the difficulty of defining philosophy that Russell elsewhere describes it as arising from 'an unusually obstinate attempt to arrive at real knowledge'[14] —though in fairness one should add that the two statements are not necessarily inconsistent.) Ludwig Wittgenstein saw philosophy as 'a battle against the bewitchment of our intelligence by means of language'.[15] Professor A. J. Ayer in *Language, Truth and Logic* predicts that 'philosophy must develop into the logic of science', and denies that it is the philosopher's task to construct elaborate explanations of the whole of reality.[16]

Can any core of agreement be traced amid these views? It would be agreed by philosophers of all kinds and of all historical periods that philosophy involves a peculiarly stringent and orderly use of reason, that

[6] *Science and the Spiritual* (Sheldon Press, 1942), p. 11.
[7] *Introduction to the Philosophy of Education* (University Tutorial Press, 1958), p. 46.
[8] *Religion and Philosophy* (Macmillan, 1916), p. 17.
[9] *An Introduction to the Philosophy of Education* (Routledge, 1957), p. 45.
[10] *Some Problems of Philosophy* (Longmans, 1911), p. 15.
[11] *Democracy and Education* (New York, Macmillan, 1916), p. 381.
[12] *An Outline of Philosophy* (Allen & Unwin, 1927), p. 233.
[13] *Unpopular Essays* (Allen & Unwin, 1950), p. 43.
[14] *An Outline of Philosophy*, p. 1.
[15] *Philosophical Investigations*, trans. G. E. M. Anscombe (2nd edn, Oxford, Blackwell, 1963), § 109.
[16] 2nd edn, Gollancz, 1946, p. 153.

3

whatever conclusions are reached must be logically valid, and any system of conclusions logically coherent. It would be generally accepted, too, that there is no field of knowledge which is automatically excluded from philosophical scrutiny. But there are also deep cleavages of view. Most fundamental of all, perhaps, is that between philosophers who deny the capacity of philosophy to answer the deep, 'ultimate' problems which have been traditionally posed for its solving, and those who believe that it can still help us to answer such questions as: Does God exist? What is the nature of man? What is the purpose of human existence? What ought I to do? There are some contemporary philosophers who hold that questions like these arise from a misunderstanding of the use of words; they are to be solved, therefore—or dispersed—by accurate analysis of linguistic usage, of how we use words in the context of actual situations.

It seems, then, that except in the most general terms agreement about the nature, function and scope of philosophy is likely to be impossible. This conclusion may distress those who expect to find in philosophy an agreed body of subject-matter and methods similar to that which exists in the sciences. But they should bear in mind, first—and this too would be generally agreed among philosophers—that philosophy is not primarily a subject but an activity; it consists not so much in the conclusions, if any, which it reaches, as in the search for them. Second, philosophy, like all other human activities, is partly determined by the social context in which it is exercised and partly by the temperament of the individuals who exercise it. Despite the most strenuous efforts to achieve objectivity and absence of bias, a philosopher can never entirely shed either his own self or the conditioning to which he is subjected by the intellectual and cultural climate of his age. 'The history of philosophy', says William James, 'is to a great extent that of a certain clash of human temperaments.'[17] It is also a clash of cultures; Descartes was as much the child of his age as is A. J. Ayer today. Differences in philosophical outlook reflect differences in social and historical situation; they also reflect the personal differences, preferences and idiosyncrasies of those who philosophise. It should not be surprising, therefore, if men of different periods and even of the same period have conflicting views about the scope and function of philosophy.

If philosophy cannot be defined, it can at least be described, and this we shall proceed to do. However, there is one minor problem which, for clarity's sake, must first be examined. It is frequently stated that 'everyone must have a philosophy', that one cannot live without subscribing to a 'philosophy of life'. Thus, Dr S. J. Curtis: 'In the widest meaning of the term, every person has a philosophy of life.'[18] W. E. Hocking writes:

[17] *Pragmatism* (Longmans, 1907), p. 6.
[18] *Introduction to the Philosophy of Education*, p. 35.

4

'When in the vernacular we speak of a man's philosophy, we mean simply the *sum of his beliefs*. In this sense, everybody, or at least every mature person, necessarily has a philosophy, because nobody can manage a life without an equipment of beliefs.'[19] Admittedly both Dr Curtis and Professor Hocking qualify their statements by distinguishing a more rigorous meaning of the word: the former remarks that the name of philosopher is usually applied to 'a person with a disciplined mind who approaches ultimate problems in a special way';[20] the latter distinguishes philosophy 'as a science', by which is meant 'the *examination of belief*—thinking one's way to a well-grounded set of beliefs'.[21] Nevertheless, the view that 'everyone has a philosophy'—or ought to have—is widespread and leads to misconceptions about what philosophy is and can do.

It is true that everyone possesses a number of established habits and attitudes, partly innate, partly acquired, which in sum constitute an outlook on life. The more individually-minded a person is, the more likely is this outlook to be distinctive; in many it is little more than a reflection of social conventions and the values inculcated by the mass media. To use the word 'philosophy' of this often vague and incoherent ensemble of attitudes is surely misleading; it would be better to reserve the word for that peculiarly rigorous and critical kind of thinking, and the conclusions it leads to, which marks out the philosopher from his fellows. Moreover, this popular sense of the word obscures an important difference of meaning between 'philosophy' and 'a philosophy'. The former suggests that philosophy is an activity, and with this, it can safely be said, all philosophers would agree. The latter implies that the activity can lead to a coherent, logically justifiable system of conclusions which offers guidance for daily living—a view from which a large number of philosophers would vigorously dissent. If we avoid this use of the word, we are less likely to be misled into expecting more of philosophy than it can give.

To understand philosophy one must see it in action: one must examine at first hand the kind of problem philosophers set themselves to solve and the methods they use in trying to solve them; one must study their arguments and conclusions, their criticisms of other philosophers and the criticisms these other philosophers make of them. This is what the present book is about; its aim is to pose for the reader a number of important philosophical problems and to show how each of these was tackled by one major philosopher (in chapter 11 by a group of philosophers). From this it is hoped there will emerge some insight into the nature and scope of philosophical activity. The extensive quotation from philosophical works

[19] *Types of Philosophy* (New York, Scribner's, 1929), pp. 3-4.
[20] *Introduction to the Philosophy of Education*, p. 2.
[21] *Types of Philosophy*, p. 4.

is intended partly for obvious explanatory purposes, partly as an incentive to read the works themselves—a far more profitable exercise, when the student is ready for it, than reading about them. There follows in the remainder of this chapter a statement of the principal characteristics of philosophy, an estimate of its value, an account of the two differing approaches to philosophy referred to earlier (commonly known as rationalism and empiricism), and a brief description of the four main traditional branches of philosophy: logic, epistemology, ethics and metaphysics.

Disinterestedness

When Thales, the first of the Greek philosophers, visited Egypt, he found the Egyptians using elementary geometry to redivide their land after the annual flooding of the Nile. What interested him, however, was not the practical application but the theory behind it—the lines, angles and figures in themselves, and the relations between them. Similarly his observation of Babylonian astronomy led to an interest in the heavenly bodies and their movements, not, as with the Babylonians, for predicting the future, but for their own sake. In each case his motive was disinterested, devoid of practical or utilitarian application. This disinterestedness has been a characteristic of philosophy throughout its history.

The philosopher is not impelled primarily by the desire for gain or comfort, by ambition or the practical affairs of life; the impulse to philosophise springs from wonder and curiosity, from a sense of puzzlement and a deep intellectual disquiet. The philosopher is a man who lives, as it were, in a perpetual state of mental insecurity induced by living in a world of unsolved problems; his work is an attempt to banish insecurity by achieving intellectual satisfaction. But he would be the first to admit that the attempt is illusory; for either the problems prove insoluble or their solving leads to other problems, and these again to others. Certainly the philosopher has an uncanny sense for the problematic; what the ordinary man sees as straightforward, the philosopher, probing behind the plausibilities of common sense, discovers to be full of unanswered questions. 'The genius of the philosopher', writes Friedrich Waismann, 'shows itself nowhere more strikingly than in the new kind of question he brings into the world. What distinguishes him and gives him his place is the passion of questioning.'[22]

But it is not questioning for the sake of it (as is sometimes supposed) or to be awkward or to appear clever. It is for the sake of understanding.

[22] 'How I see philosophy' in *Contemporary British Philosophy*, ed. H. D. Lewis, 3rd series (Allen & Unwin, 1956), p. 464.

The questions are honestly asked, the problems sincerely felt as such. What the philosopher seeks is order, coherence and relatedness in the world as he experiences it. Because he sees more deeply than his fellow men, he finds in experience unsuspected irregularities and inconsistencies, gaps and hiatuses intolerable to reason. He cannot, therefore, like other men, content himself with accepting experience; he must question, analyse, reflect upon it in order to comprehend it. He is possessed, as A. N. Whitehead puts it, by a 'craving of reason that the facts discriminated in experience be understood'.[23] This is not to say that the philosopher does not enjoy philosophising; in fact, despite the mental sweat involved and the inconclusiveness of much of his work, he derives from it intense and lasting pleasure, a pleasure, however, which is not the goal but a byproduct of his activity.

What kind of problem does he seek to solve? This will become apparent in the pages that follow, but some brief indication may be helpful here. In fact *any* problem offers material for the philosopher—at least initially. The Greek philosophers explored first the physical world and its structure; the field of enquiry was then rapidly extended to include religion and mathematics, problems of knowledge and existence, ethics and politics, until finally it became clear that no area of human experience was closed to philosophic questioning. But let us look at three particular problems as examples of how the philosopher probes below the surface and jolts our everyday complacency by his disturbing questions.

The existence of a world external to us is normally taken for granted; it seems evident enough that the origin of sensations of sight, touch, hearing, taste and smell is outside and distinct from our own selves. The belief seems amply justified when, for instance, we burn a finger or are knocked down by a car. But the existence of such a world of external objects has been seriously questioned, most eminently by George Berkeley in his *Principles of Human Knowledge*; objects exist, he argues, only in so far as they are perceived: 'Their *esse* is *percipi*, nor is it possible they should have any existence out of the minds or thinking things which perceive them.'[24] Berkeley's arguments will be examined in chapter 7; meanwhile it is not unfair to say that they have never been conclusively answered and that anyone who set out to prove beyond all doubt the existence of external objects would have a very formidable task.

Again, 'facts' are familiar items of daily life. The lawyer asks for the facts of the case, politicians exhort us to face economic facts, and scientists are supposed to discover facts in their laboratories. But what are facts? 'Facts', it might be answered, 'are things in themselves, objective realities

[23] *Adventures of Ideas* (Penguin edn, 1942), p. 167.
[24] Part I, § 3; ed. G. J. Warnock (Collins, 1962), p. 66.

independent of human beings.' To this the philosopher might reply: even supposing there are such things (and we have no right to take it for granted), can we ever know them *as they are in themselves*? For the sensory and intellectual equipment of man determines both what he sees and how he sees it; what he sees he sees *through* his senses and interprets *through* his mind; the world he observes, therefore, is not the world as it is in itself, but the world as it is pictured by human senses and structured by the human mind. Hence there are no facts in the popular sense, but only, as it were, opinions, that is, things *as we perceive them*.

Finally, there is the problem of 'truth'. This, too, is something whose existence and nature is normally taken for granted. But a closer examination suggests that truth, in the sense of something independent of ourselves to which we can appeal (and often spelt with a capital 'T') is far more elusive than is supposed. For it seems clear that truth is not one thing but several, and which it is depends on the context. If one counts accurately the number of apples in a dish and then states the result by saying, 'There are six apples in the dish', this is a true statement—one has spoken 'the truth', for the statement corresponds with the actual situation. However, if in a geometry lesson a pupil states that the sum of the internal angles of a triangle is 180°, he is speaking 'the truth', not because his statement corresponds with an observed factual situation (factual in the normal sense of objective and external to oneself), but because it fits in with, coheres with, the axioms of Euclidean geometry; for it is not fact but human contrivance that these angles add up to 180°, and in a non-Euclidean system they would not necessarily do so. A further meaning of 'truth' is suggested by the statement that punishment (or leniency or psychotherapy) is effective; here the implication is that punishment works, that it produces results in reducing crime and deterring criminal acts; the statement is true because it is supported by the consequences.[25] Furthermore, not only does 'truth' lack the simplicity which is popularly ascribed to it, but it is also often highly charged with emotion, as, for instance, in the words that St John puts into the mouth of Jesus, 'I am the way, and the truth, and the life,' or in the lines of Keats:

> Beauty is truth, truth beauty—that is all
> Ye know on earth, and all ye need to know

When this happens, far from being a final standard of appeal, 'truth' becomes highly relative to the subjective experience of the person who originally utters or later quotes the statement in which the word occurs.

It can hardly be maintained that these three problems have any obvious

[25] These examples illustrate respectively the correspondence, coherence and pragmatic theories of truth.

practical or utilitarian relevance. Yet for the philosopher they are intensely interesting and an enormous amount of thought and writing has been devoted to their elucidation. His interest in them, however, is without strings; he sees a problem and is restless until he has tried to solve it. Admittedly, a psychologist might question whether any human activity is entirely disinterested. Are there not within us springs of motivation of which we are unaware and which, did we but know it, are the source of even the most apparently objective enquiry? It might also be suggested that the impulse to philosophise has sometimes sprung from motives associated with religion or politics, that philosophers have been known to adopt a certain position—a religious doctrine or an ideology—and then build their reasoning round it, seeking to demonstrate what in fact they had already decided. For instance, it could be argued that much of Plato's thought was a development, even a rationalisation, of a view of life inherited partly from earlier thinkers, partly from the aristocratic society in which he himself grew up, partly from an aversion from years of war and revolution; and that all these combined to produce in him a contempt for the world of ordinary experience and a yearning for a certainty which he could find only in the assured results of the activity of pure intellect. Was not the philosophy of George Berkeley—to take an example nearer home—an attempt to defend the principles of the Christian religion to which he was already committed? And was not J. S. Mill's philosophy a prolonged search for a respectable intellectual basis on which to establish his socialistic ideals? There is some justification for this objection; yet granted that human thought has roots too deep for our knowing, it can still be said with some assurance that the philosopher's activity is *primarily* disinterested, that his *conscious* purpose is the solution of problems which cause him intellectual disquiet. To philosophise is to engage in a strenuous activity of thought and to pursue it with no other aim than to satisfy the importunate questioning of the human mind.[26]

An activity of reason

Philosophy is characteristically an activity of reason, of the human mind at its most rational level; not of practical reason, aimed, that is to say, at results which are useful or pleasurable, but of reason dissociated from motives external to itself. It is not, like music, poetry and the other arts, primarily or dominantly emotional; though in common with all human activities it has some springs in emotion—in wonder, curiosity, in the passion for order and consistency. It is rational in the sense that it

[26] A vivid account of the philosopher, contrasting him with the man of affairs, occurs in Plato's *Theaetetus* 172c ff.; cf. *Republic* 474b ff.

aims at objectivity, at examining every problem in a non-personal, dispassionate manner. It is true that there are limits to objectivity, but the philosopher, like the scientist, makes it his consistent aim to avoid the prejudices, the emotional bias and the unexamined assumptions which are so liable to distort argument and predetermine the results of reasoning. Philosophy is rational, too, in that it relies on logic as its main instrument, and logic is pre-eminently a rational activity, objective and detached, which seeks to subdue all argument to the laws of inference and rejects as invalid all conclusions which are not strictly entailed by the premises.

Yet there is a sense in which philosophy transcends reason. All human progress depends ultimately on creative insight, on the imaginative 'jump' which sees new patterns in familiar data, new possibilities of exploration and experiment. Reason, it might well be argued, is merely a tool for elaborating the suggestions offered to it by imagination. 'What is essential in philosophy', writes Friedrich Waismann, 'is the breaking through to a *deeper insight* . . . the flashing of a new aspect which is *non*-inferential.' He continues:

At the heart of any philosophy worth the name is vision and it is from there it springs and takes its visible shape. . . . From Plato to Moore and Wittgenstein every great philosopher was led by a sense of vision; without it no one could have given a new direction to human thought or opened windows into the not-yet-seen.[27]

This, as Dr Waismann warns, is not to be interpreted too romantically; philosophic vision is neither haphazard nor uncontrolled; it is the culmination as well as the inspiration of intensive thought. But his words are a reminder that reason is not the whole of philosophy.

One of the perennial, and perhaps the most deeply dividing, of all philosophical problems is how far reason, even assisted by imagination, can provide its own material for reflection and how far it depends on material provided through sense perception; and, further, whether the conclusions argued from reason's own material have any factual validity. More simply, can reason alone give us knowledge about reality or does it, when severed from sense perception, merely spin out patterns, elaborate and often pleasing, but devoid of reference to the real world? This is the great source of division between rationalism and empiricism which will be examined later in this chapter.

It is pertinent to ask by what method philosophy pursues its activity. The answer to this is that it has no one method but adopts whatever method is appropriate to the problem in hand. The puzzlement from which philosophy springs can take many forms. Sometimes the root of a problem lies in logical fallacy which can be exposed by careful application of logical

[27] 'How I see philosophy', *loc. cit.*, pp. 470, 488, 483.

laws. Sometimes it lies in linguistic confusion, as was the case with Parmenides and the verb 'to be' (p. 57 below), and linguistic analysis can dissolve it. Sometimes the correct procedure is to adopt an attitude of scepticism and by relentless questioning to force an opponent to clarify his position or relinquish it. Sometimes the analysis of a problem reveals either that it is no problem or that it belongs, not to philosophy, but to one of the sciences. Moreover, individual philosophers have developed methods of their own. Socrates, for instance, in his analysis of concepts followed a process which has been called 'definition under criticism':[28] a definition is suggested for, say, courage; it is examined, found inadequate and rejected; another definition is substituted, examined, rejected and so on until either a conclusion is reached or the argument terminates without one. Descartes (see chapter 5) applied what he called 'the method of doubt' and thus was led to his famous *cogito ergo sum*. In modern times Professor G. E. Moore confronted statements such as 'time is unreal' and 'there is no external world' with the view of common sense which holds that lunch comes after breakfast and that there are objects external to us.[29] To speak of 'philosophic method', then, is misleading; instead we must think of a variety of methods differing with the problem at issue and the techniques of the individual philosopher.

Comprehensiveness

Philosophy has regularly been regarded as characterised by a certain quality of 'comprehensiveness'. Plato, in the fourth century B.C., pictures the philosopher as 'reaching out for all truth from his earliest years' and engaged in 'the contemplation of all time and all existence'.[30] In the twentieth century Dr Joad assigns to him the task of 'cosmic correlation';[31] and Professor Moore declares that philosophy's most important problem is 'to give a general description to the *whole* of the Universe'.[32] What is meant by comprehensiveness and how far is it correctly ascribed to philosophy?

It has already been remarked that no problem, at least initially, is outside the scope of philosophy; in this sense it is certainly all-embracing. Problems from every field of human experience have been examined by

[28] W. Boyd, *The History of Western Education* (A. & C. Black, 4th edn, 1947), p. 28 (quoting Aristotle).
[29] See, for example, *Philosophical Studies* (Routledge, paperback, 1960), ch. vi, 'The conception of reality'; and 'A defence of common sense' in *Contemporary British Philosophy*, 2nd series, ed. J. H. Muirhead (Allen & Unwin, 1925). [30] *Republic*, 485–6.
[31] I have not been able to track down the precise source of this quotation.
[32] *Some Main Problems of Philosophy* (Allen & Unwin, 1953), p. 1.

philosophers at one time and another, originally without distinction between problems of different kinds. The Greeks, both pre-Socratics and later, gave their attention to questions whose solution would now be properly assigned to special sciences like physics, astronomy and biology or to mathematics. But the history of philosophy has involved gradually shedding off on to these and other disciplines those problems for the solving of which they have developed their own particular equipment and techniques. Yet new problems are constantly arising, and it can fairly be said that, until their nature has been determined and their appropriate province assigned, they belong to philosophy.

There is another and deeper sense, however, in which philosophy can be said to be comprehensive. Because the philosopher is not himself committed to a limited sphere of intellectual activity, as is the mathematician, say, or the theologian or the physicist, he can take his stand, as it were, above and apart from all other mental disciplines and survey them in their relationship to one another.[33] For instance, he can compare their differences of procedure—the scientist relying on observation, hypothesis and experiment, the mathematician on deduction from initial axioms; he can compare their results, sifting them for any trace of an overall pattern of interpretation or pointing out apparently irreconcilable differences—between, say, the *credo ut intellegam* of the theologian (commitment prior to understanding) and the non-committed objectivity of the scientist (no commitment prior to verification). Whether any such overall pattern will emerge it is impossible to say in advance; it may well be, however unpalatable to our reason, that there is no pattern, that reality or our experience of it is necessarily fragmented; the philosopher will accept whatever conclusion the facts of the case suggest. In this way, as Dr Joad has pointed out, philosophy may act as a kind of clearing-house for human knowledge: 'Philosophy is . . . most appropriately to be conceived as a clearing-house to which the results of all other human enquiries are brought and in which the records of all forms of human experience are sifted, assessed and evaluated.'[34]

But the philosopher can not only compare the methods and conclusions of the different intellectual disciplines, he can also examine problems which arise within each of them and which they themselves are not concerned to answer. One of the most celebrated of these is the 'problem of induction' (see chapter 10). Induction is the process of arriving at general conclusions based on observation of particular data; such generalisations are never logically certain, in the sense that it can be shown with the inevitability

---

[33] The metaphors are not intended to suggest the *superiority* of philosophy to other disciplines.

[34] *Philosophy* (English Universities Press, 1944), p. 16.

of mathematical proof that they *must* be so. It is a popular misconception that science can strictly prove its own conclusions. For unless every occurrence of a phenomenon, past, present and future, has been observed, one cannot say with certainty that it always will be so. Litmus paper turns red in acid; this has been observed many millions of times and will, no doubt, be observed many millions more; the probability of its happening is so great as to leave no practical doubt that it always will happen; but probability is not certainty, and what satisfies the scientist does not satisfy the logician. For the scientist induction 'works', that is to say, his generalisations enable him to predict with all the accuracy he requires further occurrences of phenomena; but for the philosopher there remains a problem: how, he asks, can induction be justified? what logical validity do inductive conclusions possess? and why are we entitled to use them in order to predict in advance of experience?

Another and not unrelated problem concerns mathematics. Mathematics is a principal tool for the scientist in his investigation of the world; it enables him to systematise his observations and thereby facilitates generalisation from them; it enables him, further, to predict the results entailed by his hypotheses and thus to check them against phenomena. So intimately involved is mathematics with science that many have supposed that we live in a 'mathematical universe', that in some way mathematics 'reflects' or 'pictures' reality. Many contemporary philosophers, however, argue that mathematics is a system of tautologies; that there comes out of it, though in a different form, only what is put into it; it is a product of pure thought, and though in practice it is a tool of great value to the scientist in his investigations, yet in its own right it tells us nothing about the real world. Here again is a problem, as yet unsolved, which the scientist and the mathematician can for practical purposes ignore; for the philosopher, with his wider view, it remains a disturbing problem.

In the past it has often been required of philosophy that it present a comprehensive account of the whole of human experience, bringing within a single perspective the entire range of the known. Today this can hardly be expected; for the extent of knowledge is so vast that no single mind can comprehend it. What can and must be expected, however, is that the philosopher should ignore no relevant aspect of experience in arriving at his conclusions. The temptation exists in all of us, philosophers and non-philosophers alike, to adopt a partial and blinkered view which excludes what does not accord with our own position. Thus the logical positivist dismisses as non-meaningful the value judgments of religion, morals and the arts because he cannot accommodate them within his particular criterion of meaning—an exclusion which rightly leads us to suspect the validity of the criterion (chapter 11). The blinkered view is unphilosophic;

there is no area of human experience, however seemingly trivial or fantastic, which the philosopher can afford to ignore.

But if philosophy cannot present us with a comprehensive account of the whole of human experience, may it not, perhaps, offer a single unitary principle of interpretation which will include all that is known and knowable? The attempt to find such a principle has been made repeatedly and has resulted in the great 'systems' of the history of philosophy. Plato offered one such in the Form of the Good (p. 47); even before Plato, Heraclitus had proposed his *logos*, a formula of cyclic change which governs the universe.[35] In a later age Descartes divided the world into mind and matter (chapter 5); Spinoza presupposed the essential unity of things, Leibniz their unique individuality; for Hegel reality was a spiritual whole evolving to complete consciousness of itself by a dialectical movement between extremes. Unfortunately, none of these particular principles has secured more than a partial and temporary acceptance by other thinkers, and if in fact there exists any such interpretative key to the universe, it must be said that no philosopher has yet found it. In the history of philosophy no Newton or Einstein has yet appeared to bind all that is within a single law.

In some senses, then, it can certainly be said of philosophy that it is comprehensive, in others not. It is not only comprehensiveness, however, that the philosopher seeks, but relatedness; the former alone might signify only an aggregation of separate items; the latter implies coherence, a mutual entailment by which each item is linked to every other within the whole. There is something deep within human nature, or in the rational part of it, which impels us to seek such a coherence within experience. Whether it arises from the instinctive desire for security or from the unconscious wish to impose on experience the unity which already exists in the experiencing self or from some aesthetic sense which demands a pattern in what it knows—this is of little consequence. The urge exists and must be satisfied, if not in some vast, all-inclusive system like Spinoza's or Hegel's, then on a smaller scale within a limited area of experience. In this rather special sense, too, of striving for logical cohesion between the

---

[35] Heraclitus ('the riddler', as he was called because of the obscurity of his writings) taught that everything is in a state of change or flux; not haphazardly, however, for the process of change is governed by definite laws. Essentially it consists in a circular movement of transformation through the three elements: fire—water—earth—water—fire. To the law which governs this cyclic change he gave the name of *logos*. The Greek word has a variety of meanings (calculation, proportion, formula, reason, speech, word, story) but the dominant ones here are 'formula' and 'proportion'. The *logos* is the sum of the principles of order and balance which govern the changing universe; it is that which gives coherence and pattern to the totality of existing things, including man. See p. 42.

various items of experience, it may be said that philosophy is comprehensive.

The subject matter of philosophy

The heading of this section involves two questions, related but distinct: If philosophy is an activity of reason, upon what subject-matter is it exercised? And is there a body of philosophic knowledge, as there may be said to be of historical or scientific knowledge? The answer to the first of these questions will become apparent in the chapters that follow; for the present a very general indication must suffice.

It could be said that the subject-matter of philosophy is anything; but this, though in a sense correct, is unhelpful. For instance, philosophy is not now concerned to answer problems of an empirical kind; these belong to the scientist and are investigated by observation and experiment. When, therefore, the philosopher finds that a problem is such, he hands it on to the appropriate science; the result has been a constant unloading from philosophy of problems which have been found not to belong to it, so that, as Dr Joad remarks: 'Philosophy is thus in the unfortunate position of a schoolmaster, who loses his pupils directly they show promise.'[36] But the results of empirical investigation, when they are forthcoming, may well prove of great importance to the philosopher because of the evidence they provide for him in pursuing his own enquiries. Nor does the history of philosophy constitute the subject-matter of philosophy. This may be interesting in itself and a fertile source of illustration and argument, but it is not philosophy. For it is not so much an activity of reason exercised on problems and sources of puzzlement as an empirical investigation into what past philosophers have thought and written.

The subject-matter of philosophy, as was suggested in the previous sentence, consists of problems, enigmas, and intellectual perplexities thrown up anywhere throughout the whole field of human experience, in so far as they do not belong to the empirical sciences or to some other established discipline like mathematics or theology. There is, however, no clearcut line of division; and it is often difficult to decide when a problem is philosophical and when it belongs elsewhere. For instance, the existence of God and the possibility of proving it are questions both for the theologian and the philosopher, which each approaches in his different way. Similarly the use of mathematics to predict the results of observation is a problem both for the mathematician, in the adaptation and refinement of techniques, and for the philosopher, in explaining the relation between mathematics and 'reality'. But in general it may be said that philosophy concerns

[36] *Return to Philosophy* (Faber, 1935), p. 206.

itself with problems which do not obviously belong elsewhere, problems for which no means of solution has as yet been found. It may be likened to a sieve which sorts out different kinds of material; and, like a sieve, what it retains is often the least attractive and digestible.

Philosophy examines and criticises the assumptions of other disciplines: the scientist assumes in experience a uniformity which enables him to predict future experience—the philosopher asks why and how this can be so; the theologian assumes the primacy of commitment over intellectual understanding—again the philosopher asks why. In everyday life we take for granted a world of external objects and of other persons—the philosopher challenges the assumptions of common sense and asks on what they are based. He ferrets out the fallacies and misconceptions involved in our thinking; he seeks the grounds for believing this or that, the justification for intellectual assent. He is particularly interested in the procedure by which problems are investigated, since this determines not only the likelihood of a solution but also who should look for it. In recent years it has been found that language is a rich source of intellectual confusion, and attention has been concentrated on how we are misled by it into conjuring up problems which do not exist (chapter 12). Values, too, their origin and justification, are another current problem of great interest to the philosopher. There is also, as we have seen, the problem of finding relatedness in experience, a pattern of interpretation and explanation; and this leads to the search for synthesis, whether over the whole or only a limited part of experience. Such are a few of the many problems to which philosophers devote their attention.

There is a special class of problem traditionally and popularly associated with philosophy and often referred to as 'ultimate'. They are ultimate in the sense that all enquiry leads to them; they stand like interrogation marks on the horizon of human questioning. Why is there a world and why am I in it? Is there a God? Is good the final reality? Or evil? What is man's destiny? Is it predetermined? Is there purpose in the universe? Human beings have asked such questions since thought began, and they ask them still. Often they have turned to philosophy for an answer; but it must be admitted that no certain answer has been forthcoming, and it is doubtful whether philosophy can supply one. If they are answerable at all, they are answerable, it would seem, not by reason but in the commitment of the whole personality—reason, emotion, will—to a particular view of life and the testing of it in practice; that is, in religious faith rather than by philosophy. This is not to deny that the philosopher can perform a valuable service in clearing away some of the confused thinking which frequently obscures such questions and in testing the validity of arguments used to support one or another answer to them.

Whatever may be said about the capacity of the philosopher to answer 'ultimate' problems, it can be agreed that he seeks understanding at a deeper level than that of common sense or practical needs or even of scientific enquiry. For instance, in daily life we accept that germs or viruses 'cause' disease or that frost 'causes' pipes to burst; there is no need to pursue the matter further. The scientist goes on to ask how germs produce disease and frost the burst pipe; he looks for causes in terms of general explanation. The philosopher goes deeper still and examines the whole concept of causation; in so doing he finds it a great deal more complicated, less tidy than the simple one-to-one relationship of cause and effect that satisfies us in daily life (chapter 8). 'Ulterior' problems, then (in a neutral sense of the word), if not 'ultimate', may rightly be assigned to him. Or one can say that he is concerned with 'second order' problems as distinct from the 'first order' problems of daily life and of empirical investigation.

The second question involved in the title to this section—whether there is an agreed body of philosophical knowledge—can be answered more briefly. Opinions differ even among modern philosophers. Dr Joad, for instance, writes: 'Definite knowledge has no place in philosophy, and it is in this aloofness from brute fact that men have found much of its charm.'[37] Professor O'Connor states that: 'Philosophy is not in the ordinary sense of the phrase a body of knowledge but rather an activity of criticism and clarification.'[38] Hans Reichenbach, on the other hand, insists that there is a body of philosophical knowledge; after citing a number of instances he continues: 'This is a collection of philosophical results which have been established by means of a philosophic method as precise and dependable as the method of science.'[39] Obviously the answer to the question depends in part on what is meant by 'knowledge'; but leaving this aside, it is clear that philosophy does not offer a body of knowledge of the kind to be found in scientific or historical textbooks and described as 'chemistry' or 'medieval history'; fact-finding is not the philosopher's task. Yet knowledge of a kind he surely does provide.

Philosophy is an argument conducted over the centuries from generation to generation and within each generation. The conclusions of one philosopher are examined and criticised, rejected, modified or developed by his successors. New problems arise, old ones are examined again in the light of new knowledge. In the course of the argument agreement is reached at least temporarily and within limited areas. For instance, it is

[37] *Return to Philosophy*, p. 206.
[38] *An Introduction to the Philosophy of Education*, p. 4.
[39] *The Rise of Scientific Philosophy* (University of California Press, paperback edn, 1956), p. 308.

unlikely that any philosopher today would accept Plato's Theory of Forms as an explanation of universal terms like beauty and justice (chapter 2); or Aristotle's theory of causation in terms of final, efficient, formal and material causes (p. 63); or Descartes' strict dualism of mind and matter (pp. 98–9); or would dissent from the view that language is a source (not the only one, however) of confusion in thought. In particular, there has been built up within the field of logic and methodology a large measure of agreement between philosophers of different views which comes closer than anything else, perhaps, in philosophy to a body of knowledge. It seems unreasonable to deny all this the name of knowledge because it lacks the apparent conclusiveness of scientific or historical knowledge.

The inconclusiveness of philosophy is sometimes made the ground for denying it any claim to knowledge. Now philosophy is not entirely inconclusive, as we have seen; but it cannot be denied that, compared with other disciplines, its activities often lack 'results'. The reasons for this are not far to seek. First, the philosopher relinquishes problems which he finds do not belong to him; he makes no claim, for instance, to empirical problems, but hands them on to the scientist. Hence, as William James has put it, philosophy becomes 'the *residuum* of problems unsolved by science'[40] (but not only science), and of these not a few, at least in our present state of knowledge, appear to be insoluble. Second, much of the work of the philosopher lies in the careful analysis and clarification of problems, terms and concepts in order to reveal their meaning and show up sources of error; the early Socratic dialogues afford many illustrations of this. The results of such philosophising consist in the disclosure of prejudice, misconception and logical fallacy; they are preparatory to the work of constructive thought; but they are no less valuable for being intangible. Third, philosophers, as has already been stated, are not uninfluenced by personal temperament and inclination and by social climate; it should not be surprising, therefore, if philosophers differ among themselves or philosophers of one generation from those of the next. Fourth, there belongs to the very nature of philosophy a refusal to take for granted, an attitude of scepticism which regards no conclusion as final and every matter, however apparently closed, as open to further question. This may be annoying to the non-philosopher, but it has value; for 'final' conclusions have regularly been shown to be mistaken. Last, it is fair to point out that science itself lacks the conclusiveness popularly attributed to it. The history of science, it has aptly been said, is 'strewn with the wreckage of discarded concepts'.[41]

[40] *Some Problems of Philosophy*, p. 23.
[41] F. M. Cornford, *Before and After Socrates* (Cambridge University Press, 1932), p. 31.

The value of philosophy

Socrates, in defending himself before the Athenian courts, compares the city with a large and lazy horse and himself with a horse-fly:

And all day long I never cease to settle, here, there and everywhere, rousing, persuading, reproving every one of you. You will not easily find another like me, gentlemen, and if you take my advice you will spare my life. I suspect, however, that before long you will awake from your drowsing and in your annoyance you will . . . finish me off with a single slap; and then you will go on sleeping to the end of your days, unless God in his care for you sends someone to take my place.[42]

In its picturesque way the passage describes a notable service which philosophy can perform for society.

Most of us, most of the time, live in a world of convention, of assumptions uncriticised and values uncritically acquired, of closed questions and dogmatic answers. The good is either what we want or what we are used to or what we have the power to get; truth falls victim to prejudice and suggestion. We are content to make our way, comfortably and complacently, through a world whose mysteries, perils and perplexities should shock us into vigilant and inquisitive awareness. To all such smug and incurious complacency philosophy is unendingly hostile. It strips off the subterfuges of habit and hypocrisy, lays bare the assumptions behind thought and action, and insists on keeping questions open. It attacks all forms of shoddy thinking and intellectual dishonesty; it demands care in the use of words and strict attention to meaning; it establishes criteria of evidence and compels us to examine the grounds of our beliefs. All this is no small service in a world where men are lulled into deception by the siren voices of the mass media, where thought is bastardised by commercial interests and opinion directed by competing pressure groups. It is a service which would be more effectively performed if philosophers could be persuaded to forsake more often their academic seclusion and reveal their philosophising for the disturbing, challenging, stimulating activity that it is.

But the value of philosophy is more than negative. By offering new interpretations, new syntheses, of experience, by the creation of new concepts and by the analysis, refinement and modification of existing concepts philosophy is continually expanding the horizon of human thought. It provides new ways of looking at experience, new starting-points for investigation; thus it promotes the growth of human consciousness and assists humanity in its exploration of the total context of life. For the universe is

[42] *Apology* 30e–31a, trans. and ed. H. Tredennick, *The Last Days of Socrates* (Penguin, 1954), p. 37.

not simply 'given'; it answers only the questions that are put to it; each new idea, therefore, each new scheme of interpretation is potentially 'another root struck deep into the infinite fertility of the world'.[43] Every great philosopher contributes something to the enrichment of human thought. The *logos* of Heraclitus, the Forms of Plato, the idea of substance in Aristotle, Hume's scepticism, the 'common sense' of G. E. Moore and Wittgenstein's preoccupation with language—all these have given new insights and revealed new lines of enquiry. For centuries ideas may lie dormant (like that of evolution, first conceived by the Greek Anaximander some two and a half thousand years ago), but in ways unpredictable they flash into vivid and compulsive meaning in the imagination of later thinkers. It is no objection to say that all this is remote from the common man; for even the most abstruse of philosophical ideas filters ultimately into the culture of a civilisation and influences its character and outlook. As David Hume has written: 'Though a philosopher may live remote from business, the genius of philosophy, if cultivated by several, must gradually diffuse itself throughout the whole society.'[44] Finally, it can be said that philosophy, by keeping before us life's deep unanswered problems, preserves in us the spirit of wonder, of humility, and thus prevents us lapsing into sterile indifference or preoccupation with the obvious.

Philosophy is also valuable within the more restricted sphere of specialised studies. It acts, as has already been noted, as a clearing-house; not only for evaluating established knowledge, but also for analysing and clarifying problems as yet unsolved, problems whose nature is still unclear and whose solution is not yet seen obviously to belong to one of the established disciplines. Nor is philosophy concerned only with problems in the more usual sense of the word, but with questions and concepts, arguments and conclusions, investigating their meaning, testing their clarity and validity. In this way it can help the scientist, the theologian, the historian, the educationist to see their way more clearly, to ask the right questions, to avoid pursuing false trails and being misled into error by confused concepts or faulty arguments. For instance, the analysis of causation and induction by successive philosophers has been of great value to the scientist; so too, in the early years of the formulation of scientific method, were such general principles of investigation as Ockham's 'razor', *entia non sunt multiplicanda praeter necessitatem*, and the doctrine, *nihil in intellectu quod non prius fuerit in sensu*,[45] which goes back through

[43] B. A. G. Fuller, *History of Greek Philosophy* (Cape, 1923), p. 13.
[44] *Enquiry concerning Human Understanding*, I, 5; p. 10.
[45] 'One must not assume the existence of more entities than are necessary to account for experience'; 'There is nothing in the mind which was not previously an object of sensation.'

Aquinas to Aristotle. Descartes's dualism of mind and matter, which reduced the concept of the physical world to matter-in-motion, facilitated the great advances in physics which came in the three following centuries. The 'absolute idealism' of nineteenth-century European philosophy may well have helped to create, by its emphasis on total interrelatedness, the intellectual climate in which Einstein could conceive his theory of relativity.[46] The theologian has profited from the philosophical examination of his arguments for the existence of God, of the concepts of truth and reality, and of the problems of evil and free will. The educator, too, has been helped to clarify his thinking about the nature and aims of education and to use more carefully such concepts as freedom and discipline.

Finally, what can philosophy offer the individual man and woman? It is part of the traditional view of philosophy that it is a source of ethical guidance, that it can help in making practical decisions about right and wrong and what we ought to do. Within limits this is true: philosophy can certainly clarify ethical problems by sorting out the issues involved and by distinguishing factual from valuational elements within them; it can elucidate the meaning of terms like 'good' and 'ought'; it can point to alternative choices within a situation and suggest the probable consequences of choosing one or another; it can thus ensure that moral decision, when it comes, is based on good evidence and sound reasoning. Philosophy can also suggest the logical consequences for action of ethical premises such as 'the individual person is intrinsically valuable', or 'self-advancement is right in all circumstances'. But what philosophy cannot do, apparently, is justify these initial premises themselves. Nor can philosophy recommend a particular way of life or set of beliefs; for, as Dr Joad has said, it carries 'no specific message'.[47] It is true that in the past some philosophers have tried to make it do so, but their recommendations have rarely carried conviction much beyond their own lifetime.

Philosophy offers more than this to those who practise it. It induces valuable habits of mind like tolerance, impartiality and suspension of judgment; it protects against precipitancy of both assent and dissent; it encourages a resolute aversion from all forms of intellectual shoddiness. It brings, too, a serenity which springs from insight into and acceptance

[46] 'Even from the point of view of the special sciences, philosophic systems, with their ambitious aims at full comprehensiveness, are not useless. They are the way in which the human spirit cultivates its deeper intuitions. Such systems give life and motion to detached thoughts. Apart from these efforts at co-ordination, detached thoughts would flash out in idle moments, illuminating a passing phase of reflection, and would then perish and be forgotten.' A. N. Whitehead, *Adventures of Ideas* (Penguin edn, 1942), p. 171.
[47] *Return to Philosophy*, p. 201.

of the situation as it is. Philosophy is not, of course, without its drawbacks; there is no money in it save for those who hold university chairs and lectureships; books on philosophy are seldom best-sellers.[48] Suspension of judgment can degenerate into an inert and cowardly scepticism, and philosophic criticism into a tedious analysis of verbalities. Nevertheless, the lively and earnest practice of philosophy can add greatly to the strength, vitality and sincerity of the life of the individual, and through him to that of the community.

Rationalism and empiricism

Reference has already been made to a broad division between two types of or approaches to philosophy, namely rationalism and empiricism; it is now time to examine them more closely. For the moment and in anticipation of the fuller account which follows, the difference between them can be summarised thus: while rationalism (Latin, *ratio*: reason) upholds the primacy and independence of reason in human thought, empiricism (Greek, *empeiria*: experience) puts experience first as the starting-point of knowledge. The two sides represent distinct and apparently incompatible views on the nature of knowledge and on the scope and function of philosophy; for this reason alone it is important to know something of them; they have a further importance for an understanding of the attacks which have been made during the present century on that branch of philosophy known as metaphysics.

The origin of both positions can be found in the Greek pre-Socratic philosophers; of these, Pythagoras (pp. 42–3) and Heraclitus (p. 42), the one by his number theory, the other by his *logos*, opened the way to rationalism; they were followed by Parmenides, who asserted uncompromisingly the power of pure thought divorced from experience to discover truth. In the so-called 'pluralists', however, who include the founders of atomic theory, Leucippus and Democritus, there is an interest in sense perception and a willingness to allow at least a partial validity to the knowledge which it supplies.

From the fourth century B.C. to the time of the Renaissance the dominant view was that of rationalism. The chief reason for this was the powerful influence on subsequent thinkers of Plato and Aristotle, reinforced by Christian theology and the authority of the medieval church. For Plato the material, sensible world was illusory and unreal; the intellect alone gave access to reality and genuine knowledge. Aristotle, though he had strong empirical leanings and can be said with some justice to be the founder of scientific method, never entirely shook off the strongly ration-

[48] Ayer's *Language, Truth and Logic* is a notable exception, and so too is Lee's translation of the *Republic*.

alist outlook of his master. To Christian thinkers the otherworldliness and non-materialism of Plato were deeply congenial; and since they believed that all essential knowledge was given in divine revelation, they were little inclined to seek it by investigating the natural world. Moreover, the prevalent belief in a tiny, compact, geocentric universe exaggerated man's importance and encouraged the view that human reason was adequate to produce from its own resources the whole picture of reality.

In all the centuries between Aristotle, who died in 322 B.C., and the Renaissance, the empirical outlook, though often submerged and regularly subordinated to its rival, was never entirely lost. Aristotle's successors at his philosophical school, the Lyceum, criticised and developed his proposals for a method of scientific investigation, themselves recommending the techniques of impartial observation and experiment. Their work enabled the Greek scientists in Alexandria and other cities of the Graeco-Roman world to make important discoveries in astronomy and the practical sciences. But the experimental outlook was ultimately eclipsed by the authority of Plato, Aristotle and Christian theology, and reappeared only fitfully until the thirteenth century. From that time it was recognised again with increasing insistence that knowledge, at least of the natural world, comes, not from imposing on nature human preconceptions, but from patient observation, supported by experiment, of nature herself. Among the foremost names in this revival of empiricism are two Englishmen, Roger Bacon and William of Ockham. The former deplores subservience to authority in the pursuit of truth, upholds experience as a source of knowledge, and, like his better-known sixteenth-century namesake Francis, suggests methods of experimental investigation. William of Ockham, whose dictum of method was quoted above, also emphasises the need for direct experience as the foundation of our knowledge of the natural world.

It was another three centuries before empiricism firmly penetrated philosophy, for the struggle against long-established rationalist dominance was long and hard. Late in the seventeenth century John Locke, who is often regarded as the founder of modern empirical philosophy, set himself the fundamental task of re-examining the sources of knowledge; it is in experience, he concluded, that 'all our knowledge is founded, and from that it ultimately derives itself' (chapter 6). This is a conclusion directly opposed to Platonic rationalism, which regards as illusory the world of ordinary experience. The empirical theme was developed by George Berkeley and David Hume, the latter of whom adopted an extreme form of empiricism which brought him to the verge of total scepticism. In the nineteenth century another wave of rationalism swept over Europe, to be followed at the beginning of the twentieth by another empiricist reaction.

At the present time rationalism, at least in its extreme form, is out of fashion in much of Europe and emphatically so in Britain. The need to look directly at the world and test observation by experiment is no longer disputed; the successes of science have justified its methods, and the philosopher has accepted boldly, sometimes rashly, the implications of this for his own work. It is not the case, however, that all argument has ceased about the nature and sources of knowledge and about the part played by human reason in acquiring it. Both 'reason' and 'experience' are indeterminate concepts: the meaning of the former, together with the nature and function of what it refers to, needs further exploration; and to say that knowledge derives from experience leaves unanswered the question what constitutes experience. But these are enquiries which cannot be pursued here.

The position of the rationalist philosopher may be stated as follows. There are, he would say, certain truths or principles which human reason, unaided by sense experience, can discover for itself. Such truths, whether they are regarded as self-evident to reason or as apprehended by some special faculty of intuition, are independent of and prior to experience; they are, to use the technical language of epistemology, *a priori*. The human intellect is thus a source of knowledge in itself, and the 'truths of reason' which it apprehends are different from, and most rationalists would add superior to, the knowledge given us through our senses. In support of this alleged superiority it is argued that truths of reason are 'necessary', that is to say, we know in advance of experience that they must be true of experience. Some examples will help to make this clear.

It has sometimes been claimed that the law of causality, i.e. that every effect has a cause, is a truth of reason. If this be granted for the sake of argument, then, before the occurrence of an event x it can be asserted that, if x occurs, it must have been caused. The law does not indicate the actual cause of the particular event, but affirms that there must be one. The same claim has been made for the fundamental laws of logic, the Laws of Identity, Contradiction, and Excluded Middle (p. 30). Again, if this claim be granted, then by virtue of the last of these it can be asserted in advance of experience that an object y is either on the table or not—we know without looking that one or the other, but not both, must be true. Other principles which have beeen claimed as truths of reason are Parmenides' dictum 'it is and cannot not be' (p. 57), which is equivalent to the Law of Contradiction, the dogma of the medieval philosophers that the idea of perfection includes the idea of existence,[49] and Descartes's famous *cogito ergo sum* (chapter 5).

[49] On this they based the ontological proof of God's existence; see pp. 74–5, 93–4.

Truths of reason are of great importance to the rationalist. Their necessity and certainty raises them, in his view, to a level of reality higher than that of sense experience. Truths of fact or experience are all contingent; that is to say, there is no logical (nor, so far as one can see, any other) necessity for their being as they are; logically at least they could be otherwise. This the rationalist regards as deeply unsatisfactory—that there should be anything in the universe exempt from the coherence and explicability that are the mark of reason. Moreover, truths of reason, if they can be discovered, offer a firm foundation for the building of metaphysical systems; for every such system, if it is not to appear arbitrary and insecure, must have an established point of origin, an initial premise or premises from which the rest of the structure can be deduced. Again, truths of reason have been used to justify ethical conclusions; for if, as the rationalist supposes, they give insight into the very nature of reality, it is a reasonable inference that they also imply certain modes of behaviour in the human beings who are involved in that reality. Thus the *logos* of Heraclitus and the Platonic Form of Good, because (in their authors' view) they constitute the basic pattern of the universe of which we are all a part, embody ethical as well as metaphysical implications.

We must now examine the empiricist's position. This, briefly, is that all knowledge, or at least all knowledge of matters of fact, is derived from sense experience; the limits of knowledge, therefore, are the limits of sense experience. (By sense experience he means, of course, to include the various instruments, such as telescopes and seismographs, by which the very limited range of the human senses is extended.) The empiricist, since he believes that all truth is factual, based ultimately on experience, denies that there are truths of reason; the more extreme empiricist dismisses them as fabrications, fictitiously devised to satisfy the human desire for security. That there are *a priori* principles, such as the laws of logic and mathematics, he does not deny; but these, he argues, are either generalisations from experience or prescriptive statements which tell us how we must think or act *if* we wish to do so correctly within a chosen system. It follows from this that the empiricist has no regard for metaphysical system-making of the traditional kind such as can be seen in Plato, Aristotle and Descartes. If there are no truths of reason, there is no basis for the kind of metaphysics which creates comprehensive systems by deduction from so-called first principles. Or at least, while still possessing aesthetic and imaginative value and suggesting ways of exploring experience, they have no foundation in fact. We should not, therefore, look to the great system-makers for ultimate explanations of reality and the purpose of life; or if we do, we must **not be** disappointed if we find their conclusions at variance.

In its simplest terms, then, the issue between the rationalist and the empiricist is this: the former, while admitting that some, perhaps most, of our knowledge comes to us via sense experience, affirms that part—and this the most important because consisting of the very principles on which knowledge is founded—is the creation of unaided human reason; the latter, while admitting that reason contributes to the creation of knowledge, declares that reason, by its very nature, is incapable of initiating knowledge and is idle without material supplied by the senses. The resolution of the issue, even if it is possible at all, is certainly not within the scope of this book; but it may be helpful to indicate some of the arguments on either side and to suggest a tentative conclusion.

The empiricist's case against the rationalist centres on the status of the so-called truths of reason. If the human reason discovers these truths independently of experience, from what sources does it derive them? Apart from bare potentialities which await external stimulus to growth, is there anything in the mind itself which it could draw on to formulate them? Unless one adopts the seventeenth-century theory of 'innate ideas', long since discarded (p. 105), or accepts the Platonic view that the mind recalls truths apprehended in some previous existence (p. 49), it is very difficult to suppose that it has any such material prior to experience. Reason, the empiricist argues, is instrumental; its function is not to create but to exercise a purely logical faculty on the data of sense experience. Even imagination, which admittedly has a creative function, can exercise it only on what is given from outside. Truths of reason, the empiricist maintains, are either empirical generalisations disguised to conceal their origin or prescriptive rules deliberately chosen, like those of logic or Euclidean geometry, to apply within certain areas of experience. Close to the latter alternative is Kant's view that for experience to be possible at all the mind must prescribe certain conditions or categories which serve as a framework for experiencing; they are 'conditions of the possibility of experience' and include, for instance, unity, plurality, negation, cause and necessity (chapter 9). If there are no truths of reason as the rationalist understands them, his claim that the mind is an independent source of knowledge is untenable.

But, the rationalist would retort, neither is sensation, which is the basis of sense experience, an independent source of knowledge. For sensation, before it can be apprehended as anything more than simple sense impressions, must first be perceptualised, that is, incorporated with other sensations into a pattern of meaningful relationships; to become knowledge it must then be conceptualised, that is, generalised and reduced to concepts which the mind can use in its processes of thought. That reason plays some part, therefore, in the creation of knowledge is beyond dispute. (With this the empiricist can agree without yielding his case; for the fact that reason contributes to knowledge does not make it an independent source of knowledge.) Moreover, the search for knowledge must always start with assumptions of some kind: the early Greek philosophers had to assume the rationality of the universe and man's capacity to understand it; the modern physicist assumes a space-time world of external objects which can be expected to exhibit uniformities in their behaviour; to make sense of daily life we must all assume the existence of selves other than our own. In other words, as Kant said, the mind must prescribe in advance of experience the conditions of experiencing. (To this again the empiricist can assent; for he has already argued that truths of reason are prescriptive in just this way, not, as the rationalist would have it, immutable truths which reason somehow discovers.) Finally, in the contingency of empirical fact the rationalist finds an inconsistency with reason's demand for intelligibility, and from this he argues the essential superiority of the rational over the empirical. To which the empiricist's reply would be that the rationalist, like ordinary folk, must learn to accept the givenness of life instead of seeking refuge from its apparent arbitrariness in ideal creations of his own.

The present writer is inclined to the empiricist's position, for he is not persuaded that the simple faculty of reason is capable of conjuring truth from its own resources. He would agree on the other hand that reason plays an indispensable part in the creation of knowledge, first by conceptualising the raw material of experience, second by suggesting principles (for instance, causality, uniformity, coherence and economy) which help to explore and interpret experience. Knowledge, therefore, is the joint product of reason and experience; without sense data reason has nothing on which to exercise its powers; without the organising and conceptualising power of reason sense data would remain momentary and unrelated impressions.

The main branches of philosophy

Within the total activity which constitutes philosophy there have come to be recognised certain broad distinctions of subject-matter, areas of more specialised attention within the general field. These are: logic, which is regularly linked with methodology; epistemology, or theory of knowledge; ethics, which examines problems of right and wrong and conduct; aesthetics, which is concerned with principles of taste and judgment, particularly, but not only, within the arts; and metaphysics, perhaps the most difficult of them all to understand. To these can be added philosophy of science, political philosophy, philosophy of religion, philosophy of history and philosophy of education, each of which (together with other 'philosophies' which might also be mentioned) is a further particularisation of attention within the total field. None of these divisions is self-contained or rigorously exclusive of the rest; logic, for instance, as the study of the principles of valid reasoning and of the methods of investigation, underlies them all; epistemology raises within each of the separate branches the problem of what constitutes knowledge and how it can be attained; aesthetics overlaps with ethics, and political philosophy with ethics and metaphysics. Within the compass of this book it is impossible to give any detailed account of the various subdivisions of philosophy; for this the reader must turn to the works listed for further study (pp. 37–8 and chs 3, 6, 9, 10). All that can be attempted is a summary description, sufficient to guide through the chapters that follow, of logic, epistemology, ethics and metaphysics.

1. *Logic.* Since the time of Aristotle, who first made of it a systematic study, logic has been recognised as of fundamental importance not only to philosophy but to all intellectual activity which aims at what is called the truth; it is the arbiter of all human reasoning. Now reasoning is a process whereby we pass from data to conclusion; whether the data are supplied by physics, theology, mathematics or some practical problem of everyday life makes no difference to the general nature of the process, which is characterised by 'inference'. Inference is the drawing of conclusions; it is a mental or psychological act whereby we move from what is given to what is concluded from the given. Logic is concerned with the validity of inference—whether or not we are justified in inferring a particular conclusion from the data at our disposal. It tests the validity of the inference by examining the implications of the data. Implication, as distinct from inference, is not a mental act but a logical relationship. If A implies B, it may be possible validly to infer B from A; if A never implies B, the inference would be false. Logic may thus be called the science of valid inference or, more correctly, the science of implication.

Within logic a distinction has traditionally been made between deduction and induction. Deduction, it has been said, is a process of reasoning from a general statement or axiom to a particular conclusion, from a premise to what is necessarily implied by it; induction, on the contrary, is a process of arriving at generalisations from particular instances (illustration can be found in the first part of chapter 10). However, this account of deduction and induction as contrasted types of inference moving in opposite directions is neither complete nor wholly accurate as a description of the actual processes of reasoning. A more appropriate contrast might perhaps be between the *necessity* of deductive conclusions and the *probability* (combined with predictive power) of induction.

It is important to note a further distinction, namely between 'true' and 'valid'. Logic is concerned primarily not with truth but with validity. It is perfectly possible to infer a valid but untrue conclusion; it is equally possible to infer a conclusion which is true but invalid; for instance:

(*a*) All vehicles have four wheels; lorries are vehicles; therefore lorries have four wheels.

(*b*) Some Englishmen write poetry; Masefield is an Englishman; therefore Masefield writes poetry.

In (*a*) the conclusion is valid but untrue (because the initial premise is false); in (*b*) the conclusion is true, but it cannot be validly inferred from the two premises. What interests the logician is not so much the factual content of a proposition or statement as its implications, not truth but logical relations. This does not, of course, mean that he is indifferent to truth; indeed his work often contributes indispensably to its discovery. This characteristic of logic is sometimes expressed by saying that logic is a formal study; that is to say, it is concerned with such relationships between propositions as exist independently of their content. Thus, if A includes B and B includes C, then the inference that A includes C is valid whether A, B and C are Easter eggs, glass bottles or biscuit tins. It should not be assumed from this that logical relations are entirely unaffected by the factual content of propositions; but it is sufficiently true to enable logicians to express them symbolically, and in the past hundred years there has been developed a 'symbolic logic' which is wholly expressed in symbols.

An important part of deductive logic is the syllogism, the study of which has occupied an enormous (some would say a disproportionate) amount of attention throughout the history of philosophy. It was Aristotle who first distinguished and analysed syllogistic reasoning; basically it is a form of reasoning which consists of three statements or propositions, the last of which (the conclusion) is necessarily implied by the other two. It can exist in many different forms, but the following will serve as examples:

All Englishmen are Europeans;
Smith is an Englishman;
Smith is a European

No fishes are mammals;
Whales are mammals;
∴ Whales are not fishes.

It is generally accepted that there are four basic varieties or 'figures' of the syllogism, though Aristotle recognised only three of them; and there are further varieties within each of these. The syllogism is a difficult and

complicated subject, the details of which need not detain us; more will
be found on this too in the chapter on Mill.

Reference will be found in textbooks of logic to the so-called 'laws of
thought'; the phrase refers to three rules of right reasoning first enunciated
by Aristotle and traditionally regarded as of fundamental importance;
they are the Law of Identity, the Law of Contradiction, and the Law of
Excluded Middle. The word 'law' is used metaphorically, of course, and
signifies chiefly how we must think if we are to think correctly, that is, its
significance is normative or regulative rather than descriptive (as is the
case with 'laws of nature'). The Law of Identity states that A is A, that a
thing is what it is and must be clearly and unambiguously conceived as
what it is. The Law of Contradiction can be stated in two ways: A is not
not-A, or, A is not both B and not-B; that is to say, contradictory propositions cannot both be true—a tree cannot be both oak and ash, oak and not-
oak. This is the negative formulation of the first law. The third law
asserts that A is either B or not-B, thus excluding any third (or middle)
possibility. Just as the second law asserts that contradictory propositions
cannot both be true, so this asserts that they cannot both be false. These
three laws do not constitute an exhaustive statement of logical principles,
nor are they immune from criticism; but they are valuable guides to clear
and consistent thinking.

(The reader will not, of course, assume that these few paragraphs do
more than graze the fringe of a vast and intricate area of study; the same
comment applies to the sections that follow. All that is intended here is a
minimal orientation to assist him in finding his way through the chapters
that follow.)

2. *Epistemology.* Epistemology, as its derivation suggests (Greek,
epistémé: knowledge), is concerned with knowledge and its associated
problems. It is commonly regarded as the most fundamental of all philosophical studies, since until some answer has been given to the questions
what and how and how far we know, indeed what is *meant* by knowing,
philosophy is likely to be a somewhat vacuous activity.

When a person says that he knows, what does he intend to be understood and how does this assertion differ from saying that he believes?
Perhaps he has an overwhelming sense of assurance that what he says he
knows is true; he is *certain* that this is the case, as Descartes was certain
of the fact of self-consciousness—*cogito ergo sum*. But, as we are all aware,
it is quite possible to have this psychological certainty of the truth of what
we affirm and yet be mistaken. If, then, psychological certainty is not the
basis of knowledge or knowing, what else might it be? Logical certainty,
perhaps—the ability to *prove* what one says one knows? However, proof

is harder to come by than is commonly thought, and in some fields of knowledge is quite impossible in the sense, at least, of conclusive demonstration. In geometry or where in logic one can argue deductively from general premises to particular conclusions, proof of this kind is possible and the claim to know is legitimate. But what of historical events long past or the empirical generalisations of science? To prove conclusively that Julius Caesar landed in Britain in 55 B.C. is simply not possible, powerful though the evidence may be in favour of it; nor can the scientist prove the truth of a general statement or theory, however widely held, for there is always the possibility that further observation may falsify it. It would seem, then, that there are substantial areas of experience where, if proof is required for knowledge, we cannot be said to know the truth of what we affirm but only to believe it.

Suppose, however, we used 'know' and 'knowledge', not as signifying a kind of certainty, whether logical or psychological, but as indicating evidence strong enough to support acceptance of a statement. The difference between knowledge and belief would then be one of the amount and nature of the available evidence; knowledge would still be falsifiable by further observation—it would make sense to say, 'I thought I knew, but I was mistaken'—but it would indicate at least a justifiable claim to commit oneself to the particular proposition in question; 'believe' would indicate a certain hesitation, an inadequacy in the evidence. (This conclusion is in line with the view put forward by some contemporary philosophers that 'know' is simply a token that the person who uses it commits himself to a statement, backs its truth by his personal authority.) But the question remains, What constitutes evidence? What criteria are required to support the claim to know? Agreement would be necessary on this before such a claim could be regarded as established.

Another group of problems centres, as Locke was aware (chapter 6), round the sources of knowledge. Can reason alone, unaided by sensory experience, provide knowledge from itself or must it have the cooperation of the senses? And how far are these latter reliable? The great religions of the world have affirmed that revelation is a source of knowledge, while some philosophers have made a similar claim for intuition: by one or the other means the human consciousness is capable of direct insight into reality. Plato suggested that knowledge is a remembering of what was known to the soul in a previous existence; others that knowledge is somehow innate in the mind and must be nurtured into actuality by careful education. All these suggested sources of knowledge engender problems of singular perplexity. Still further problems arise from a consideration of sense perception and its function in presenting to us what we call the external world: it is obvious that what we perceive depends in part on the

31

nature of our sense organs, and that these are easily deceived or misled; it depends too on space and time—we see the night sky not as it now is but as it was many centuries ago. Some discussion of these problems will be found in the chapters on Berkeley, Hume and Kant.

So perplexing are the difficulties of epistemological enquiry that a number of philosophers have resorted to scepticism, which casts doubt on the whole enterprise of knowledge by questioning its possibility. Traces of scepticism can be found in Socrates, who decided that he was wiser than other men, not because he knew more, but because he was aware of his own ignorance while they were unaware of theirs. This avowal of ignorance was a constructive attempt to clear the way for an approach to genuine knowledge; so too in more recent times we find Descartes using systematic doubt as a means to discovering the one, incontrovertible certainty from which to begin the construction of his philosophical system (chapter 5). But the best known of sceptics is the Scotsman, David Hume (chapter 8): 'In all the incidents of life', he tells us, 'we ought still to preserve our scepticism. . . . Nay, if we are philosophers, it ought only to be upon sceptical principles.'[50] Yet Hume found, as others after him have found, that complete suspension of judgment is a practical impossibility: life demands decision—intellectual, moral, political and many another; moreover, a true sceptic, he admits, will question the validity even of his own scepticism.

The ordinary person is apt to be impatient with epistemology; unlike logic or moral philosophy it seems to have no obvious practical value and to consist largely in splitting hairs about matters which the vast majority of us are content to take on trust. However, there are two things at least which can be said in its defence: first, it is not entirely without practical value, for by dispersing superficial intellectual confidence it can, as Socrates showed, prepare the way for a more fundamental attack on a wide range of philosophical problems; second, the very perplexity of its problems makes it a subject of peculiar fascination for the philosopher, who, as was pointed out earlier, is motivated primarily by the intellectual disquiet and insecurity which spring from his confrontation with puzzlement and paradox.

3. *Ethics*. Ethics examines certain problems which arise within the sphere of human conduct, and of all the branches of philosophy it is thus the one which touches us most closely; in particular it is concerned with three concepts, 'good', 'ought', and 'right', and their practical application.

Like so many other concepts these three, in their everyday usage, are

[50] *A Treatise of Human Nature*, ed. L. A. Selby-Bigge (Oxford, Clarendon Press, 1888), I, iv, 7; p. 270

full of ambiguity; part of the ethical philosopher's task is to clarify them by sifting one meaning from another. 'Good', for instance, can mean instrumentally efficient, that is to say, conducive to a particular end or purpose (and in this sense the instrument can still be said to be good even if the purpose is bad—for instance a sharp knife used for murder); it can also mean 'in conformity with certain agreed standards'; sometimes it refers to the consequences of an action—the latter is good if its results are beneficial; sometimes 'good' means little more than simple approval—'What a good idea!' The attempt at clarification raises numerous questions which ramify into still further questions: is there a supreme good, a *summum bonum* pursued simply for itself and never as a means? If so, what is it?—health, wealth, pleasure, happiness, intellectual activity, serenity? And what do any of these mean? How far is 'good' the expression of a personal or subjective view and how far objective?

The concept 'ought' is similarly ambiguous. 'I ought to do this' can mean at least three things: first, 'if I wish to act consistently with a choice or commitment already made, then this is what I must do'; second, 'the laws of the universe and the circumstances of my own life being such as they are, I am bound to act in such a way' (a combination, this, of necessity with obligation, 'must' with 'ought'); third, 'it is my absolute duty always to do this' (e.g. tell the truth, love my neighbour, etc.). Here also further questions arise: is there (as the third meaning suggests) an 'ought' which transcends time, place and circumstance, and is somehow written into the structure of the universe? Why ought I to do what I ought? Is my 'ought' the same as yours?

'Right' is closely related to 'good' and 'ought', but is not synonymous with either. A proposed action may in itself be good, in that, say, it would relieve distress or bring obvious benefit to numerous people; but it may not be right, whether because it is inopportune at the particular time or inappropriate to a particular person (beyond his competence or financial means) or for some other reason. 'Right' is more often equivalent to 'ought'; what we ought to do is always the right thing to do, but the converse is not necessarily true: a particular action may be right in the sense of unobjectionable or not-wrong (eating a bar of chocolate or staying in bed ten minutes longer), yet there may be no element of obligation attached to it—it is morally indifferent. Again, 'right', like 'good', can be defended in a number of ways; what is right may be said to be what God wills, what conscience demands, what most people approve, what the law requires, or what is in accordance with a rule or rules. The meaning of the concept is complicated by an extension of its use to include 'right' in the sense of entitlement—human rights, political rights, parental rights and so on.

But ethics is concerned not only with the meaning of words and concepts such as these, but also with how we judge in any particular situation *what* is good, *what* is right, *what* we ought to do, that is to say, with the criteria of ethical judgment and their application. This is far from being the simple matter it might appear from the ease with which in daily life we make such decisions. For instance, it is clear that there is a certain amount of relativity in all ethical judgment: because societies and individuals differ in their views of what is good and right, so their ethical judgments differ in regard, say, to chastity, honesty and justice. Philosophers have given many different answers to this question of ethical criteria; two of them are examined in the chapters on Kant and Mill. Numerous other questions arise within the sphere of ethics: are we genuinely free to choose or are our wills wholly or partly determined? is there a distinct faculty of moral judgment—conscience, perhaps—and, if so, how can it be trained? can ethical propositions about good and bad, ought and ought not, be said to be true or false like statements of fact? If not, then how can they be justified or refuted? This last one, the problem of the justification of value judgments, is crucial, and has occupied much attention in recent years; so too has the associated problem of whether it is possible to argue from statements of fact to assertions of value, from 'is' to 'ought'.

It is commonly supposed that the philosopher can show what one ought to do and that this is part of his task; it is further supposed that ethical judgments are demonstrable in the sense that they can be proved. Both these assumptions are dubious; many philosophers would urge that they are altogether wrong. 'The answers to ethical questions', one of them has said, 'can neither be logically demonstrated nor experimentally verified';[51] hence, in the words of another, 'ethics cannot serve practice in more than an advisory capacity'.[52] It would be widely agreed, however, that philosophy can contribute to ethical decision by the clarification of moral concepts, by showing the logical implications of accepted ethical premises, by distinguishing elements of fact and value within the context of ethical choice, and in general by its characteristic antipathy to prejudice and dogma.

4. *Metaphysics.* The origination of this branch of philosophy is usually credited to Aristotle; to him also, quite accidentally and as a sort of historical quirk, we owe the name 'metaphysics' (which, unfortunately, gives no clue to the thing itself). He wrote a book known to us as the

---

[51] C. E. M. Joad, *Guide to the Philosophy of Morals and Politics* (Gollancz, 1938, 5th impr. 1945), p. 148.

[52] A. C. Ewing *Ethics* (English Universities Press, 1953), p. 10.

Physics and another which we now call the *Metaphysics* but to which he himself gave no title; had he done so, it would probably have been 'Fundamental Philosophy' or 'Basic Philosophical Principles'. An early editor of Aristotle's works, Andronicus by name, placed the second of these books after the former in serial order; the Greek for 'after' is *meta*, and the book was therefore referred to as the 'meta-physics'. In origin the word 'metaphysics' means no more than this; it does not, except as a result of later accretion of meaning, signify 'beyond physics', 'ultra-empirical', 'transcendental' or anything similar.

The traditional account of metaphysics is that it is the science of 'being', of 'reality', or of 'ultimate reality'. This also derives from Aristotle, who (though the word itself, of course, was unknown to him) describes metaphysics thus:

There is a science which investigates being *qua* being and its essential attributes. This science differs from all the so-called special sciences in that none of the latter deals generally with being as such. They isolate one part of it and study the essential attributes of that one part.[53]

As William James has said, 'the question of being is the darkest in all philosophy'[54]—not only, one should add, because of its intrinsic obscurity, but also because of the linguistic pitfalls that beset it. There is the fundamental problem of why anything exists at all, ourselves included, and associated problems such as: are there different levels or qualities of existence (substance and attribute, mind and matter, appearance and reality)? is 'reality' one or many, coherent or discrete? is it fundamentally mechanical or personal? There is the problem of time, of change, of cause and effect, development and decay. There are the various concepts which we use in thinking about existence, such as 'same' and 'different', 'quantity' and 'quality', 'absolute' and 'relative', 'finite' and 'infinite', 'accidental' and 'necessary', 'whole' and 'nothing'—all of which require analysis to render them intelligible both in themselves and in their mutual relationships. None of these problems belongs solely to metaphysics; it shares them with the sciences and with other branches of philosophy; its peculiar function, however, is to view them all in the light of the central problem of existence. Nor are they easy problems; indeed they are baffling and obscure. But metaphysics, whatever one's account of it, is a difficult pursuit, and to pretend otherwise would be dishonest.

Associated with this account of metaphysics as concerned with existence or being is the view that its subject is 'reality' as against 'appearance'; for by 'existence' is surely meant that which is essentially and fundamentally

[53] *Metaphysics*, 1003a 21; ed. Warrington, p. 115.
[54] *Some Problems of Philosophy*, p. 46.

real as contrasted with the illusory and deceptive. Since the picture of the world presented by our senses is neither clear nor unambiguous, the instinct for security compels us to look for a certainty which is undistorted by the limitations of human experience. A further offshoot of the traditional view of metaphysics is the belief that it investigates 'ultimate problems'. It has been said above that one function of philosophy is to examine the problems and perplexities thrown up by experience; any such problem is apt to lead to another and deeper one, and this in turn to a problem profounder still. Hence there is a kind of recession to an ultimate point of questioning which marks the apparent limit of enquiry. It is the examination of such terminal problems which, on this view, is the peculiar province of metaphysics.

It has been the custom of metaphysical philosophers to construct 'systems', that is to say, logically coherent, comprehensive accounts of reality aimed at explaining experience. Such systems vary in rigour and complexity from the simple *logos* formula of Heraclitus (p. 14 and note) and the loose, imaginative constructions of Plato, to the more stringent logical coherence of Descartes. They have the common aim, however, of displaying the basic structure or pattern of 'ultimate reality' and of offering in terms of this an all-embracing formula of explanation. In some an additional aim has been to find a convincing basis for morality or, as it has been expressed, 'to get morality transcendentally underwritten',[55] to find sanctions for moral conduct somewhere 'outside' or 'beyond' the world of everyday experience.

The validity of these metaphysical systems (indeed of metaphysical systems of any kind) has been severely attacked by David Hume (pp. 141, 206–7) and more recently by the logical positivists (see chapter 11); the current fashion is to dismiss them as imaginative structures of no more than aesthetic value. Thus Hans Reichenbach: 'Many a philosophical system is . . . a masterpiece of poetry, abundant in pictures that stimulate our imagination, but devoid of the power of clarification that issues from scientific explanation.'[56] Kant also rejected metaphysics of the traditional kind, but was willing to allow a metaphysics which concerned itself with the presuppositions of knowledge, that is, with the conceptual framework which (in his view) the human mind imposed from within itself on the data of experience (p. 163).

There is no space here to attempt a defence of metaphysics, but this much, perhaps, may be said in conclusion: human experience is conditioned by the limitations of human sense and intellect; we are placed, as observers, in a definite setting—temporal and historical, geographical,

[55] D. F. Pears, ed., *The Nature of Metaphysics* (Macmillan, 1957), p. 15.
[56] *The Rise of Scientific Philosophy*, p. 9.

social, personal—which inhibits the answering of the questions which concern us most deeply; there is, moreover, an element of mystery in experience which experience itself cannot dispel. Hence there is in man a natural urge towards metaphysical explanations which transcend the limits of experience; 'the heart's unrest', it has been remarked, 'is not to be stilled by logic'[57]—nor, it may be added, by scientific enquiry. These considerations do not constitute a justification of metaphysics, but they may incline us to regard it more sympathetically.

[57] F. Waismann, 'How I see philosophy', *loc. cit.*, p. 460.

Further study

Readers who wish to extend this introductory survey of philosophy and philosophical problems will find the following helpful: E. R. EMMET, *The Use of Reason* (Longmans, 1960), and *Learning to Philosophise* (Longmans, 1964). Both these books are designed to encourage the practice of philosophical thinking and include numerous exercises together with solutions and/or comments. Similar in purpose, and including lists of topics for discussion and essays, is F. VIVIAN, *Thinking Philosophically* (Chatto & Windus, 1969). Another valuable introduction, much longer and at a deeper level, is J. HOSPERS, *An Introduction to Philosophical Analysis* (Routledge, 1956); there is also a companion volume to this, *Readings in Introductory Philosophical Analysis* (Routledge, 1969).

A. C. EWING, *The Fundamental Questions of Philosophy* (Routledge, 1951) has an initial chapter on the nature and value of philosophy, and then surveys many of its traditional problems. An older book, and now a classic of its kind, is BERTRAND RUSSELL, *The Problems of Philosophy* (Oxford University Press, 1912 and often reprinted). *Reconstruction in Philosophy*, by the American pragmatist JOHN DEWEY (Beacon Press, enlarged edn, 1948) is an interesting survey from his particular viewpoint of the mood of philosophy in the early twentieth century.

Among more recent books are: S. KÖRNER, *What is Philosophy?* (Allen Lane, The Penguin Press, 1969)—a wide-ranging book and in parts difficult for the beginner; K. BRITTON, *Philosophy and the Meaning of Life* (Cambridge University Press, 1969); J. HARTNACK, *Philosophical Problems* (Copenhagen, Munksgaard, 1962); and R. J. HIRST, ed., *Philosophy* (Routledge, 1968). The last of these introduces philosophy through its major traditional branches—logic, epistemology, etc.; it has a final chapter on social and political philosophy. Many others less recent are referred to in the notes above.

For the history of philosophy and for reference to specific topics the reader may consult: F. C. COPLESTON, *A History of Philosophy* (Burns & Oates, 8 vols, 1947–66); A. G. N FLEW, *An Introduction to Western Philosophy* (Thames & Hudson, 1970); and D. J. O'CONNOR, *A Critical History of*

Western Philosophy (New York, The Free Press of Glencoe, 1964). Invaluable for its summary critical accounts of philosophers and philosophical problems is *The Encyclopedia of Philosophy*, ed. P. EDWARDS (New York, Macmillan Company and The Free Press, 8 vols, 1967). G. J. WARNOCK, *English Philosophy since 1900* (Oxford University Press, 2nd edn, 1969) is a very helpful survey of contemporary and near-contemporary English philosophy; wider and far more detailed is J. PASSMORE, *A Hundred Years of Philosophy* (Duckworth, 1957).

Articles on the various issues examined in the present book can be found in the philosophical journals such as *Mind, Analysis, Philosophy*, the *Aristotelian Society Proceedings* and *Supplements*, and *The Philosophical Quarterly*; but these articles are not written primarily for the philosophical novice! There are further articles and an extensive bibliography in the Macmillan 'Modern Studies in Philosophy' series; this series now includes all the philosophers who head the chapters below except (at the time of writing) the Logical Positivists.

2   Plato

Universals

Biographical note

Plato was born about 427 B.C., a member of a distinguished and ancient Athenian family. Little is known of his early life, but presumably he received the education normal for a boy of his class; in addition he was privileged to attend and, no doubt, to take part in the discussions between Socrates and his friends which Plato illustrates in his early dialogues. The result of this was a profound admiration for Socrates and an equally profound shock when the Athenian democracy put him to death in 399 B.C. on charges which were obviously manufactured for the occasion. It was the consequent disillusionment that, more than anything else, turned Plato from politics, to which he was originally committed, to philosophy. Throughout his youth and early manhood Athens was engaged in a war which ended disastrously in military defeat and occupation; Plato served in the Athenian army and according to tradition was decorated for valour. The end of the war brought political chaos, with now one party now another in power; intrigue and violence were its natural accompaniment. Equally evident was the moral chaos due partly to the sufferings of war, partly to the collapse of the traditional religion and the sanctions of conduct that it had supported, partly to the work of the sophists (p. 50 and note). The death of Socrates and the political and moral circumstances of his time were powerful influences in determining the purpose and direction of Plato's thought.

In later years Plato travelled abroad, probably visiting many parts of the Mediterranean world and certainly southern Italy and Sicily; in the former he would meet the followers of Pythagoras, who were strongly established there; in Sicily he made more than one attempt at different times to interfere in the politics of the town of Syracuse, but to no avail. The main work of his life, apart from his writings, was the founding in Athens of a philosophical school called the Academy (after the district of Athens in which it was situated). Despite the modern implication of 'academic', Plato's school was no ivory tower of seclusion from the realities of life. His experiences in Athens and abroad had shown him

that all existing states were badly governed, and that their constitutions were incapable of reform without drastic treatment and a great deal of good luck. I was forced, in fact, to the belief that the only hope of finding justice for society or for the individual lay in true philosophy, and that mankind will have no respite from trouble until either real philosophers gain political power or politicians become by some miracle true philosophers.[1]

Thus, though research was prominent in the activities of the Academy, its initial purpose may well have been the training of 'philosopher-kings' for the purpose of reforming the internal politics of the Greek city-state.

Almost all Plato's writings are in dialogue form; the exceptions are the Apology, *which gives an account of Socrates' answer to the charges brought against him at his trial, and a number of letters of which some, including the important* Seventh Letter, *are believed to be authentic. Of the dialogues, the best known, perhaps, is the* Republic, *which begins with a discussion of justice or right conduct and proceeds to an account of the ideal society; the* Phaedo, *set in an Athenian prison on the day of Socrates' execution, is concerned with the immortality of the soul. Other well-known dialogues are the* Symposium (Drinking Party), *whose subject is love and beauty, and the* Timaeus, *which describes the creation and structure of the universe; those which are most relevant for the Theory of Forms are mentioned in the suggestions for further study. Plato was not only a great philosopher but also a talented writer; his dialogues display a high order of imagination, dramatic skill and command of language; of their kind they are unsurpassed in European literature. Clearly there was much in him of the poet and the artist, and when he tells us in the* Republic *that poetry and philosophy are in perpetual conflict with each other he is revealing a struggle within his own nature.*

The world of daily experience appears to consist of a vast number of separate items—chairs, trees, dogs, men and women, ships, stars and so on; such, presumably, is how it impinges on the mind of an infant, though he is not, of course, consciously aware of this manifold separateness or capable of thinking about it. But the growing child soon learns to distinguish and to express in language resemblances, differences and other relations between the objects he perceives; he learns that 'dog' can refer not only to the family pet but also to the one next door or up

---

[1] *Seventh Letter*, 326a–b; quoted in H. D. P. Lee, *Plato: the Republic* (Penguin, 1955), p. 14.

the road, that other children have mummies and daddies, houses and gardens, that a number of quite different things can be called 'red', and that 'hot' describes fires, kettles, storage heaters, electric irons and other household articles. To think and speak thus in general terms instead of referring to every object of experience as a distinct and unrelated item is essential to the child's mental development and to civilised life; without this capacity for generalisation it would be impossible for thought to range beyond the immediate here and now, impossible to communicate with other people except in a most rudimentary manner, impossible to understand what had not come within the orbit of direct personal experience. If 'flower' meant only *this* flower in *this* corner of *my* garden, I could never appreciate my friend's description of his own garden or of his visit to Kew; if 'hot' referred only to *this* electric fire, a child could never understand (and it would be impossible to warn him) except by actually touching them that irons and kettles are also hot and to be avoided. In fact general words—verbs and adverbs as well as nouns and adjectives—compose by far the greater part of any advanced language, the remainder consisting almost entirely of proper names like John and London.

Yet common and necessary as these general terms are, they have been a constant source of philosophical perplexity. In the room in which I am writing there are three kinds of chair, different in shape, size and the materials of which they are made; despite their differences, however, they are all recognisably chairs, for they have in common certain distinguishable features, such as legs and a seat and are used for the same purpose. One might perhaps say that they all have the quality or nature of 'chairness'. Again, there are many things in the world which might be described as beautiful—a flower, a sunset, a picture, a woman, a dress; all have (or seem to have) something in common which prompts us to attribute to them the same quality of beauty. So too with actions: we speak of this or that or another deed as just or generous, for there seems to attach to all of them a certain common quality of justice or generosity which enables us to describe them all by the same adjective. Such general qualities or natures—'chairness', beauty, justice, generosity—are known as universals, and the philosophical problem they raise is this: what kind of thing is a universal? what is it we refer to in using general words of this kind? It is all very well to speak of 'chairness', 'beauty' and the rest, but no one has actually seen or experienced them apart from a particular chair or a particular object of beauty. Do universals, then, exist separately from the objects that embody them? and, if so, do they exist in our minds or quite independently both of our minds and of objects? or are universals merely a trick of thought and language to enable us to apprehend and to communicate intelligibly about the world we live in?

For a number of reasons Plato had a special interest in the problem of universals. One of these was the influence of Socrates, for whom he evidently had a great admiration. Socrates made a point of discussing with his friends and acquaintances (of whom Plato was one) such moral qualities as courage and justice and goodness, trying by careful interrogation and argument to elicit their essential nature: we point to this or that particular deed as courageous, but what is courage itself? What is the essence of the quality which in all its particular manifestations distinguishes it as courage and not some other quality? These were questions that Socrates never answered—such indeed was not his purpose, but rather to stimulate in those who argued with him the desire for clarity and precision and the humility that comes from awareness of ignorance. On Plato at least he impressed the desire to investigate further these and other universals, and to explore the whole question of their relationship to the objects or actions that seem to embody them.

Another important influence was the earlier philosopher Heraclitus, one of whose principal doctrines was that the whole universe is in a constant state of change or flux; nothing is the same from one moment to the next; one cannot literally step into the same river twice, for its waters have moved between the first occasion and the second (p. 14 and note). This has disturbing epistemological implications, for how can one be said to *know* what is for ever shifting and changing and never the same? Knowledge, surely, is secure; knowledge is of the permanent, the fixed, the dependable; in a world of flux, therefore, knowledge has no place. Plato was inclined to accept the Heraclitean doctrine of flux; on the other hand he was firmly convinced that knowledge was both necessary and possible. What, then, can be known? If not the ever-shifting objects of the everyday world, the manifold mutable variety of particular things, then perhaps the universals, which seem to offer a permanence and stability secure enough for genuine knowledge.

Pythagoras was another who shaped the direction of Plato's thinking about universals. A strange mixture of mathematician and mystic, he had founded a religious society in southern Italy towards the end of the sixth century and engaged in mathematical research; apart from the well-known geometrical theorem associated with his name he also discovered that the chief musical intervals or consonances can be expressed in simple numerical ratios—the octave 2 : 1, the fifth 3 : 2, the fourth 4 : 3;[2] from this he went on to suggest that the whole of reality is explicable in mathematical terms

[2] A piece of taut string gives a certain note when plucked; a piece half the length at the same tension gives a note an octave higher; a piece three-quarters of the length gives the fourth note in the octave; a piece two-thirds of the length gives the fifth.

and even that numerical patterns spatially extended in three dimensions compose the basic structure of the physical universe. From Pythagoras Plato derived both a special interest in mathematical universals—triangle, square, circle, etc.—and also a mystical turn of thought which encouraged him to suppose (as we shall see) that universals exist quite independently of the objects that manifest them and of the human minds that conceive them.

A further and personal incentive to investigate universals sprang from Plato's own experience of Athenian life and politics in the tragic years of war and its aftermath of revolution and intrigue. Not only was there a lack of political and social stability, but the questioning of traditional values and conduct, begun long before Plato was born, had quickened to the point where ethical norms were in danger of complete collapse, leaving the individual at best in deep perplexity as to right and wrong, at worst in a condition of moral licence. The desperate need was for assured standards in both personal and social life, so that order, stability, security and decent behaviour might be re-established in an eminently diseased society. In ethical universals like goodness and justice, thought Plato, such standards might indeed be found, permanent exemplars which we should strive to emulate in our individual lives and to embody in the ordering of society.

We turn now to Plato's own account of universals, generally known as his Theory of Forms or of Ideas; but two words of caution are necessary first. The Greek word *eidos*, of which 'Form' is a translation, means 'outward appearance', 'form', 'shape', 'pattern'; it is linked etymologically with the Latin *video*, 'I see' and the English 'visible', 'vision', etc. Plato also uses the word *idea*, which in Greek means more or less the same but to the English reader suggests a mental concept or idea existing only in the mind; since this was certainly not Plato's view of universals, the word 'idea' is best avoided in this context and we shall use, therefore, the term 'Theory of Forms'. Second, it need not be supposed that the theory was a permanent and unalterable part of his philosophy; much of what Plato wrote was tentative and hypothetical, suggestions for discussion rather than dogmatic conclusions; and although the theory was for a long time central to his thought and profoundly influenced it, yet in view of the difficulties it raises (which Plato was far too intelligent to overlook) it seems unlikely that he held it unmodified to the end of his life.

In some respects Plato's answer to the problem of universals was clear and specific: a universal (or Form, to use his own word) is something which exists quite independently not only of its manifestations in particular objects or actions but also of the human mind; it is neither an idea (in the modern sense) nor a concept; nor is it simply a word which describes what is common to a number of different entities. A Form exists actually, substantially and in its own right; furthermore it is only Forms that are fully real, fully existent—the particulars which manifest them belong to the fleeting, impermanent world of Heraclitean flux. Forms are also non-sensible; they cannot be apprehended by sight or hearing or any other of the human senses, but only by the intellect in complete isolation from any kind of sensory interference. Plato is emphatic on this point; not only is it an essential element in his Theory of Forms, but his rejection of sense perception in favour of pure intellectual cognition is fundamental to his whole philosophy. Again, since Forms are the very essence of the nature or quality with which they are identified—beauty, goodness, etc.— it follows that they are permanent and immutable; being already perfect of their kind—*absolute* beauty or beauty *itself*, in Plato's words—they cannot change for the better nor without ceasing to be Forms can they change for the worse: they are eternal patterns of perfection. Finally, the Forms 'share' their peculiar essence with the objects and events of sense perception, so that these latter, by 'participating' each in its appropriate Form, take on its quality and display it (though imperfectly and fragmentarily) in themselves.

Plato nowhere gives us a complete and coherent exposition of his Theory of Forms, but the description in the previous paragraph emerges with reasonable consistency from the various passages in the dialogues where he discusses it. Yet there is much that he leaves unclear, and a number of uneasy questions spring at once to mind. If Forms have a separate existence of their own apart from the human mind and from the sensory world, *where* do they exist and *how*? What are there Forms of—all general terms or universals without exception, including mud and stone, artifacts like chairs and tables, and organic creatures like birds and worms, or only of ethical, aesthetic and mathematical universals? How do particular objects 'share' in the Forms whose qualities they display? Plato has no satisfactory answer to any of these questions, though he was undoubtedly aware of the difficulties they raise and thought seriously about them; the Theory of Forms, it should be remembered, was not a finalised and coherent philosophical scheme but rather a tentative blueprint to be improved and no doubt amended by prolonged and meticulous examination. To the first of them—where and how do Forms exist?—his answer would be that they exist in a transcendent, suprasensible world which is never fully accessible to the human mind so long as it remains embodied, though before birth and again after death that which is immortal in us, when unencumbered by bodily impediment, may succeed in approaching them. As to how they exist or what kind of existence they enjoy, Plato could only say that it is existence of the purest and most absolute kind, the very quintessence of existence such as the mind, whether embodied or not, is incapable of apprehending. Clearly Plato was aware that he was pushing into regions unknown and unintelligible to human reason; hence so often in writing of this transcendent world he uses myth and metaphor borrowed from contemporary religious cults and the mystical doctrines of Pythagoras.[3]

To the second question a more definite yet still incomplete answer can be given. Of the existence of ethical, aesthetic and mathematical Forms (goodness, beauty, circularity) Plato had no doubt at all; and he was aware that logically his theory required the existence of Forms for universals of every kind, including artifacts, organisms and negative or contrary qualities like ugliness and evil. In one of his dialogues, the *Parmenides*, he admits both this logical implication of his theory and his own uncertainty on the matter. Parmenides, a fifth-century philosopher considerably older than Socrates, asks him whether he thinks there are Forms of man or of fire or water, and Socrates confesses his perplexity; Parmenides presses the point by asking whether there are Forms of hair, mud, dirt and other such commonplace or worthless items, and to this Socrates replies:

No . . . it would be quite absurd to think there are Forms of these. Yet I am sometimes harassed by the thought that possibly the same principle applies to everything; then, when I have arrived at this position, I shy off for fear of coming to grief by falling into some pit of nonsense. So when I reach the things which I have already admitted have Forms [the beautiful, the good, etc.] I stop there and busy myself with them.[4]

On the other hand, in the *Seventh Letter* (generally accepted as authentic) Plato seems to admit a far wider range of Forms, including those of artifacts and natural objects, fire and water, animals, qualities of character, and actions and passions of every kind.[5] Beyond this we cannot go; it must be admitted that Plato never worked out his Theory of Forms to logical completeness, but his intense interest in morals and mathematics convinced him of the existence at least of Forms within these areas, and with this he was content as a working basis.

The last question—how do particulars participate in Forms?—must also be left open, though it constitutes one of the greatest difficulties in the theory and for that matter in Plato's whole philosophy. Plato is quite sure that particular things derive both their being and their quality from participation in the appropriate Forms; he uses numerous expressions to describe this relationship—participation, sharing, partnership, imitation, resemblance and others—but nowhere does he clarify its precise nature.

---

[3] As, for instance, in the Myth of Er in *Republic* X, and Diotima's account of the ascent of the soul in the *Symposium*.

[4] *Parmenides*, 130c–d.

[5] 342d.

In fact so great is the gulf which he places between sensible objects and the transcendent world of Forms that it is difficult to see how any bridge can be made to cross it; difficult, too, to see how things of fundamentally different natures—the absolute essential being of the Forms and the partial, transitory existence of sensible objects—can ever be brought into a genuine mutuality of relationship. Aristotle, a pupil of Plato and his strongest critic, was quick to seize on this weakness: 'To call the Forms "patterns" and to assert that other things "participate" in them is to talk in empty metaphor.'[6] Metaphors, certainly; but how far they are empty is something Plato would no doubt want to argue further.

We turn now to the part played by the Forms in the overall context of Plato's philosophy. Apart from offering a solution to the problem of universals, their function, briefly, is metaphysical, epistemological and ethical. These roles overlap and it would be mistaken to regard them as rigidly distinct, but for exposition and illustration it will be simpler to take them separately and in that order. In the dialogue *Timaeus*, where Plato attempts an account of the origin and structure of the universe, the Forms play an essential part in creation; they are one of three main elements in reality, the others being Soul and Matter.[7] Soul is the dynamic, organising principle responsible for such order, coherence and purpose as the physical universe possesses; it is a principle of change and growth, though itself uncreated and imperishable; and in view of the uniformity and regularity of natural processes Soul must also be regarded as rational. But Soul needs a pattern to guide its operations, and this pattern is provided by the Forms; they are the perfect types or models of all that can exist; themselves also uncreated and immutable they constitute, as it were, the ultimate blueprint of perfection which Soul must try to embody in its cosmic architecture. The nature of the third element, Matter, is not clear, for Plato describes it only in metaphor. It was obvious, however, that something was needed on which the purposive activity of Soul could impose the pattern of the Forms; what he has in mind is a kind of indeterminate space which lacks form and quality but is capable of receiving them. This third element is also, in Plato's view, the source of evil and imperfection in the world as

---

[6] *Metaphysics* 991a 20–22, trans. Warrington, p. 77.
[7] 'Soul' and 'matter' are liable to mislead because of their modern associations. The basic meaning of the Greek *psyche*, translated 'soul', is 'life', 'life-principle', the source in all organisms of their unity, identity and power of growth, and in man of consciousness; later it came to mean 'personality', 'character', then 'soul' in a sense akin to our own use. Plato's 'matter' is no more solid than that of modern atomic physics; he calls it 'receptacle of becoming', 'nurse of becoming' and *ekmageion*, 'towel', meaning by this last something which passively receives the impress of any object applied to it.

we know it; for it is essentially non-rational, governed only by blind forces operating with mechanical necessity.

In cosmic creation the Forms are only one of three elemental constituents, and the work of world construction is shared with Soul, which figures almost as a senior partner selecting and organising patterns which the Forms supply. However, in an earlier dialogue, the *Republic*, the position of supremacy is occupied by the Form of Good, in writing of which Plato uses language comparable with that used by religious writers of God. Through the mouth of Socrates he is arguing that the rulers of the ideal state must be thoroughly imbued with the highest form of knowledge and that this is knowledge of the essential nature of goodness which is 'the end of all endeavour, the object on which every heart is set'.[8] This essence of goodness is, of course, the Form of Good. He continues:

What gives the objects of knowledge their truth and the mind the power of knowing is the Form of the Good. It is the cause of knowledge and truth, and you will be right to think of it as being itself known, and yet as being something other than, and even higher than, knowledge and truth. . . The Good . . . may be said to be the source not only of the intelligibility of the objects of knowledge, but also of their existence and reality; yet it is not itself identical with reality, but is beyond reality and superior to it in dignity and power.[9]

Thus, over and above the particular Forms, each of which, of its kind, is a unique and absolute reality, there reigns the Form of Good, the ultimate, transcendent source of all being and all knowledge.

Elsewhere Plato uses the Forms as the basis for a theory of causation (of which there are hints in the passage just quoted). In the *Phaedo*, for instance, after discussing other theories of causation, particularly that of Anaxagoras who said that 'it is Mind that produces order and is the cause of everything',[10] he says (again through the mouth of Socrates):

I cannot understand these other ingenious theories of causation. If someone tells me that the reason why a given object is beautiful is that it has a gorgeous colour or shape or any other such attribute, I disregard all these other explanations—I find them all confusing—and I cling simply and straightforwardly and no doubt foolishly to the explanation that the one thing that makes that object beautiful is the presence in it or association with it (in whatever way the relation comes about) of absolute Beauty. I do not go so far as to insist on the precise details; only upon the fact that it is by Beauty that beautiful things are beautiful.[11]

Similarly, 'it is also by largeness that large things are large and larger things larger, and by smallness that smaller things are smaller'.

[8] 505e; trans. Lee, p. 269.   [9] 508e–509b; *ibid*., p. 273.
[10] 97c; H. Tredennick, *Plato: the last days of Socrates* (Penguin, 1954), p. 129.   [11] 100c–d; *ibid*., p. 133.

Finally, the Forms are essentially and absolutely real; they are the very acme and criterion of reality, existence, being. The everyday world of objects and events is in a state of constant change or flux; in organic natures there is the familiar process of growth and decay; in material substance there is change of shape and position, the transformation of elements, the movement of wind and water, sun and stars; in man there is the fickleness of shifting desires which dart unsatisfied from one enticement to the next. All this belongs to the realm of non- or partial reality; for Plato the real is the eternal and immutable; all else is but a shadow or reflection of the actuality of existence; whatever of limited reality there is in ordinary things is due to the Forms (and to them also, of course, is due the fact that things occur in groups or classes). He illustrates this in the *Republic* by two famous analogies, the Line and the Cave, in which metaphysics and epistemology are closely intervolved.

In the analogy of the Line all existing things are divided into four levels according to the degree of reality they embody; corresponding to these are four levels of knowledge. At the bottom of the scale of existence are shadows, images and dreams, next above them the world of physical objects; in the scale of knowledge the former belong to illusion, the latter to opinion or belief. The third level is that of mathematical objects; the fourth is that of Forms, which enjoy the purest existence and are apprehended at the culmination of the most intense intellectual endeavour. The lower two levels belong to the physical world, the world of matter; the higher belong to the world of genuine existence and genuine knowledge; highest of all in the scale both of existence and of knowledge is the Form of Good, the source of all knowledge and the ultimate goal of human aspiring.

The analogy of the Cave carries the same message in more picturesque form. Imagine, says Plato, a long cave, at the far end of which and in almost total darkness is a row of prisoners bound and chained so that they can look only straight ahead at the end-wall of the cave in front of them. Behind and above them, but still far from the entrance, is a raised path which crosses the cave from wall to wall and is bordered by a parapet on the side nearest the prisoners. Along the path walk men carrying in their upstretched arms puppets whose shadows are cast by a light on to the end-wall of the cave; the shadows of the men themselves are intercepted by the parapet. All that the prisoners can see is the shadows of the puppets; this is all that they can know of reality—mere images of images, the insubstantial outlines of things which themselves are only copies. The goal of human endeavour for those who can achieve it is to secure liberation from the darkness and passivity of ignorance into the full light of day, whose sun is the Form of Good. In these two analogies reality and knowledge are bound together; the level of one is the level of the other. Especially noteworthy in the Line is the place of mathematics, for it is a bridge between two worlds: both in arithmetic (at first) and in geometry tangible and visible objects are used to assist intellectual effort—nuts to count with, lines and circles for problems in geometry. These objects, as such, belong to the world of partial reality; yet from the former the mind abstracts pure number, from the latter the perfect form of line and circle, and thus proceeds to the Forms themselves.

Epistemologically the Forms provide the only secure basis for knowledge, as the analogy of the Line has already suggested. Just as Plato draws a firm distinction between the suprasensible world of genuine existence and the illusory world of sense perception, so also he sharply divides knowledge from belief. The former is certain and infallible, the latter tentative and liable to error. Even *true* belief does not constitute knowledge; for it is characteristic of knowledge that it can give an account of itself; it is based on understanding, insight and causal explanation; once attained it persists unchanged. True belief, on the contrary, is the result of conditioning or persuasion and can be modified by the same means as produced it; its truth involves no insight but is secondhand, fortuitous. So too with the objects of knowledge and belief; the former must have the same permanence and stability as knowledge itself; to be fully intelligible they must be fully real; the latter share the same features of mutability and impermanence as their corresponding mental state. Clearly only the Forms can satisfy the requirements of knowledge; it follows that those who are capable—pre-eminently, of course, the philosophers—must strive by arduous intellectual endeavour to climb the Line from one stage to the next until, at the level of the Forms, they emerge into the light of genuine knowledge.

Yet strictly speaking knowledge in this life is not so much acquired as re-acquired. For Plato believed that man has something immortal in him which includes the faculty of intellectual insight. Birth is the incarnation of a pre-existing soul and involves forgetting knowledge already acquired. (In this, Plato reveals the influence of Pythagoras and his followers, who believed in some kind of successive reincarnation.) Knowledge for the embodied mind is therefore more properly called reminiscence or recollection. How seriously Plato expects his readers to take him is difficult to say, but leaving this question aside, knowledge as recollection equally assumes the existence of Forms; for these are an abiding reality, the only possible source of a knowledge which transcends the vagaries of birth and death. This is how (through Socrates) he reasons in the *Phaedo*, linking the existence of Forms with knowledge as recollection and using both to support his arguments for the immortality of the soul.

The ethical importance of the Forms must already be obvious: they supply absolute standards by which particular choices, actions or qualities of character can be objectively assessed; and they constitute ideals of perfection which provide stimulus and direction for human aspiration. Because the Forms actually exist as transcendent realities, they give to moral judgment an objectivity and a reliability which it must otherwise lack; and because they are perfect of their kind, they are the ultimate objects of human desiring, compared with which all else pales into triviality. Individuals differ in their moral judgments; they are swayed by passion and self-interest; considerations of right and wrong yield place to expediency and the authority of superior power. Especially was this true in the Athens of Plato's time; prolonged and total war had left its inevitable mark on the character of her citizens; conduct was debased, motives constricted by opportunism and the demands of self-preservation. Traditional values were further undermined by certain professional teachers called sophists,[12] of whom many encouraged their pupils to question accepted norms of behaviour without offering them any substitute. The decline of religion had left it with little more than a formal hold on the majority of educated people. From two directions, therefore, there was impressed on Plato the need for moral absolutes: philosophically, to explain the universal element in all particulars of the same ethical quality and to establish objective criteria for ethical judgment; socially, to counteract moral drift by substituting the guidance of positive ideals. Both these purposes are combined in the Form of Good: not only is this the essence of being, the ground of all knowing and the ultimate ethical universal; it also provides the necessary pattern for the construction of the ideal state and the regulation of individual conduct within it. Hence the central purpose of the utopia which Plato sketches out in the *Republic* is to reflect in a temporal setting the transcendent world of Forms; this is achieved, as far as may be, by a system of education which, for the elite who receive it, culminates in the vision of the Good:

When they are fifty, those who have come through all our practical and intellectual tests with success must be brought to their final trial and made to lift their mind's eye to look at the source of all light and see the Good itself, which they can then take as a pattern for ordering their own life as well as that of society and the individual.[13]

Some indication has already been given of the weaknesses in the Theory of Forms and reference made to Aristotle's criticism of it (his own solution

___

[12] Not originally a derogatory term, though it rapidly became so. In the following century Aristotle described a sophist as a man who makes money by the appearance of knowledge without the reality (*Sophistical Refutations*, 165a).   [13] 540a; trans. Lee, p. 310.

will be found in the following chapter). Its gravest defect, undoubtedly, is the dualism it creates between Forms and the particulars which 'participate' in them, between the real and the unreal, between objects of knowledge and objects of belief. Here are two distinct categories of existence and of intelligibility which are nevertheless united in our experience of the every-day world; yet this union of incompatibles Plato leaves wholly unexplained. It could also be objected that the theory is unnecessarily complicated: Plato has tried to make the Forms do too much. In daily experience universals make at least practical sense; they perform a recognisably important task by giving generality to thought and language. Admittedly this raises problems of logic—the meaning of general terms and their relationship both to each other and to particulars; of language—the linguistic origin of general terms and their function in actual use; and of psychology— why the mind needs universal concepts for its interpretation of experience and how they are formed. By elevating universals to an implausible transcendent status and associating them with far wider issues of meta-physics, ethics and cosmology Plato has made an already difficult set of problems far more intractable. Equally it might be argued that his solution is incomplete: his interest is restricted to a narrow range of universals derived in the main from nouns and adjectives, and these predominantly ethical and mathematical; but general terms include also verbs, adverbs, prepositions, conjunctions—indeed virtually all words save proper names —but the Theory of Forms is little concerned with these. Despite its defects, however, the theory marked an important philosophical advance: it affirmed that the world is more than physical matter (thus contradicting the conclusions of some of the early Greek scientists)—there is a realm of spiritual entities which is not wholly inaccessible to man; and the world is more than a flux of indeterminates—there is real being, real knowledge, objective values. Bertrand Russell has found it possible to describe the theory as 'one of the most successful attempts hitherto made' to solve the problem of universals;[14] the degree of its success is arguable, but that the attempt was notable and widely influential can readily be conceded.

The problem has remained since Plato's time a major, and still open, philosophical issue. Three main solutions have been proffered, known technically as realism,[15] nominalism and conceptualism. The first of these asserts that universals exist independently of the mind; their existence is

[14] *The Problems of Philosophy* (Oxford University Press, 1912, repr. 1946), p. 91.
[15] Realism in the present context must be distinguished from two other uses of the word: to indicate belief in the independent, extra-mental existence of physical objects; and, popularly, to refer to an attitude of hard-headed matter-of-factness.

real, actual, substantial, and in no way derived from human intellectual activity. For universals to be *known* there must indeed be a mind or minds capable of knowing them; but this is not true of their existence. Clearly, Plato was a realist; but so too was Aristotle, and this points to an important distinction within the realist position. Aristotle rejected the doctrine of the Theory of Forms that universals enjoy a transcendent existence which is independent both of the mind and of their manifestation in particulars; for him, universals exist surely enough, whether or not there are minds to apprehend them, but only as elements common to particulars of the same class; in other words, there can be no universals without instances of them, and Plato's transcendentalism is a metaphysical extravagance. We shall see more of Aristotle's views in succeeding pages.

The nominalist position is that universals do not exist in their own right; admittedly, there are resemblances between different objects—lemons are yellow, stones hard—but every occurrence of yellow or hardness is a separate localised instance peculiar to the object which it qualifies, not a common factor identical in every one. The universality of general terms is a convention embodied in language: we make a particular instance represent or stand for all others of the same kind, or else we attach this kind to a certain word or term—'yellow', 'hard'—and use the word of whatever possesses it—'yellow' of sunflowers and egg yolks as well as lemons, 'hard' of wood and iron as well as stone. On this view, whatever there is of universality belongs, not to the particular instances, but to the word or name (hence 'nominalism') which we use to describe it. Conceptualists agree with nominalists in refusing to universals an existence independent of minds and objects, but part from them in asserting that they are more than linguistic or terminological conventions; they do actually exist, but as general ideas or concepts in the mind that knows them.

It is difficult to see how any of these solutions can be accepted as it stands. Platonic realism creates an impassable division between two worlds; Aristotle's, though more amenable to common sense, leaves us in doubt as to the precise nature of the element which is common to particulars— what *is* the yellowness that lemons have in common, and how do they share in it? what is meant by 'common quality'? Extreme nominalism would reduce general terms like 'yellow' or 'dog' to arbitrary convention: if there is *nothing* universal in particulars themselves but only in the words we use to describe them, it would seem to be a matter only of agreement or of personal choice whether a particular animal is classed as a dog or a cat. A similar argument can be brought against conceptualism: if universals exist only in the mind, why should we suppose that these mental entities correspond to any reality outside the mind? Why then should we include only dogs within the conceptual category of 'dog' and not also animals of other species? To the present writer some degree of realism seems inescapable: if universals had no existence in particulars, neither thought nor language would correspond to the actual world—we could not be sure that we had knowledge of that world; it must surely be more than an arbitrary decision that classifies groups of objects under the same heading—is there not some property in dogs which *inclines* us to include them under the same name, or something common to all falling objects which brings them universally within the law of gravity? 'Dog' and 'gravity' are more than words, more than concepts; they refer in some way to what exists outside of both language and thought. To say this does not, of course, solve the problem of universals; it merely states a conviction which any solution must take into account. Meanwhile the problem remains open, and argument seems likely to continue for some time yet to come.[16]

[16] It may be that progress towards a solution will come from further research in psychology and linguistics, for it would seem reasonable to suppose that universals in part reflect the nature both of the mind and of the medium which mind uses to communicate its ideas.

Further study

Plato

F. M. CORNFORD, *Before and After Socrates* (Cambridge University Press, 1932, repr. 1950), is an excellent introduction to Platonic philosophy in its context; so too is W. K. C. GUTHRIE, *The Greek Philosophers from Thales to Aristotle* (Methuen, 1950). Also useful as introductory reading are: G. C. FIELD, *The Philosophy of Plato* (Oxford University Press, 1949); R. S. BRUMBAUGH, *Plato for the Modern Age* (Collier Books, 1964); and, as intermediate to the books that follow, I. M. CROMBIE, *Plato the Midwife's Apprentice* (Routledge, 1964).

For more advanced study there are: A. E. TAYLOR, *Plato, the Man and his Work* (Methuen, 4th edn, 1937); G. M. A. GRUBE, *Plato's Thought* (Methuen, 1935); and I. M. CROMBIE, *An Examination of Plato's Doctrines* (Routledge, 1962/3, 2 vols). There are numerous articles in the volumes on Plato (ed. G. VLASTOS) in the Macmillan series referred to on p. 38.

Of Plato's longer dialogues the most rewarding for the general reader are the *Republic* (on which there is the excellent commentary by R. C. CROSS, and A. D. WOOZLEY, *Plato's Republic* (Macmillan, 1964)), *Phaedo* and *Symposium*; to these may be added such shorter works as the *Apology* (Socrates' defence at his trial), *Crito* and *Meno*. Translations of these can be found in either the Penguin Classics or the Dent Everyman's Library (EL) editions, but the Penguin edition of the *Republic* by H. D. P. LEE is particularly recommended.

Universals

The main Platonic sources for the Theory of Forms are: *Phaedo*, 95e–107b (Penguin, pp. 127–143); *Republic*, 471c–541b (Penguin, pp. 231–311) and 595a–608b (*ibid.*, pp. 370–86); *Symposium*, 201d–212c (Penguin, pp. 79–95); *Parmenides*, 127d–136c (EL, pp. 2–13); *Timaeus*, 27c–31b and 51b–52d (EL, pp. 13–21, 59–62). However, these are not the only dialogues in which the Forms appear; and there is the passage in the *Seventh Letter* referred to on p. 45 above. For Aristotle's criticisms see *Metaphysics* A, 990b–993a (EL, pp. 75–83).

Some account of the Forms will be found in the books mentioned in Section A; reference should also be made to SIR DAVID ROSS, *Plato's Theory of Ideas* (Oxford, Clarendon Press, 1951) and J. E. RAVEN, *Plato's Thought in the Making* (Cambridge University Press, 1965).

There are chapters on universals in A. C. EWING, *The Fundamental Questions of Philosophy*; BERTRAND RUSSELL, *The Problems of Philosophy*; A. D. WOOZLEY, *Theory of Knowledge* (Hutchinson, 1949); G. E. MOORE, *Some Main Problems of Philosophy* (Allen & Unwin, 1953); A. G. N. FLEW, ed., *Logic and Language* (2nd series, Blackwell, 1959); and G. N. FINDLAY, ed., *Studies in Philosophy* (Oxford University Press, 1966). For more extended study there are R. I. AARON, *The Theory of Universals* (Oxford University Press, 2nd edn, 1967) and H. H. PRICE, *Thinking and Experience* (Hutchinson, 1953). Among useful articles are these three in *Mind*: F. P. RAMSEY, 'Universals' (vol. 34, 1925), R. I. AARON, 'Two senses of the word "Universal"' (vol. 48, 1939), and N. LAZEROWITZ, 'The existence of universals' (vol. 55, 1946).

3   Aristotle

The analysis of 'being'

Biographical note

Aristotle was a native of northern Greece, born at Stagira in 384 B.C. His father had been a physician to one of the kings of Macedon, but he had died early, leaving his son in the care of a guardian. At about the age of eighteen Aristotle moved to Athens to continue his education in Plato's Academy; here, so far as is known, he remained for twenty years engaged in scientific and philosophical study and in writing a number of dialogues, now lost, on the model of Plato. When Plato died in 348 B.C. Aristotle moved to Assos, on the coast of Asia Minor, where a branch of the Academy had been established. However, the overthrow of the local ruler forced him to flee to the island of Lesbos; here he remained, actively pursuing his studies, until about 342 B.C., when King Philip of Macedon invited him to undertake the education of his son, known to us as Alexander the Great. This task finished, Aristotle returned to Athens and founded there a philosophical school of his own which was known as the Lyceum (from its position near the temple of Apollo Lyceus) or the Peripatos (from the covered walk, peripatos, which was a feature of its buildings); hence the name 'Peripatetics' by which the followers of Aristotle were often known. The school flourished and its renown equalled that of the Academy. Aristotle remained its head until, on the death of Alexander the Great, a political revolution in Athens brought a change of government; specious charges were brought against him on the grounds of sympathy with Macedon, to which the Athenians were virtually subject; forced again to flee, he settled in the island of Euboea and died there at the age of sixty-three.

Aristotle wrote on logic, ethics, metaphysics and aesthetics, on politics and education, and on a host of subjects within the field of natural science. Catholic in his interests and indefatigable in his pursuit of learning, he was among the most erudite men of all time; he outlined a geography of knowledge which later centuries have laboured to complete, and within certain areas of enquiry, notably the three first named above, he formulated problems and principles whose importance is undiminished by the passage of time. His writings have come to us in a form which suggests that they are either notes for lectures or outlines for books; this has the unfortunate result of making him one of the least readable of all great philosophers. The Ethics and Politics (especially the sections on education in the latter) are perhaps the best starting-point for the general student, but he must still be prepared for close reading and strenuous thought.

At heart Aristotle is a rationalist and, like Plato's, his philosophy is one of aspiration. Despite a strongly empirical bent of mind (for which, no doubt, his father's profession was partly responsible—it is in biology that Aristotle's empiricism is most conspicuous), he believes powerfully in the sovereignty of reason: 'Small in bulk it may be, yet in power and preciousness it transcends all the rest. We may in fact believe that this is the true self of the individual.'[1] Yet, quite unlike Plato, he never scorns the sensible world or doubts its reality; on the contrary it is an endless stimulus for his insatiable curiosity and arouses in him feelings which merge at times into reverence.

The problem of 'being' can be traced back to the earliest speculations of Greek philosophers about the nature of the universe. At the start of the sixth century B.C. an Ionian Greek named Thales from the island of Miletus, off the coast of Asia Minor, had asked what was the basic stuff of which the world was made and concluded that it must be water. A later thinker gave the answer 'air', and another that it was an indeterminate something which he called 'the unlimited'. All agreed that, underlying the obvious change and movement characteristic of the world as we know it, there is a fundamental reality which persists throughout. From the deliberations of these and succeeding philosophers there emerged two pairs of contrasted concepts—permanence and change, and 'the one' and 'the many'. All four of these correspond to something observable in the sensory world: children grow into manhood and men mature and die, yet they remain the same person—permanence within change; the same substance, water for instance, is found in different forms, and the unity of a social community is composed of numerous individuals—one and many. It seemed that any theory about the fundamental constitution of the universe must account for them all; especially must it account for the existence side by side within each pair of what are apparently incompatible: if there is permanence in experience, how can there also be change? And how can the one also be the many? In a sense they are the same question,

[1] *Ethics* 1178a, trans. J. A. K. Thomson (Penguin, 1955), p. 305.

for permanence can be regarded as a form of unity, and there is an evident relationship between change and plurality. Thinkers tended to range themselves at one or another pole within each pair of opposites; thus, on the one hand are the 'single-substance' philosophers, like Thales, who asserted that everything was water, and on the other the atomists, like Democritus, who believed that the world was composed of different kinds of tiny particles.

There were two in particular, Heraclitus (p. 42) and Parmenides, who took extreme and opposing views. The former believed that change was the fundamental reality; nothing is constant; everything is in process, moving from one transient state to another. The latter declared in powerful and emphatic verse that all is one and that change and plurality are impossible. (Each of them, it should be noted, allowed some modification of his extreme position: Heraclitus argued—not without an element of self-contradiction—that change is cyclic and is governed by what he calls the Logos;[2] Parmenides concedes that, though reality is incontrovertibly one, there is nevertheless a world of appearances which admits plurality.) Since the latter poses the problem of 'being' or reality in a specially challenging way, it will be helpful to examine his thought a little further. He begins with the assertion, 'That which is *is*, and it is impossible for it not to be'; 'being' cannot be converted into 'non-being'; change, therefore, is impossible, for it implies that what is has become something else and ceased to be itself. Of previous philosophers some had supposed that a basic world stuff could be transformed into different substances, others that the varied materials of the universe were composed of different configurations of atoms in empty space or nothingness; both views imply the existence of 'non-being' and are therefore mistaken. Now there is a fallacy in Parmenides' argument which is obvious enough to us but could not have been so in the fifth century B.C.; it arises from his failure to see that the verb 'to be' in Greek has two distinct uses—as a simple connective or copula ('the cloth is white') and as signifying existence ('God is'). If a piece of white cloth is dyed red, one must say of it, 'The cloth is not white'. It does not follow, however, as Parmenides assumed, that non-existence is being ascribed to the cloth; what is now being said is: 'the cloth is not-white', not 'the cloth is-not . . . ', i.e. does not exist. Had Parmenides understood this, he would have realised that his argument against transformation and change would not carry the weight he required of it. It was Plato, a century later, who distinguished, in his dialogue the *Sophist*, between the predicative and existential uses of the verb 'to be' and so brought the error to light.

However, granted that 'being' is all there is, what sort of 'being' must it

[2] 'word', 'reason', 'pattern', 'proportion'—the Greek can mean all of these.

be? From the only permissible premise, 'it is', he proceeds to deduce that
'being' is uncreated and imperishable, continuous, indivisible and total
(i.e. there is nothing beyond it; it is all there is); he further concludes that
it is motionless, finite and spherical. This, he argues, is the picture of
reality to which, once the initial premise of existence is granted, we are
driven by the sheer force of reason. Yet the finality of Parmenides' stand on
the immutability of 'being' was unconvincing—quite apart from its logical
weakness; there *is* multiplicity in the world, and there *is* change, and to
dismiss these as illusory is an affront to common sense. The problem for his
successors, therefore, was to give such an account of 'being' or reality as was
consistent with logic, with common sense and with the observed phenomena
of change and multiplicity. This was the task that Aristotle set himself.

First, however, we must glance back at Plato. The Theory of Forms
was an attempt to solve the problem of universals, but Plato also saw it
as a means of explaining the relationship between unity and plurality—
the Form and its numerous manifestations—and of accounting for change
—the aspiration of material and organic nature towards the ideal of the
Good. Aristotle rejected the theory: it placed an impassable barrier between
sense and intellect, belief and knowledge; it gave no convincing explanation of the movement, growth and decay of physical objects and organisms;
and the 'participation' of particulars in the Forms was 'empty metaphor'.
In effect it evaded the real issues by rejecting as unintelligible the world of
ordinary experience. To Aristotle such rejection was totally unacceptable,
for he had a strongly empirical bent of mind and an intense interest in
the natural, and especially the biological, world; he was, in fact, the first
genuine scientist. What was needed, so it seemed to him, was a new and
fundamental re-examination of the nature of reality, which, besides
accounting for plurality and change, would give due recognition to the
place of the phenomenal world in human experience. This he made the
task of a special kind of research to which he gave the name of 'first
philosophy', now known as metaphysics (for the origin of the word see
pp. 34–5).

'First philosophy' is the highest of all intellectual activities, for it is
practised simply for its own sake; it is a disinterested, but none the less
ardent, pursuit of knowledge. It has two main areas of subject-matter. One
of these is 'being' or 'reality', the fundamental nature and causes of things:
'There is a science which investigates being *qua* being and its essential
attributes' (see p. 35 above).[3]

The concern of 'first philosophy' is with the *whole* of 'being' *as such*,
not with any particular area or determination of it. Its second main province is that of the axioms or principles which other branches of knowledge

[3] *Metaphysics*, 1003a, trans. Warrington, p. 115.

require as starting-points or rules of procedure, but which they assume without proof; such are, for instance, the Laws of Contradiction and Excluded Middle (p. 30), and the principle of causation—that any effect must have some preceding cause. These axioms, though they are used by particular sciences for their own purposes, are common to all the different kinds of 'being'; it is the task of 'first philosophy' to examine them, justify them (or, if necessary, repudiate them), and to defend them against attack. The *Metaphysics* (the book in which he expounds this 'first philosophy') also includes what may be called Aristotle's theology—his proofs of the existence of a kind of deity which he calls 'the unmoved mover' and his account of its nature; as the highest and purest form of 'being' the 'unmoved mover' is properly included within the scope of 'first philosophy'.

Although he examines the Laws of Contradiction and Excluded Middle, as basic presuppositions of all intellectual enquiry, and devotes a section of the *Metaphysics* to the 'unmoved mover', the purpose to which he chiefly addresses himself in this book is the analysis of 'being' together with the numerous subsidiary problems that arise from it. Because of his strongly empirical leaning Aristotle did not, like Plato, question the reality of the ordinary world of objects, people and events which constitutes our daily experience. It is here, in fact, that his thinking starts: for the purpose of his investigation the primary reality is not the universal or the ideal, but the individual thing, animate or inanimate; this is where knowledge has its origin—in the particular objects that we perceive with our senses. Each such object is what he calls a substance;[4] that is to say, it exists in its own right and, though superficially it seems to change, there persists in it a 'substantial' element which remains unaltered, its very existence as an individual. From the logical point of view 'substance' may be described as that which is qualified by predicates but cannot itself qualify anything else; 'horse', for instance, may be qualified by 'male', 'brown', 'fast', but cannot itself be nsed as a qualifying predicate. Metaphysically, 'substance' is that which persists unaltered through superficial change, just as a man grows older and changes in appearance while remaining the same person. It has, too, an application to the physical world, since a material body may change in shape and colour yet retain its essential material nature, its 'substance'. 'Substance' is not the only kind of 'being'; there are, for instance, 'quantity', 'quality', 'relation' and several others which Aristotle

[4] This, of course, is a Latin substitute for the Greek. Aristotle's word is *ousia*, 'being', 'essence'; the more exact equivalent of the Latin *substantia* is *hypokeimenon*, 'that which underlies', but Aristotle tends rather to use this of the material component of an object as distinct from its 'form' (see pp. 60–61).

enumerates both in the *Metaphysics* and in his logical works; any particular 'substance' may be of a certain size or kind and will stand in various relationships to other 'substances'. But 'substance' itself is prior to all these, since without it none of the others can have meaning or function.

The western world owes no small debt to Aristotle for his formulation of the concept of substance, which has played a long and honoured, though often perplexing, part in the history of philosophy. It was used by Aquinas, Descartes, Spinoza, Kant and a host of other philosophers from the Middle Ages to the twentieth century. Even empiricists like Locke could not escape from it, since it was an essential part of their contemporary conceptual vocabulary. Presentday philosophers, however, tend to regard it with suspicion; its usefulness, they suggest, is over, and where it lingers on it is an increasing source of error and confusion. One criticism is especially worth noting, that the concept of substance merely reflects the structure of language and of one group of languages, the Indo-European, in particular; it is simply an extension into metaphysics of the grammar of language—the noun qualified by its adjective—an example, therefore, of imposing on reality an alien structure imported from outside, of what Wittgenstein would regard as an illusion born of linguistic misunderstanding (p. 239 ff.). One answer to this is that language may itself be a reflection of reality and that Aristotle was merely conceptualising a reality whose structure was already embodied in language. This is a question that cannot be pursued here.

Although Aristotle believed that it is the particular thing, the individual, that is the primary reality and the starting-point of knowledge, he nevertheless agreed with Plato's view that genuine knowledge is concerned, not with particulars, but with universals; there must therefore be within each particular 'substance' something which is distinguishable, at least in thought, and which is the proper object of knowledge. Moreover 'substance' is permanent, but individuals are observed to change. How does this happen? How can the individual be modified while retaining unaltered its substantial self? The solution to this double problem is found in Aristotle's doctrine of matter and form and in the distinction he draws between potential and actual 'being'.

Once again we must be careful about the meaning of words. Aristotle is here using 'matter' neither in the modern sense of solid stuff—the metal, wood, flesh and bones of which particular objects are composed—nor in the Platonic sense of a basic constituent of the universe; rather he is using it to describe that in 'substance' by virtue of which it has the bare possibility of being something or other; it is a potentiality not yet realised, but able to be apprehended by the mind and logically abstracted. By 'form' he does not mean a transcendent pattern belonging to a suprasensible world—this he emphatically rejected—but that in 'substance' which gives it reality, its actual character as an individual of a certain kind; form is the essence of the individual, the sum of its defining characteristics, that which makes it this kind of thing and not another. The form of a man is his 'manness'; matter is his potentiality for being a man, actualised and individualised for the time being by its association with his form. Neither form nor matter can exist by itself or separately from 'substance';[5] in isolation they are only logical abstractions, but together and joined with 'substance' they compose the concrete individual thing. Now although form belongs to the individual, yet because it is repeated in many individuals of the same kind, it is also in a sense universal; this element of universality makes form the proper object of knowledge.

There are two related difficulties here which we may pause to note. What is it that gives to particular things their individuality, and how can this individuality be known? Form is universal and is the same in all members of the same class; it cannot be form, then, that gives to a particular 'substance' its distinctness as an individual. Matter on the other hand is unqualified by any characteristics whatever; it is pure recipiency, a potentiality for being, and cannot of itself differentiate individuals from one another. How, then, can the union of form and matter produce that individuality of objects and persons which we actually experience? Aristotle's answer is that matter is, in fact, the principle of individuation, though quite how this is so he does not make clear. But he also held that matter in itself is unknowable; it is form that is the intelligible element in 'substance'. It would seem to follow that 'substance' can never be known in its unique individuality and can never be an object of science; yet experience contradicts this—we *do* know individual men and women, and particular 'substances' can be brought, as individuals, within the orbit of scientific knowledge. Again, Aristotle gives no firm answer; there would seem here to be an unresolved conflict between the Platonic view, inherited from his years in the Academy, that knowledge is of the universal and his own empirical interest in particular things as the starting-point for scientific enquiry.

'Substance' as a permanent substratum combining matter and form provides the answer to what can be known; there remains the problem of change. Another way of describing matter and form is by means of the terms 'potentiality' and 'actuality'—indeed it has already been found necessary to use them (or related words) in the preceding explanation. Each individual substance, Aristotle maintains, although it is now a particular entity, yet contains within itself further possibilities, potentialities

[5] But Aristotle does grant the possibility of pure form existing by itself; such is the 'unmoved mover'; such, too, is what he calls *nous poietikos*, the highest of human intellectual faculties.

either temporarily in abeyance or not yet actualised. A builder who is asleep or playing bowls is not actually building, but the potentiality is in him and when he returns to work it will be actualised in the construction of a house. An acorn, though it bears no resemblance to the mature tree, is nevertheless potentially an oak, and given the appropriate conditions this is what it will become. A block of stone of no recognisable shape may nevertheless become under the sculptor's hand the statue of a man; it possesses a potentiality (by contrast with the two previous examples an entirely passive one) of becoming something different. It is by means of form that potentiality is brought to actuality; indeed actuality *is* the full realisation of form in a particular 'substance'—the activity of building, the mature oak, the statue shaped by the artist's hand and imagination; and matter is the element of potentiality, that which is capable of being actualised into form.

It is important to note that for Aristotle form or actuality is always logically prior to potentiality and in one sense also temporally prior: it is logically prior because it is the end or goal towards which potentiality develops and is therefore presupposed; it is temporally prior in that the builder's skill, the mature oak and the sculptor's 'blueprint' exist before the actualisation. (In another but for Aristotle less important sense the reverse is true: we *observe* first the acorn then the oak.) In this his thought is typically Platonic, but it is reinforced by his own biological studies. Plato's philosophy was essentially one of aspiration—there is an ideal of perfection which the whole universe strives to attain; it is not a question of evolution gradually unfolding hitherto non-existent types, but of increasing approximation to an end which does already exist. (The idea is foreign to the modern mind, yet can we be certain that the goal of evolution, whatever that may be, is not somehow encapsulated, like a genetic pattern, in the movement towards it?) The same conception is supported by observation of the organic world, where again and again we observe the process of development towards pre-established goals.

Here then is Aristotle's answer to the problem of change and to Parmenides' denial of its possibility. The opposition of 'is' and 'is not' is false and misleading; except perhaps in logic there is no abrupt gulf between the two. Potentiality for change is a factor built into every existing 'substance', and in the process of change it does not cease to exist but takes on a new actualisation. An acorn is *actually* an acorn, *potentially* an oak tree; an oak is *actually* a tree, *potentially* a ship, a table, a door; the passage from one to the other is not a ceasing-to-exist but a new actualisation of existing potentiality, matter taking on a new form. However, the importance of this pair of concepts does not lie simply in its being an answer to a contemporary problem; it has become an important part of the furniture of European thought. Especially has the concept of potentiality been of value in fostering an attitude of mind which looks for the latent possibilities in people and situations, and seeks to develop them; such, for instance, is the educational principle of the realisation of individual aptitude.

The analysis of 'being' is not yet complete, for although Aristotle has explained how change is possible, he has not shown why it takes place; in other words, he has still to analyse the concept of cause. How and why, he goes on to ask, does a particular thing come to be what it is—the living plant or animal at its maturity, the finished product of the craftsman? He identified four different causal elements: matter and form (which we have already met), and the 'efficient' and 'final' causes. To become what it is, anything must have matter in the sense of the bare possibility of becoming something at all; it must also have form to give it its characteristic nature and identity. In addition, however, there must be a goal towards which its becoming moves, and a source for initiating the process of change. In living things the final cause or goal of becoming is the mature specimen of its kind; thus the acorn grows to an oak tree, the baby to an adult. In artifacts it is the pattern of the finished product in the mind of the craftsman. The efficient cause in organic growth is initially another individual of the same species, secondarily it is the natural force or drive within the living thing which impels it to the full realisation of its form; in the artifact it is the craftsman or artist whose labour fashions the article towards its goal. (It is not easy to distinguish the formal and final causes, and Aristotle does not always do so: the form of a thing, its full realisation, is also the goal of its development.) This analysis of causation will no doubt seem strange to those whose idea of cause is restricted to that of *a* effecting *b* and *b* effecting *c*, like billiard balls successively communicating their motion;[6] but this picture does less than justice to the concept of cause, and though we may disagree with Aristotle over details, he was right to insist on its complexity. And here too he has contributed concepts of immense importance to European thought.

'First philosophy' is concerned with the whole of 'being' in all its varieties; of these, 'substance' is fundamental: 'The ancient and everlasting question "What is being?" really amounts to "What is substance?" '[7] There are others, however, such as 'quantity' and 'quality', which are manifestations or determinations of 'substance' and depend on it for their

---

[6] The word 'cause' may also be misleading; it might be better, as A. H. Armstrong suggests, to speak of 'the four Reasons Why the thing exists and is what it is' (*An Introduction to Ancient Philosophy*, 4th edn, Methuen, 1965, p. 82).

[7] *Metaphysics*, 1028b, trans. Warrington, p. 168.

own existence; these Aristotle calls 'categories'.[8] Now so far in his analysis of 'being' Aristotle has been chiefly concerned with the problems of knowledge and change in relation to natural objects; but he distinguishes in the *Metaphysics* between two kinds of 'substance', that which belongs to the sensible world, is involved in change, and is properly the subject-matter of physics, and that which is eternal and immutable; this latter is the province of theology or metaphysics. It seems, then, that there is a superior kind of 'being'—superior because it transcends time and change—and that this too must be examined before the investigation of 'being' can be regarded as complete.

That there is such a transcendent kind of 'being' is a conclusion to which Aristotle is driven by the logic of his own doctrines, by the influence of Plato and by his own scientific enquiries. Actuality, he maintained, is prior to potentiality; as the goal of change it is presupposed in the process of change. There must, therefore, exist, as a presupposition of the mutable natural world a 'being' which is utterly and completely actualised and in which there is no potentiality at all. Plato's influence is plain in the aspirational nature of this ideal perfection of 'being', which is Aristotle's version of the Form of Good. Among existing things, he argues, we observe gradations of quality—good, better, best; applying this to the whole realm of 'being', we must assume the existence of a final transcendent superlative which can only be divine. (The aspiration in this is more apparent than the logic.) Finally, his observation of the natural world suggested to him that its orderly complexity must be due to intelligent purpose (a hint of the 'argument from design' by which Christian theologians have supported their belief in the existence of God);[9] it further suggested a hierarchical ordering of things—inorganic objects, plants, animals, man—which must surely culminate in a final apex of perfection; and

[8] The full list of categories (which includes 'substance' as the primary form of 'being') is: substance, quantity, quality, relation, place, date, position, state, action, passivity.

[9] Cicero quotes Aristotle as imagining a race of men suddenly released from life beneath the earth and seeing for the first time the phenomena of earth and sky: 'When they suddenly saw earth and seas and sky, when they learned the grandeur of clouds and the power of winds, when they saw the sun and learned his splendour and beauty and the power shown in his filling the sky with light and making day; when, again, night darkened the lands and they saw the whole sky picked out and adorned with stars, and the varying lights of the moon as it waxes and wanes, and the risings and settings of all these bodies, and their courses settled and immutable to all eternity; when they saw those things, most certainly they would have judged both that there are gods and that these great works are the works of god.' W. D. Ross, *The Works of Aristotle* (Oxford, Clarendon Press, 1952), vol. xii, p. 86.

last, since change was always the result, apparently, of causes external to itself, the world as a whole requires an ultimate source of change and movement.

The 'prime mover' of the universe must itself be without movement or change: movement is a passage from the potential to the actual, but the 'prime mover' is fully actual, contains no element of potentiality, and therefore cannot itself be moved; it is an 'unmoved mover' or 'changeless changer'.[10] It is immaterial (since matter is potentiality) and can therefore be none other than pure thought; moreover, since it cannot think of what is less perfect than itself (for this would be to introduce into itself an element of potentiality), it can only think about itself; its activity is thought inwardly focussed, a thinking about thinking. Like the universe it energises, the 'mover' is eternal and uncreated; it does not *create*, but merely keeps in motion. This it does simply by being a passive object of desire, exciting in the outermost of the spheres which compose the universe a form of imitation which consists in circular motion (this being for Aristotle the perfect type of all movement); the rotation of the outermost sphere is transmitted to the rest, and from these derive the various motions of all other physical bodies as well as the processes of growth, appetition and purpose in living creatures.[11]

This 'unmoved mover' is Aristotle's nearest approach to the concept of God; but it is not an object of worship, as is the God of all monotheistic religions, nor is it a God of active, providential love, as in the Christian religion. He writes of it thus:

On such a principle, then, the whole physical universe depends. It is a life which is *always* such as the noblest and happiest that we can live—and live for so brief a while. Its very activity is pleasure. . . . Thought which is independent of lower faculties must be thought of what is best in itself; i.e., that which is thought in the fullest sense must be occupied with that which is best in the fullest sense. Now thought does think itself, because it shares in the intelligibility of its object. It becomes intelligible by contact with the intelligible, so that thought and object of thought are one. . . . Activity rather than potentiality is the divine element in thought—actual contemplation, the most pleasant and best of all things. If, then, God is *always* in that good state which we *sometimes* attain, this must excite our wonder; and He is in an even better state, which must inspire us with yet greater awe. God must also have life; for the actuality of thought is life, and God is that

---

[10] The latter expression is suggested by D. J. Allan, *The Philosophy of Aristotle* (Oxford University Press, 1952), p. 35.

[11] Aristotle's universe is geocentric: the moon, sun, planets and fixed stars are carried through the heavens by a complicated system of concentric spheres; the outermost, that of the fixed stars, derives its motion from the 'unmoved mover' and passes it on to the remaining spheres.

actuality. His essential actuality is life most good and eternal. God, therefore is a living being, eternal and most good: to Him belong—or rather He *is*—life and duration, continuous and eternal.[12]

The passage illustrates both the nobility of Aristotle's conception of deity and at the same time how far it falls short of the compassionate self-giving of the God of Christian experience. Personal relationship with him is inconceivable—'friendship . . . exists only where there can be a return of affection, but friendship towards God does not admit of love being returned, nor at all of loving'.[13] He is an impersonal and entirely self-involved quintessence of intellect, not an object of worship but a necessity of logic.

Such, then, is Aristotle's account of 'being': in the concrete individual thing 'substance' is associated with matter and form and possesses both the actuality of its present state and the potentiality of others; passage from state to state is the product of material, formal, efficient and final causes; but the ultimate origin of all change and movement is the perfect actualisation of 'being' in the 'unmoved mover'. What are we to make of this analysis? A natural reaction in many will be to dismiss it as an abstruse piece of imaginative architecture which has no practical signficance and little relevance to an understanding either of ourselves or of the world we live in; but this is less than fair. It should be remembered, first, that philosophical effort is not primarily directed towards practical ends but is undertaken to resolve the unease of intellectual puzzlement. Second, philosophy is dialogue and it is also contextual: the starting-point and to some extent the direction of Aristotle's thought was determined by his predecessors, whose inadequate analysis of 'being' had created an impasse for thought; he could neither escape their influence nor reject their terms of reference. Third, his analysis is not as remote as may seem from ordinary life—indeed it reflects with remarkable accuracy the way in which we do in fact think and speak about the empirical world: we distinguish particular objects and persons and in each of them we further distinguish something which persists ('substance') through different manifestations; we differentiate between the stuff of a thing and its shape or appearance (matter and form); and we acknowledge the possibility of growth from a less to a more developed state (potential to actual). For all this Aristotle has given us a conceptual framework and a vocabulary which is far more plausible and down to earth than the logic of Parmenides or the transcendentalism of Plato. Even the 'unmoved mover', though for many it satisfies neither religious instinct nor common sense, can be defended as a logical extension of his thought; and his arguments for its existence have been

[12] *Metaphysics,* 1072b, trans. Warrington, p. 346.
[13] *Magna Moralia*, 1208b, *Works*, ed. Ross, vol. ix.

developed by Christian thinkers to find a place among their own proofs
of God (pp. 74 ff.).

Finally, Aristotle established what was accepted for more than two
thousand years as the proper subject-matter of metaphysics—'being *qua*
being and its essential attributes'; in different guises this has been the
theme of all the great metaphysicians since his time. This is certainly true
of St Thomas Aquinas, whose great work it was to accommodate the
Aristotelian philosophy to Christian theology; it is true of Spinoza, whose
Ethics is a prolonged enquiry into the logical implications of the concept of
substance defined as 'that which is in itself and is conceived through
itself'; of Leibniz, whose starting-point is simple substances or 'monads'
as the basic items of existence; and, in the nineteenth century, of F. H.
Bradley, for whom metaphysics is 'an attempt to know reality as against
appearance'.[14] In the twentieth century metaphysics has been under a
cloud; it has been attacked by Logical Positivists on the grounds that its
conclusions are incapable of verification, and by linguistic philosophers,
who have argued that 'being', 'reality', 'existence' and the like are concepts fabricated from a misunderstanding of the workings of language—
they present only linguistic problems. Yet interest in 'being' remains; in
the philosophy of existentialism there is flourishing a renewed interest in
the meaning and nature of 'being' as it is manifested in the individual
person; and, surely, in the very fact that there *is* anything at all, that we
and the world *exist*, there is a problem, a mystery, which merits investigation by the best powers of the human intellect.

[14] *Appearance and Reality* (Oxford, Clarendon Press, 2nd edn, repr.
1946), p. 1.

Further study

Aristotle

CORNFORD's *Before and After Socrates* and GUTHRIE's *The
Greek Philosophers* are again valuable as introductions to Aristotelian
philosophy in its context; further and more specific introductory reading
may be found in D. J. ALLAN, *The Philosophy of Aristotle* (Oxford University Press, 1952); B. FARRINGTON, *Aristotle: Founder of Scientific Philosophy*
(Weidenfeld & Nicolson, 1965); M. GRENE, *A Portrait of Aristotle* (Faber,
1963); G. E. R. LLOYD, *Aristotle: the Growth and Structure of his Thought*
(Cambridge University Press, 1968); and A. E. TAYLOR, *Aristotle* (Dover
Publications, 1955, repr. of rev. edn, 1919). A more advanced and standard
work is W. D. ROSS, *Aristotle* (Methuen, 5th edn, 1949, repr. 1968; Univ.
paperb., 1966).

Aristotle is among the least readable of great philosophers; however,
there is much of interest in his *Politics* (especially at the end, where he

The Scope of Philosophy

discusses education) and *Nicomachean Ethics* (for instance, his examination of 'happiness' in Book I). Both these are available in Penguin translations.

'Being'

Aristotle's *Metaphysics*, the main source for this chapter, is an eminently unreadable book—which is a pity, for it is among the great philosophical works of mankind and has been of enormous influence in the shaping of European thought. Perhaps the best advice for the would-be reader and student is to use Warrington's edition (Dent, Everyman's Library) as a kind of handbook or companion; judicious use of the index and table of contents will guide him to the appropriate places in the text.

The whole of preceding Greek philosophy is virtually a prelude to Aristotle's analysis of 'being'—hence the value of Cornford's and Guthrie's books mentioned above. Heraclitus and Parmenides are especially important. A more detailed account of the early philosophers is in J. BURNET, *Greek Philosophy from Thales to Plato* (Macmillan, 1932), and in GUTHRIE's monumental work, *A History of Greek Philosophy* (Cambridge University Press, vols. i–iii, 1962–69); COPLESTON's *History of Philosophy*, vol. i, is also helpful. For reference and advanced study there is J. OWENS, *The Doctrine of Being in the Aristotelian Metaphysic*, a study in the Greek background of medieval thought (Pontifical Institute of Mediaeval Studies, Toronto, 2nd edn, 1963).

From Aristotle the reader may wish to proceed to a further sampling of metaphysics; to this there are numerous introductions, such as D. F. PEARS, ed., *The Nature of Metaphysics* (Macmillan, 1957; based on Third Programme talks); W. H. WALSH, *Metaphysics* (Hutchinson, 1963); and C. H. WHITELEY, *An Introduction to Metaphysics* (Methuen, 1950); more difficult are I. RAMSEY, ed., *Prospect for Metaphysics* (Allen & Unwin, 1961) and D. EMMET, *The Nature of Metaphysical Thinking* (Macmillan, 1945). A more traditional approach is A. E. TAYLOR, *Elements of Metaphysics* (Methuen, 1903; paperback edn, 1961); and in protest against metaphysics there are A. J. AYER, *Language, Truth and Logic* (Gollancz, 2nd edn, 1946), ch 1; and H. REICHENBACH, *The Rise of Scientific Philosophy* (University of California Press, 1951), Part 1.

Another direction might be towards modern existentialism; for this the following could serve as introductions: H. J. BLACKHAM, *Six Existentialist Thinkers* (Routledge, 1961); M. GRENE, *Introduction to Existentialism* (University of Chicago Press, 1959); P. ROUBICZEK, *Existentialism: For and Against* (Cambridge University Press, 1966) and M. WARNOCK, *Existentialism* (Oxford University Press, 1970).

Articles include: G. E. MOORE, 'Is existence a predicate?', *Aristotelian Society Supplement*, 15 (1936); W. V. QUINE, 'On what there is', *Review of Metaphysics*, vol. 2 (1948–49); and P. T. GEACH, A. J. AYER and W. V. QUINE, 'Symposium: On what there is', *Aristotelian Society Supplement*, 25 (1951). See also the Aristotle volume, ed. J. M. E. MORAVCSIK, in the Macmillan series.

68

4   St Thomas Aquinas

The Existence of God

Biographical note

Thomas Aquinas was born near Naples in 1224/5. When he was five, his father, the Count of Aquinas, sent him to the Benedictine Abbey of Monte Cassino to be educated under his uncle, then the abbot of the monastery. No doubt it was his parents' expectation that Thomas would eventually be raised to a position consistent with his noble rank. However, in 1239 the Emperor Frederick II expelled the monks, and Thomas, after spending a few months with his family, went to the University of Naples at the age of fourteen to continue his studies. Here he became acquainted with the friars of the Dominican Order, who had recently established a house of studies in the city; attracted by their life he joined the Order. His decision brought great consternation to his family, who regarded his membership of a mendicant order as an affront to their dignity as well as to their hopes for his preferment; but despite their pleas, which were supported by the Pope himself, Thomas remained firm. The Dominican General now resolved to take him from Naples and send him with three other friars to the University of Paris; on their way thither the party was waylaid by two of Thomas's brothers, who took him back to the family castle; here he was immured for a year in the hope that he would change his mind. In the end he escaped and made his way to Paris.

At the University of Paris he studied for three years under the famous teacher and exponent of Aristotle, Albert the Great. In 1248 he accompanied his master to Cologne, where Albert was to found a house for the Dominican Order, and stayed with him until 1252; he then returned to Paris for further study. Soon after this he began lecturing; in 1256 he received a licence to teach within the faculty of theology and in the same year he became Dominican professor a position which he held until 1259. For the next nine years Thomas was attached to the Papal Court in Italy as a teacher of theology; after this he taught again in Paris from 1269 to 1272 and for another two years in Naples. He died in 1274 while journeying, at the bidding of the Pope, to attend a council at Lyons; he was canonised in 1323.

Apart from its early years Thomas's life was outwardly unexciting; it was devoted to the service of his Order in study, writing and teaching. Yet his work involved him in notable controversies which revealed his capacity for intellectual innovation, his passion for truth, his courage in the defence of his own views and his utter fairness in presenting those of his opponents. Because of his physical size, the giant strength of his demeanour and his habit of reflective abstraction he was known as the 'dumb ox'; but he was no secluded pedant. His organising ability was recognised and used in the foundation of houses for his Order and in the business of the Papal Court. Eminent, too, was his skill as a teacher, displayed both in books and in lecture hall—he had a rare capacity for surveying, simplifying and ordering a wide and complex range of material; it is as such, no doubt, that he would most wish to be remembered, and his greatest work, the Summa Theologica, *is aptly subtitled* ad eruditionem incipientium—*'for the instruction of beginners'. Despite his sanctity he was not a man greatly given to mystical experience, but it is recorded that the* Summa *remained unfinished because of a vision during Mass; after it he said to his secretary: 'All I have written seems to me like so much straw compared with what I have seen and with what has been revealed to me.'*[1] *No more need be said of his character; a man who is elevated to sainthood only fifty years after his death must obviously be pre-eminent in this respect. 'The truths of which he wrote,' it has been said of him, 'were the realities by which he lived.'*[2]

His writings include commentaries on many of the works of Aristotle, books on science, morals, politics, and various philosophical and controversial subjects, and, of course, religion. There is no need to name them all, but his masterpiece is the Summa Theologica, *a theological account of the whole of reality in three volumes (though incomplete, as has been said). Next in importance is the* Summa contra Gentiles *in which he seeks to prove the great truths of Christianity by reason alone and to show that philosophy and religion are not necessarily in conflict. An outstanding feature of his style is its impersonality; he effaces himself completely from what he writes. Yet it is not without attraction, for it has the beauty of clarity, precision and perfect adaptation to purpose—and these qualities are apparent even in translation.*

St Thomas's arguments for the existence of God must be seen in the context, first, of contemporary discussion about the relative roles

---

[1] F. C. Copleston, *Aquinas* (Penguin, 1955), p. 10.

[2] Copleston, *History of Philosophy*, vol. ii (Burns & Oates, 1950), p. 304.

of religion and philosophy as means to truth, second, of his own epistemology. From the time of the Greek pre-Socratic philosophers to the beginning of the Christian era philosophy had rarely been far removed from
religion: in Pythagoras and Plato there are strong undercurrents of
religious mysticism; Aristotle requires an 'unmoved mover' as a source of
physical motion and as a standard of ethical perfection; Stoicism and
Epicureanism, however thinly disguised as philosophy, are basically
religious theses. With the advent of Christianity there developed two
different views of the relationship of religion and theology to philosophy:
one, which originated with the second-century theologian Tertullian,
asserted that philosophy was unnecessary; the truth as revealed in the
Christian religion was all that man required, and anything that philosophy
could offer was at best superfluous, at worst positively harmful. Another
view, more lenient to philosophy, derived from St Augustine of Hippo:
philosophy is not opposed to religion; reason and faith are not in conflict,
but the former is dependent on the latter—*credo ut intellegam*, as St
Anselm expressed it in the eleventh century—'I believe in order to understand'; man's intellect must first be illumined and then guided by
religious faith; it can thus arrive at an understanding which, though incomplete, is nevertheless genuine and can pave the way to the fuller
knowledge which awaits the Christian in the life to come.

In these two views religion takes precedence over philosophy, faith over
reason. In the twelfth and thirteenth centuries, however, a third view
came into prominence which reversed this relationship and subordinated
theology to philosophy. Its source was the Arabian philosopher Averroes;
belonging to the tradition of the Koran, not of the Bible, he held that the
proper interpreters of scripture are the professional philosophers, since
they alone have the requisite skills in logical argument and demonstration; where theology and philosophy conflict, therefore, the latter should
have the final say. Clearly, such a position was unacceptable to the
Christian Church; it was the more dangerous because it appeared to have
the support of Aristotle, on whom Averroes was a recognised authority.
A settlement of the issue became urgent, and St Thomas provided a
possible solution.

His position is that theology and philosophy are separate disciplines,
each of them autonomous in its own sphere. Yet the separation is not so
sharp as to create a dualism; there is overlap between them in that both
share a common area of knowledge and the same ultimate goal. The area
of knowledge consists of truths which are attainable both by theology
through revelation and by philosophy through the exercise of natural
reason. Some truths are known only by revelation, such, for instance, as
the doctrine of the Trinity—God in three Persons; others are known only

by natural knowledge—the data of sensory experience and the 'laws' of science; but there is also an area of truth accessible to both, and this includes our knowledge of God's existence and of some aspects of his nature. The common goal is the knowledge of God, to which all enquiry leads: 'All conscious things implicitly know God in everything they know.'[3] The fundamental difference between the two disciplines lies in the method and direction of the cognitive processes which they employ: theology starts from truths which God reveals directly to the human mind through the Bible and through Jesus Christ; accepting these in faith it proceeds deductively, elucidating them and particularising their application to the created world. Philosophy, on the other hand, cannot start from God or from truths divinely revealed, but by reflecting on the finite data of sensory experience it moves away from the created world towards transcendent truths which for theology are the content of revelation. In this way St Thomas avoids the two extremes of Tertullian and Averroes: he neither relegates philosophy to a position of triviality nor exalts it to one of sovereignty over theology. He also avoids Augustine's subordination of reason to faith—philosophical understanding does not require a prior act of theological commitment. For St Thomas there are two ways of knowing—the way of faith and the way of reason—which are proper, respectively, to theology and to philosophy. Neither is subordinate to the other; moving independently from different directions they share a common area of content and the same ultimate goal. Their independence is qualified, however, by the fact that knowledge by faith requires at least some prior grounding in the natural knowledge which comes through reason—'Faith presupposes natural cognition', we are told in the *Summa Theologica*;[4] at the same time the imperfection and incompleteness of natural knowledge imply the necessity of revelation:

Instruction by divine revelation was necessary even about truths concerning God which are accessible to the human reason. For otherwise they would have been found only by a few men and after a long time and even then mixed with many errors. And the whole salvation of man, which is to be found in God, depends on the knowledge of this truth.[5]

Theology and philosophy may therefore be said to be partners, not exactly in a common enterprise, but in activities which, though autonomous, are related in content, in purpose and by logical implication.

To understand the epistemology of St Thomas and also his need to demonstrate the existence of God it is essential to bear in mind this clear distinction which he makes between revealed knowledge, accessible by

---

[3] *Quaest. Disp. de Veritate*, 22, 2.
[4] *Summa Theologica*, Ia, 2, 2.
[5] *Ibid*., Ia, 1, 1; quoted from Copleston, *Aquinas*, p. 56.

faith and divine grace, and natural knowledge which comes through sense experience and the activity of reason. In his account of the latter he assumes, as must already be clear, an empiricist position; accepting what he believes to be the implications of Aristotle's thinking on the subject,[6] he asserts the principle, *nihil in intellectu quod prius non fuerit in sensu*—'there is nothing in the mind which was not previously in sensation'. The mind at birth he describes (using the actual words of Aristotle) as *tabula rasa in quo nihil est scriptum*—'a blank sheet on which nothing is written'.[7] Even in John Locke, who is commonly regarded as the founder of modern empiricism, there is scarcely a more emphatic statement of the origin of human knowledge in sense experience (p. 105). There are no innate ideas waiting to be roused, as Plato suggested, from a state of dormancy; nor are the mind's contents provided readymade like prepackaged goods. Knowledge is the product of intellect working from materials supplied by sense perception; the mind is dependent on sensation both for its contents and, to that extent at least, for its ability to operate.

How, then, does knowledge arise? St Thomas distinguishes two kinds of cognition, sensory and intellectual. Sensory cognition is the knowledge of the particular material objects of which we are aware in sense perception; within the area of natural knowledge it is the only direct or immediate cognition available to the human mind; but it is a knowledge of particular things merely and includes no general or universal element. From this sensory knowledge of particulars and their properties the universal elements are abstracted by the mind and formed into intellectual concepts; hence come the conceptual structure of knowledge—'existence', 'substance', 'matter', 'form' and the rest—and the possibility of intellectual judgment and understanding. It follows that the origin of all philosophical and scientific enquiry lies in sensation, and that sensation is a prior condition also of the knowledge of God in natural, as opposed to revealed, theology. Now there is an obvious difficulty here: if intellectual cognition is dependent on sense perception, which itself gives knowledge only of material objects and their sensory qualities, the mind is barred (in this life at least) from direct knowledge of what is immaterial. But God is immaterial and cannot be an object of sense perception; granted, then, that *nihil in intellectu quod prius non fuerit in sensu* and that God cannot be *in sensu*, how can we, apart from direct revelation, ever know him in this life, and how can there be a 'natural theology' or a metaphysical knowledge of non-material reality? And how can St Thomas vindicate his assertion that philosophy is an autonomous discipline with its own independent approach to the knowledge of God and his nature?

[6] e.g. *De Anima*, III, 8, 432a: 'No one can ever learn or understand anything in the absence of sensation.'   [7] *Summa Theologica*, Ia, 79, 2.

His answer is that sense perception is not the sole cause of intellectual cognition; it provides it with material, with content, with occasions for its operation, but the mind's natural inclination is towards 'being' in general not sensory 'being' in particular; as an *embodied* mind it must start from sense perception, but as *mind*, with intrinsic capacities and inclinations of its own, it tends beyond sense perception towards the immaterial; it is enabled to do this by the fact that the material world, being the creation of God, manifests the immaterial and points towards it. Thus the human mind *can* achieve some knowledge of God and of non-material reality by natural means, though the knowledge remains indirect and imperfect. For instance, it can know God analogically; that is, it can argue from the wisdom or goodness of human beings to a divine wisdom or goodness which, though beyond man's understanding, can yet be assumed to belong to God. It can approach him, too, along the *via negativa* or 'negative way'; for instance, we can know that God is *not* material, *not* limited, *not* spatial or temporal, and thus by elimination we can construct, however inadequately, some conception of God's nature and on the basis of this formulate a natural theology.[8] In particular it is possible for the mind to demonstrate the existence of God, and we turn now to the arguments by which St Thomas thought this could be done.

Before starting his own arguments he disposed of others with which he disagreed. First, he rejected the view advanced by some theologians that the existence of God is self-evident: it is logically impossible to think the opposite of what is self-evident; but there are atheists and agnostics who do in fact deny the existence of God; this cannot, therefore, be self-evident. Next, he dismissed a form of the ontological[9] argument put forward by St Anselm. According to this the idea of God is the idea of a being 'than which no greater can be thought', that is, of the supremely perfect being; now if such a being existed only as a mental idea, it would not be supremely perfect, since it would lack an existence outside our minds; we could then conceive of a greater being, namely, one which existed apart from our idea of it; the idea of God therefore implies his existence. St Thomas makes several objections to this argument. First, the conception of God as that 'than which no greater can be thought' is by no means universally accepted; God has been defined or conceived in other terms than these. Second, to define God in this way—or at all—presumes

---

[8] Though ultimately God remains a mystery to the embodied mind: *Illud est ultimum cognitionis humanae de Deo, quod sciat se Deum nescire,* 'Human knowledge of God culminates in knowing that it does not know God.' *Quaest. Disp. de Potentia Dei,* 7, 5, ad. 14.

[9] 'Ontological' means 'concerned with being'; Greek *einai,* 'to be', pres. partic., *on, ontos,* 'being'.

a knowledge of his essential nature which is inaccessible to human reason, relying as it must on the data of sense experience; for it is not given to us to know him directly through sense experience, nor even through revelation fully and entire—God alone, in fact, can know his own essence; the starting-point of the argument is therefore unacceptable. Finally, to argue from the idea of God to his existence is logically invalid, since it involves an illicit transition from the conceptual order to that of existence—from idea to fact: St Anselm is saying that the idea of perfection includes actual existence, but the idea of something and its existence belong to different orders of reality and it is impossible for one to include or entail the other; the definition of God as 'supremely perfect being' can only imply, not his *actual* existence, but the *idea* of it. (It might perhaps be said in reply to St Thomas that he gives less than due acknowledgment to the unique character of God, which might be supposed capable of bridging the gulf between the conceptual and the existential.)

St Anselm's argument is *a priori*; its premises are not taken from experience but from concepts and principles formulated by the intellect independently of experience. St Thomas, on the other hand, follows the empiricist leaning of his thought by arguing *a posteriori*; all his proofs begin with some fact or feature of the universe as we observe it. There are five of them—the Five Ways, he calls them—of which the first is for him the *via manifestior*, 'the clearer way'. None of them is entirely new; the ideas from which they are developed can be found in the writings of Aristotle (p. 64), whence they were taken and enlarged by later thinkers, including St Augustine, St Anselm, the Persian philosopher Avicenna, and Thomas's teacher, Albert the Great.

The first proof is based on the idea of motion and change, not in the narrow sense of locomotion or physical transformation, but in the Aristotelian sense of movement from potentiality to actuality. Such movement, he argues, always requires an agent which is itself in a state of actuality; thus, 'whatever is in motion is set in motion by another';[10] but since an infinite series is impossible, there must be a first mover—'and all understand this to be God'. The second proof is similar: we observe in the sensible world a chain of causation in which every effect has an efficient cause; nothing can be the cause of itself, for it would then have to exist before itself—which is impossible; since there cannot be an infinite series of efficient causes, there must be a first cause, 'which all men call God'.

The third proof is more difficult to follow:

We observe in our environment how things are born and die away; they may or may not exist; to be or not to be—they are open to either alternative.

---

[10] *Summa Theologica*, Ia 2, 3; trans. and ed. T. Gilby, *St Thomas Aquinas: philosophical texts* (Oxford University Press, 1951), p. 48.

All things cannot be so contingent, for what is able not to be may be reckoned as once a non-being, and were everything like that once there would have been nothing at all. Now were this true, nothing would ever have begun, for what is does not begin to be except because of something which is, and so there would be nothing even now. . . . Therefore all things cannot be might-not-have-beens; among them must be something whose existence is necessary.[11]

Observation shows that some things come into being and later cease to be; it is possible, therefore, for them to exist or not to exist—they do not exist *necessarily*; now assuming infinite time there must come an occasion when the possibility of their non-existence is fulfilled; if all things were of this contingent nature, there would then be nothing at all, and if there had ever been nothing, nothing could now exist; to avoid this, there must be something which exists necessarily, and this is God.

The fourth proof starts from the degrees of goodness, truth, beauty, etc., that we observe in things and which allow us to make comparative judgments—'*x* is better (truer, etc.) than *y*'. St Thomas argues that such degrees of quality imply the existence of a supreme good, truth, etc., which is the cause of the lower degrees and shares its quality with them; now goodness and being are convertible terms—goodness *is* being and vice versa: 'Therefore there is a real cause of being and goodness and all perfections whatsoever in everything; and this we term God.'[12] (Although St Thomas refers in his argument to Aristotle's *Metaphysics*, the line of thought is nearer that of Plato in the *Republic* and *Symposium*—the Forms sharing their quality with the objects which display it.) Finally, in the fifth proof—again borrowing from his predecessors—St Thomas anticipates what is now known as the teleological argument or the argument from design:[13]

We observe that things without consciousness, such as physical bodies, operate with a purpose, as appears from their co-operating invariably, or almost so, in the same way in order to obtain the best result. When diverse things are co-ordinated, the scheme depends on their directed unification, as the order of battle of a whole army hangs on the plan of the commander-in-chief. The arrangement of diverse things cannot be dictated by their own private and divergent natures; of themselves they are diverse and exhibit no tendency to make a pattern. It follows that the order of many among themselves is either a matter of chance or it must be resolved into one first planner who has a purpose in mind. What comes about always, or in the great majority of cases, is not the result of an accident. Therefore the whole of this world has but one planner or governor.[14]

---

[11] *Summa Theologica*, Ia 2, 3; trans. and ed. T. Gilby, p. 56.

[12] *Ibid.*, p. 58.

[13] Greek *telos*, 'end', 'purpose'. There are hints of this in Aristotle, who also uses the analogy of an army: *Met.*, 1075a; trans. Warrington, p. 351.

[14] *Summa Theologica*, Ia, 2, 3, and I *Contra Gentiles*, 42; trans. Gilby, p. 63.

The crux of the argument is the unconscious cooperation of diverse material things in producing and maintaining an orderly universe; this can only be the result of a purposive intelligence which directs them.

It should be noted that when St Thomas rejects the possibility of an infinite series he is not thinking of mathematical infinity nor of a series receding through time. What he has in mind is a chain of dependence within the order of 'being', the ontological order; what he denies is that there can be, here and now, an infinite succession of dependence for motion or cause; without a first mover or causal agent—first *ontologically*, not in time—there can be no explanation of movement or change. This idea of ontological dependence is a common element in all five proofs: movement, change, contingency, qualities like goodness, and the cosmic order as a whole—all these derive ultimately from a cause which transcends them. It is this ontological dependence, revealed by careful metaphysical analysis rather than strict logical entailment, which St Thomas regarded as the cogent element in his proofs. It should also be noted that when he speaks of 'cause' he means by it something real; it is not, as Hume later asserted, a psychological disposition representing merely an observed uniformity in the sequence of events (pp. 145 ff.); it is something which not merely precedes an effect but *produces* it. (This metaphysical conception of cause was one of the things which Hume set out to destroy.) Of the five proofs he himself expressed a preference for the first, but the modern philosopher would be more inclined to favour the third; for the fundamental problem that St Thomas is here posing is how it is that anything exists at all; it is the attempt to resolve this apparently insoluble mystery that suggests, perhaps more powerfully than anything else, the existence of a Creator.

What can be said of these proofs? Are they proofs in the strict sense or merely a form of reasoned persuasion which falls short of logical cogency? First, although the proofs all start from some observed feature of the world around us, they also incorporate *a priori* principles which many would regard as open to question. For instance, the first proof employs the metaphysical concepts of potentiality and actuality; the second assumes an account of causation which is not now generally accepted; and both require as a premise the impossibility of an infinite ontological series—the proof of which itself depends on further *a priori* principles. Similarly, the third proof uses the concepts of contingency and necessity, the fourth that of perfection together with the assumption that goodness and being are convertible terms, and the fifth that of purpose; in other words all the proofs depend on presuppositions acceptable to an Aristotelian or Thomist philosopher but not necessarily to any other. Moreover, against the rejection of an infinite series it could be argued that, distasteful though it may be to a certain type of mind, yet this is how the world is—a world in which there is, in fact, no end to the series, no first mover or efficient cause, no ultimate ontological explanation. Indeed such a world might even be preferable in that it would relieve the human mind of at least a part of its metaphysical burden. Questionable, too, is the validity of the statement which concludes the proofs: 'And all understand this to be God.' Even granted that they indicate the existence of a being of some sort, it does not follow that this is God in the Christian sense of a personal being. However, the fourth proof assigns to God personal qualities like goodness, and the fifth affirms the existence of a transcendent intelligence; the five together, therefore, may be said to point to a God who is recognisably Christian, while in later sections of the *Summa Theologica* St Thomas argues for divine attributes which complete this tentative picture. To the present writer it seems doubtful whether proof of God's existence is either possible or desirable; the former, because it is inconceivable that the human mind should find definitive proof in a matter which surely must exceed its grasp; the latter, because the essence of man's relationship with God is not knowledge but commitment—faith, not fact—and because a God who could be so reduced to the span of logical demonstration would not be a God worthy of commitment.

However, leaving aside these personal views we must look more generally at the main traditional arguments for God's existence and consider some of the principal objections to them. The arguments belong to one of three main types—ontological (p. 74 n.), cosmological (Greek, *cosmos*, 'universe', 'world order') and teleological (Greek, *telos*, 'end', 'purpose'). The ontological argument was first formulated by St Anselm in the eleventh century and was also used in modified form by Descartes in the seventeenth; it is a purely *a priori* argument, making no reference to our actual experience of the world; on this partly depends its simplicity and apparent cogency, but St Thomas was right to reject it. Some of its weaknesses have already been indicated; of these the most important is the logically illicit transition from idea to existence, concept to actuality: from the definition of a thing we can deduce only what is contained within the definition; the definition of God as the perfect being has logical implications which may well include the *idea* of his existing, but the idea of existence does not entail its actuality—if it did, one could equally well argue from the idea of the perfect woman to *her* existence and so with any other idea of perfection. Another way of expressing this is by means of the distinction made by Kant between analytic and synthetic statements: the former are true because of the meaning of the words which compose them—'All bachelors are unmarried' is true because 'unmarried' is part of the definition of 'bachelor'; it is included in the meaning of the subject and adds nothing to what it already contains. A synthetic statement adds to the subject something which cannot logically be deduced from it. Now on the basis of the ontological argument 'God exists' is true only because 'God', as defined by St Anselm, implies 'exists'; it purports to be a synthetic statement adding something from outside the definition, but in fact it is analytic; it does not therefore prove the existence of God as a matter of actual fact external to the definition. Another grave weakness in the argument is that it assumes that 'existence' is a predicate which can be attached to subjects in the same way as can 'good', 'true', etc.; by assuming that existence is a 'perfection', a necessary attribute of God, it puts it on the same logical footing as qualities like 'goodness'; but 'existence' is not an attribute—to say that unicorns are existent is very different from saying that unicorns are one-horned.

Of St Thomas's Five Ways the first three are cosmological; they argue the need for a 'first cause' in order to explain certain features of the universe—change, efficient causation, and existence. The core of this kind of argument is its demand for an ultimate reason for, or explanation of, the universe such as does not itself require a further reason to account for it; the alternative to such a self-explanatory explanation or self-causing cause is an infinite regress of causal explanation which is both difficult to understand and repugnant to the human mind. The appeal of the argument is twofold: it is not so obviously *a priori* as the ontological argument but appears to start from our knowledge of the empirical world and the observed facts of change, cause, and existence, and therefore to have some scientific standing; second, it satisfies the desire of human reason for ultimate explicability. However, it has already been shown that St Thomas uses *a priori* concepts like potentiality and contingency which are not, or not wholly, derived from experience, and that infinite regress and the absence of ultimate explanation, albeit unpalatable to reason, may yet be features of the universe as it is.

A more fundamental objection, also hinted at above, is the use which the argument makes of the concept of cause; here we must anticipate briefly what will be said in later chapters. David Hume subjected the concept to an exacting analysis which concluded with a denial of any necessary connection between cause and effect: an event x (my throwing a stone) is followed by event y (a broken window), but x does not cause y in the sense that y follows x by logical necessity; y does in fact follow x with consistent regularity, but what we have here is not the operation of some occult causal agent but simply a uniformity of sequence whose very consistency impels the mind to regard y as the necessary effect of a cause x; the necessity, however, is not logical but psychological. Such an interpretation of cause undermines the whole concept of an infinite causal regress and of a primal uncaused cause.

The German philosopher Kant starting from Hume's analysis went on to argue that, although the causal concept is an indispensable means of interpreting experience and that scientific understanding is impossible without it, yet its application lies in *this* world, the world of experience; as soon as we extend its use beyond actual or possible experience, we are involved in contradiction: 'The principle of causality has no meaning and no criterion for its application save only in the sensible world. But in the cosmological proof it is precisely in order to enable us to advance beyond the sensible world that it is employed.'[15] If we accept Kant's argument, it follows that in attempting an explanation of the whole cosmos we pass beyond the limits of science and scientific proof; science is concerned with experience, but in postulating a first cause we transcend experience into realms where scientific concepts no longer operate. It is idle, therefore, to defend the cosmological argument by supposedly basing it on science and the facts of experience.

St Thomas's Fourth Way does not fit readily into any of the three main types of argument for God's existence; nor is it particularly impressive, for there is no logical justification for supposing that because we discern comparative degrees of quality in the world around us there must necessarily be a transcendent superlative which is also the cause of these lesser degrees; moreover, here too the concept of cause is suspect. The teleological argument, however, which the Fifth Way exemplifies has long enjoyed a considerable prestige. The orderliness and apparent purposiveness of the universe, in both its physical and its biological aspects, have always held a peculiar fascination for the human mind. 'The heavens declare the glory of God,' the psalmist assures us, 'and the firmament showeth his handiwork.' In fifth-century Greece the philosopher Anaxagoras conjectured that Mind is the initiator and guide of cosmic processes: 'Mind has power over all things that have life, both greater and smaller. . . . And Mind set in order all things that were to be, and all things that were and are now and will be.'[16] Precisely what he meant by 'mind' (*nous*) is not clear and did not satisfy Socrates and Plato, but the movement of his thought from observed order to intelligent control foreshadows the teleological argument. There are hints of it in Aristotle (p. 64) and in the Stoic philosophers of the third century B.C. Kant,

[15] *Critique of Pure Reason*, trans. and ed. N. Kemp Smith (2nd edn, Macmillan, 1933), p. 511; trans. and ed. J. M. D. Meiklejohn (Dent, 1934), p. 355.
[16] Fr. 12; G. S. Kirk and J. E. Raven, *The Presocratic Philosophers* (Cambridge University Press, 1957), p. 373.

though he denied the validity of the argument, was impressed by its force: 'This argument always deserves to be mentioned with respect. It is the oldest, clearest, and that most in conformity with the common reason of humanity.'[17] J. S. Mill, who had little regard for formal Christianity, nevertheless admitted that 'in the present state of our knowledge the adaptations in Nature afford a large balance of probability in favour of creation by intelligence'.[18]

The power of the argument is obvious enough: there is abundant evidence in nature of order, pattern and adaptation of means to end— the microcosm of the atom, the incredible intricacy of the human brain, the persistent uniformities which we call 'laws of nature'. How else could these exist save as the product of some transcendent intelligence? Furthermore, the mathematical odds against the universe being the result of chance are so astronomically great as to defy belief that this can be so. Yet despite its persuasiveness the argument is vulnerable from several quarters, as Hume has shown in his *Dialogues concerning Natural Religion*. Among Hume's objections are, first, the logical impropriety of arguing by analogy from human artifacts to divine intelligence:

If we see a house . . . we conclude with the greatest certainty that it had an architect or builder, because this is precisely that species of effect which we have experienced to proceed from that species of cause. But surely you will not affirm that the universe bears such a resemblance to a house that we can with the same certainty infer a similar cause or that the analogy is here entire and perfect.[19]

(Yet it is not clear that the force of the teleological argument lies in the analogy itself so much as in the sheer complexity of natural phenomena, which seems to put them beyond the scope of chance eventuality.) Second, it by no means follows from the argument that a *single* mind was responsible for the universe: the building of a house results from the

[17] *Critique*, trans. Meiklejohn, p. 363; on the previous page there is this memorable paragraph: 'The world around us opens before our view so magnificent a spectacle of order, variety, beauty and conformity to ends, that whether we pursue our observations into the infinity of space in the one direction or into its illimitable divisions in the other, whether we regard the world in its greatest or its least manifestations—even after we have attained to the highest summit of knowledge which our weak minds can reach, we find that language in the presence of wonders so inconceivable has lost its force, and number its power to reckon; nay, even thought fails to conceive adequately and our conception of the whole dissolves into an astonishment without the power of expression—all the more eloquent that it is dumb.'
[18] *Three Essays on Religion* (Longmans, 1874), p. 174.
[19] H. D. AIKEN, ed. (New York, Hafner, 1948), p. 18; R. WOLLHEIM, ed., *Hume on Religion* (Collins, 1963), p. 117.

activity of a number of men—bricklayers, joiners, plumbers and the like. 'Why may not several deities combine in contriving and framing a world?'[20] A further objection is the problem of evil: there is much in the world that is wasteful, cruel and, from the human point of view, irrational; is all this, too, the work of a transcendent intelligence? If so, then men may well be excused for thinking they could have done better themselves. This was a stumbling-block for J. S. Mill as well as for Hume: the former was not disinclined to believe in an intelligent ordering of the universe, but the abundance of evil suggested to him either the existence of two transcendent principles, a good and an evil, in conflict, or of a benevolent deity frustrated by obstacles he did not create.

In conclusion, then, it would seem that none of the three principal arguments for God's existence can claim logical cogency; even together they add up to no more than a possibility, at the very most a probability, that a god exists. This would suggest that in pursuing proofs of God's existence the human mind is exceeding its proper bounds and that Kant was right in saying that for the speculative reason a Supreme Being is 'a conception which perfects and crowns the system of human cognition, but the objective reality of which can neither be proved nor disproved by pure reason'.[21] On the other hand, Kant did believe that proof was possible by analysing the implications of moral experience, by *practical*, not speculative reason; but this is a line of thought the reader must be left to follow up for himself.

[20] ed. H. D. AIKEN, p. 39; ed. R. WOLLHEIM, p. 141.
[21] *Critique*, trans. Meiklejohn, p. 372.

Further study

St Thomas:

One of the best introductions to St Thomas is F. C. COPLE-STON, *Aquinas* (Penguin Books, 1955), now unfortunately out of print; as an alternative there are the chapters in vol. ii of his *History of Philosophy* (Burns & Oates, 8 vols., 1947–66). Another useful introductory book is J. PIEPER, *Introduction to Thomas Aquinas* (trans. R. and C. WINSTON, Faber, 1963). For further reading and reference there are E. GILSON, *The Philosophy of St Thomas Aquinas* (Heffer, 1924) and M. C. D'ARCY, *Thomas Aquinas* (Benn, 1930).

The best entry to St Thomas himself is through an edited selection of his writings such as T. GILBY, ed., *St Thomas Aquinas: Philosophical Texts*, and *Theological Texts* (Oxford University Press, 1951, 1955). There is also a selection by M. C. D'ARCY in Everyman's Library (Dent, 1949).

The Existence of God:

For St Thomas's arguments see Gilby's *Philosophical Texts*, pp. 36 ff.; and for discussion of them see A. KENNY, *The Five Ways*

(Routledge, 1969) and E. SILLEM, *Ways of Thinking about God* (Darton, Longman and Todd, 1961); SILLEM's *George Berkeley and the Proofs of the Existence of God* (Longmans, 1957) is also relevant. Further discussion of them can be found in the books mentioned above and in the Aquinas volume of the Macmillan series, ed. A. KENNY.

For wider reading on the existence of God and our knowledge of Him the list is almost endless. An excellent introduction is in the central chapters (each with suggestions for further reading) of H. D LEWIS, *Philosophy of Religion* (English Universities Press, 1965); LEWIS's *Our Experience of God* (Allen & Unwin, 1959) is a deeper but still very readable exploration of religious experience. There are relevant chapters also in J. L. GOODALL, *An Introduction to the Philosophy of Religion* (Longmans, 1966) and J. RICHMOND, *Faith and Philosophy* (Hodder & Stoughton, 1966). And of course JOHN ROBINSON's *Honest to God* (S.C.M., 1963) is essential reading for the current debate on God and the language we use to describe Him. An older but helpful book is A. E. TAYLOR, *Does God Exist?* (Collins, 1905 and 1961).

Philosophical discussion of these and related issues can be found in A. G. N. FLEW, *God and Philosophy* (Hutchinson, 1966); A. G. N. FLEW and A. MACINTYRE, eds, *New Essays in Philosophical Theology* (S.C.M., 1955); the Royal Institute of Philosophy Lectures 1967/8, vol. ii, *Talk of God* (Macmillan, 1969); and J. MACQUARRIE, *God-Talk* (S.C.M., 1967). A. PLANTINGA, *The Ontological Argument* (Macmillan, 1968) surveys the argument from St Anselm, through St Thomas and Descartes to Kant and Schopenhauer; the second part of the book consists of articles from twentieth-century writers on the theme. Another, more general, series of readings is G. I. MAYRODES, ed, *The Rationality of Belief in God* (Prentice-Hall, 1970). The first two books in the new Macmillan series in philosophy of religion are concerned with problems of deity: H. P. OWEN, *Concepts of Deity*, and J. HICK, *Arguments for the Existence of God* (both forthcoming).

Finally, a classic in this field is Hume's *Dialogues concerning Natural Religion* (ed. R. WOLLHEIM, Collins, 1963); with this should be read Kant's examination of the arguments for God's existence in the chapter 'The Ideal of Pure Reason' in his *Critique of Pure Reason*.

5   Descartes

The quest for certainty

Biographical note

Descartes was born in 1596, the son of a councillor of the parliament of Brittany. At the age of eight he was sent to the Jesuit College of La Flèche and stayed there until he was sixteen, receiving meanwhile an education which, judged by the tradition of his time, was firstrate. Yet he was dissatisfied with it—not with the teachers or their system of instruction, but with the content of the education itself. For it was based, so he thought, on insecure foundations, on conceptions of learning and scholarship that belonged to a bygone age. 'Books formed my education from childhood,' he tells us; but at the end of it 'I found myself hampered by so many doubts and errors that the only benefit of my efforts to become an educated person seemed to be the increasing discovery of my own ignorance.'[1] Philosophy disappointed him because 'every one of its propositions is still subject to dispute and consequently to doubt', logic because it enables one rather 'to speak without judgement of what one does not know, than to acquire knowledge'; as for history, 'a man who has too much curiosity about what happened in past centuries usually shows a great ignorance of what is happening in this one'. It was mathematics that gave him most pleasure, 'because of the certitude and evidential character of its reasonings', but he did not perceive then 'the true use to which mathematics can be put'.[2]

On leaving school he therefore put away his books for a time, and after a period of uncertainty decided to educate himself by seeing the world. The rest of his youth he spent 'in travel, in visiting courts and armies, in seeking the company of men of varying character and rank, in gathering experience';[3] and always and everywhere he reflected on the events which confronted him. He engaged in military service in various parts of Europe,

[1]*Discourse on Method*, trans. and ed. A. Wollaston (Penguin, 1960), p. 38.
[2] *Ibid.*, pp. 41, 49, 40, 41.   [3] *Ibid.*, p. 42.

serving as a gentleman volunteer and thus enjoying a measure of independence. During one such period of service, when he was staying in a small town in Germany with nothing to occupy his time save meditation, he experienced a moment of revelation which showed him what his mission was to be—to seek truth by the use of reason, and to devise methods of enquiry which would give his conclusions the same certainty as those of mathematics. For some years after this Descartes lived in Paris; but he found the life there uncongenial to study and retired to Holland in 1628, where he spent the next twenty years. In 1649 he accepted an invitation to go to Sweden in order to instruct the Queen in his philosophy. Unfortunately, the climate proved too much for him, and he died of a fever early in the following year.

The most important of his writings are the Discourse on Method, Meditations on First Philosophy, *and* Principles of Philosophy. *The first of these, after describing the intellectual malaise which impelled him to forsake the dogmatic security of scholastic philosophy and of his own teachers at La Flèche, outlines the rules of method by which he hoped to establish a new and unassailable philosophical structure; it then sets forth the basic premises on which this structure is to be founded, first of which is the famous* cogito ergo sum; *finally, it gives a brief account of the physical world as implied by his earlier conclusions. (This account is a summary of the contents of a treatise on the physical and organic worlds which he had left unfinished; the latter contained a description of the universe which implied that the earth was in motion; since Galileo had recently been condemned for asserting this, Descartes thought it prudent to abandon the work.) In* Meditations *he elaborates the main philosophical positions of the* Discourse; *in* Principles *he develops further some of the ideas of* Meditations *and presents some extremely important views on the laws of motion, the fundamental concepts of physics, the relation of physics to sense experience, and the nature of scientific hypotheses. He also wrote essays on optics, physics and geometry, and a short treatise,* Rules for the Direction of the Mind; *the last, written before the* Discourse *but published posthumously, was an early attempt to elaborate rules for intellectual procedure.*

The quest for certainty has been a constant preoccupation of the human mind. Its origin lies, no doubt, in the insecurity of man's situation in an environment which he can neither fully understand nor fully control. To live at all, still more to live happily and effectively, he must be secure against the forces that threaten him; this requires knowledge of them, a knowledge reliable enough to preclude the possibility of error and consequent disaster—the greater the certainty the greater the security. At the level of civilisation, which takes for granted an acceptable degree of physical safety, this propensity finds expression in intellectual enquiry; man is perturbed by the mysteries not only of the natural world, whose complexity baffles his understanding, but also by the problems which arise from his own transient existence and his relationship with others in the same predicament. Mystery is always unsettling—at least to those who are conscious of it; hence, when there is leisure to think, the mind addresses itself to issues now recognised as scientific and philosophical—the basic constituents of the physical universe and the forces which operate in it, the nature of 'being', of knowledge itself, of the principles which govern or ought to govern human behaviour. At this level too there is the same quest for certainty, for a knowledge which is indubitable; here it arises partly from psychological causes connected with man's primitive desire for security, partly from the mind's aesthetic satisfaction in solutions whose tidiness and coherence gives them the appearance of finality.

In Greek philosophy the quest appears in the initial tentative questionings of Thales and his successors, whose aim was to provide for the physical universe an explanation which rendered it intelligible; for intelligibility is itself a form of security—the mind is at ease with what it understands—and, as we now know, it offers also the possibility of control. It appears in Plato's Forms—the absolute, unchanging universal realities which give stability within the flux of physical change and shifting values; in Aristotle it shows itself in the analysis of 'being'—the permanent pattern which underlies existence and change—and in the eternal self-thinking of the 'unmoved mover'. The quest is typical of the rationalist position described in an earlier chapter; for in rationalism there is seen at its most intense the mind's passion for conclusions derived infallibly by logical deduction from unassailable *a priori* premises. There are, of course, traces in Greek philosophy of the other view, that knowledge has its origin in the data of sense perception—in Aristotle, for instance, who for all his rationalism could assert that 'no one can learn or understand anything in the absence of sensation';[4] but until the time of the Renaissance the dominant view was the rationalist, and for long after this, though men like Roger Bacon and William of Ockham in the thirteenth century and Francis Bacon in the sixteenth proclaimed and practised a rudimentary experimental science, it was reason rather than observation that was regarded as the proper source of knowledge.

At the Jesuit college of La Flèche Descartes received an education which was traditional in its emphasis on the centrality of reason and on the

[4] *De Anima*, III, 8, 432a.

theoretical knowledge derived from books; the logic he learned there was the syllogistic logic of the medieval schoolmen which infers by deduction from agreed premises to necessary conclusions. It was his dissatisfaction with this education that led to his resolve to seek henceforth 'for no other knowledge than the knowledge I might find in myself or else in the great book of the world'. In the course of his travels there came a moment of visionary insight which impelled him to attempt a reconstruction of his thoughts 'on foundations that belong only to me'; sweeping away, as he thought, all prior assumptions, it was his aim to build a new edifice relying only on the power of reason and his own intellectual resources; the opinions he had hitherto accepted on faith he might or might not incorporate in the structure once he had 'brought them to the level of my reason'[5]—this remained to be seen; but at least it was to be a new start in philosophy, a break from the past. In this he did not entirely succeed, for the traditional categories of thought had been so dinned into him at La Flèche and were still so essentially a part of the intellectual equipment of his age, that to escape them completely was impossible. His success was sufficient, however, to secure for him in later times the title 'father of modern philosophy'.

Descartes was a very able mathematician; he discovered, for instance, that algebraic methods could be applied to geometrical problems and was thus among the originators of what is now known as analytical geometry; he also discovered the use of coordinates in geometry to determine the position of a point in a plane, and by his work on equations he contributed to the development of the calculus. It is not surprising, therefore, that he took his ideal of knowledge from mathematics, which impressed him by its independence of empirical observation, its deductive methods and the absolute certainty of its conclusions. Deduction, so it appeared to him, moves from certain and self-evident premises, through stages of argument each of which is also certain and self-evident, to conclusions which are guaranteed by the reliability of the deductive inference preceding it. The premises, the intermediate links of argument and the ultimate conclusion are all of them apprehended *intuitively*; once they have been closely examined and the inference tested, they are *seen* to be so. The ideal of knowledge, then, is this intuitive apprehension of the truth which depends on the clear light of reason and is unaffected by the distortions of the senses and the fantasies of imagination:

By *intuition* I mean, not the wavering assurance of the senses, or the deceitful judgement of a misconstructing imagination, but a conception, formed by unclouded mental attention, so easy and distinct as to leave no room

---

[5] *Discourse*, trans. Wollaston, pp. 42, 47, 46.

for doubt in regard to the thing we are understanding. . . . It is an indubitable conception formed by an unclouded and attentive mind; one that originates solely from the light of reason. . . . Thus, anybody can see by mental intuition that he himself exists, that he thinks, that a triangle is bounded by just three lines and a globe by a single surface, and so on.[6]

Not only is intuition essential to the deductive process in providing self-evident premises from which to reason—such, for instance, as Descartes mentions here; but inference is itself a form of intuition, which is thus involved throughout the movement from premise to conclusion and may be said, therefore, to be the basis of knowledge or even knowledge itself.

Assuming, then, that intuitive insight is the only secure basis for knowledge, Descartes now felt it necessary to establish rules of procedure for scientific and philosophical investigation; these too are obviously indebted to mathematics. He describes them in detail in an early and posthumously published work, *Rules for the Direction of the Mind*; they are more succinctly stated in his *Discourse on Method*. First, he required absolute clarity and distinctness whether in the initial concepts or premises of argument or in each stage of inference or in the final conclusion:

Never to accept anything as true if I had not evident knowledge of its being so; that is, carefully to avoid precipitancy and prejudice, and to embrace in my judgement only what presented itself to my mind so clearly and distinctly that I had no occasion to doubt it.[7]

Any proposition which failed to satisfy this requirement was to be regarded with scepticism; nothing was to be accepted simply on authority; everything must be submitted to the test of personal experience and personal judgment. His second requirement was accurate analysis of the problem under examination: 'To divide each problem I examined into as many parts as was feasible, and as was requisite for its better solution.' Complex questions must be broken up into smaller ones simple enough to be apprehended by the natural light of reason, and the basic principles involved must be exposed to view. This is of obvious practical value in the clarification of problems in any sphere; accurate analysis is a first step to solution. Next he proposed the rule of orderly synthesis: 'to direct my thoughts in an orderly way; beginning with the simplest objects, those most apt to be known, and ascending little by little, in steps as it were, to the knowledge of the most complex; and establishing an order in thought even when the objects had no natural priority to one another.' What Descartes is recommending here is a process which starts from fundamental principles of

[6] *Rules for the Direction of the Mind*; trans. and ed. E. Anscombe and P. T. Geach, in *Descartes: Philosophical Writings* (Nelson, 1954), p. 155.
[7] *Ibid.*, p. 20.

great generality and, by deducing their implications and relating these to one another, gradually erects a coherent structure of knowledge. His final procedural rule is: 'to make throughout such complete enumeration and such general surveys that I might be sure of leaving nothing out'.[8] Ideas must be re-examined to ensure that each is entirely clear and distinct; the validity of every inference must be tested, so that conclusions must be shown to rest on valid objective reasoning and not on prejudice or false assumptions. In all this his purpose is to find epistemological certainty, to create a structure of knowledge as indubitable as that which is provided by the elementary, self-evident axioms of mathematics and the conclusions validly inferred from them.[9]

The basis, and also the weakness, of Descartes' ideal of knowledge and of the method by which he hoped to establish it is the clear and distinct ideas, intuitively apprehended, which he requires as indubitable starting-points for argument. He believes wholeheartedly in the efficacy of human reason and—most surprisingly—in its equal distribution. In the first paragraph of the *Discourse* he writes: 'The power of judging rightly and of separating what is true from what is false (which is generally called good sense or reason) is equal by nature in all men.' 'What the natural light of my mind shows me to be true,' he affirms, 'that I cannot doubt.' Again and again he accepts on no other evidence than 'the natural light of reason' premises for argument which surely require a more solid justification than this. 'It is repugnant to reason,' he writes, 'that the more perfect should proceed from the less perfect.' And elsewhere: 'It is something manifest to the natural light of the mind that there must be at least as much reality in the efficient and total cause as in its effect.'[10]

Descartes exaggerates the importance of man's rational faculty and its intuitive powers; the truth of an idea is not guaranteed by the clarity and distinctness with which the mind conceives it. He was right to try to break away from the syllogistic reasoning of the medieval scholars, which was quite incapable of exploring the natural world; but his mathematical genius, his passion for certainty and also, no doubt, the influence of his education obscured from him the possibility of other forms of reasoning as a means to knowledge.

However, Descartes himself became aware of the weakness of his position. Might it not be possible, after all, that he was wrong in accepting intuitive perception of a clear and distinct idea as the guarantee of its

[8] *Ibid.*, pp. 20, 21.
[9] *Discourse*, trans. Woolaston, p. 58: 'My whole object was always to achieve certainty, and to probe beneath the shifting soil and the sands to find the underlying rock or stone.'
[10] *Ibid.*, pp. 36, 121, 62, 123.

truth? He resolved therefore to 'start the whole work of construction again from the very foundation';[11] he would re-examine his fundamental beliefs, applying to each in turn the test of methodical doubt and rejecting any that appeared to be less than indubitable:

And so, because our senses sometimes deceive us, I made up my mind to suppose that they always did. Then, since there are men who fall into logical errors when they reason, even in the simplest geometrical matters, I reflected that I was as fallible as anyone, and rejected as false all the arguments I had hitherto regarded as conclusive. Finally, in view of the fact that those very same ideas which come to us when we are awake can also come when we are asleep without one of them being true, I resolved to pretend that everything that had ever entered my mind was as false as the figments of my dreams.[12]

But surely the conclusions of mathematics and deductive logic are exempt from the possibility of error? 'For whether I be awake or asleep, two and three always make five, and a square always has four sides.' Not so, however: perhaps it is God's will that I should always be wrong when I add 2 and 3 or count the sides of a square; or perhaps—an even more dreadful thought—'there is no God of goodness, the sovereign source of truth, but a malignant genius, as powerful as he is cunning and deceitful, who has used all his zeal to deceive me'.[13]

Is there anything at all, Descartes asks, which is exempt from this probing sceptical attack and may therefore be accepted as certain truth? Before examining his answer to this question it may be useful to comment briefly on this technique of methodical doubt, for it represents a quite different conception of knowledge from that which he had adopted earlier; clear, distinct and indubitable premises are still the object of his quest, but intuition alone is insufficient as a criterion of their truth. A premise can now be accepted as certain only if it is immune from doubt; but the process of doubt is continuous, so that, even though once accepted as indubitable, it may still be subjected to further questioning and eventually fail the test. The criterion of truth is thus no longer intuitive assurance but the absence of refutation; a proposition may be accepted as true, as part of knowledge, so long as it remains unrefuted; knowledge is therefore provisional, probable, and the essence of mind is not vision but enquiry. How far the implications of this technique of scepticism were apparent to Descartes is difficult to say, but it certainly accords more closely with the view of knowledge prevalent in modern science than with that of his own time, and it is part of the justification for regarding him as 'the father of modern philosophy'.

[11] *Discourse*, trans Wollaston, p. 101.   [12] *Ibid.*, pp. 60–1.
[13] *Ibid.*, pp. 104, 106.

To proceed with the construction of his philosophical system Descartes must have an assured starting-point totally immune from doubt; this he finds by persisting with his sceptical questioning till it brings him at last to one truth whose certainty seems beyond dispute:

Immediately, as I strove to think of everything as false, I realised that, in the very act of thinking everything false, I was aware of myself as something real; and observing that the truth: *I think, therefore I am*, was so firm and so assured that the most extravagant arguments of the sceptics were incapable of shaking it, I concluded that I might have no scruple in taking it as that first principle of philosophy for which I was looking.[14]

Cogito, ergo sum. In order to think, he argues, I must exist; I do think, therefore I exist. Whether my thoughts be false or not does not matter; all experience may be illusion, but so long as I am conscious of the possibility of its illusoriness, I must exist. (It should be noted that the argument is not original to Descartes; St Augustine had already thought along similar lines and formulated his conclusions in the words, *Si fallor, sum*— 'If I am deceived, I exist'; but he did not make it the foundation-stone of his philosophy.)

Is the *cogito* a satisfactory initial premise? Has it the incontestable security which Descartes requires in his first principle? It may be objected that 'I think, therefore I am' is not strictly a statement or proposition but a kind of argument; it is not a premise at all. Moreover, even as an argument it is not complete, for logically it should run: Whatever thinks exists; I think; therefore I exist. In other words, the major premise is omitted. Now Descartes nowhere fully unfolds the argument behind the *cogito*, nor does he express himself with entire clarity in expounding it; but his intention seems to be as follows: 'I think that I exist' necessarily implies 'I exist', since without existence there can be no thinking; from this he infers that it is impossible to think that one exists and be mistaken, and so concludes that he has found in 'I exist' an indubitable proposition which is beyond the reach of the malignant demon. However, granted that 'I think that I exist' necessarily implies 'I exist', it does not follow that I cannot be mistaken in *thinking* that I exist; certainly, *if* I think, then I exist, but how can I be sure that I am in fact thinking? Logical certainty is not the same as psychological certainty, and Descartes appears to confuse the two. The proposition 'I think' is just as much open to doubt as any other—I may not in fact be thinking and I may be quite wrong in supposing that I am. Moreover, Descartes had earlier suggested that even logical validity was open to doubt, since the deceiving demon could cause me to suppose that 2 and 3 are not 5 and to make errors in logical inference.

It seems, then, that the *cogito* is open to criticism on at least two counts;

[14] *Ibid.*, p. 61.

neither psychologically nor logically has it the absolute certainty he requires. A possible answer to the second of these criticisms is that *cogito* does not mean simply 'I think' but includes every mental and emotional state of which I am consciously aware. 'What am I?' Descartes asks: 'A thinking thing—a thing, that is to say, which doubts, understands, affirms, denies, wills and does not will, and which also imagines and feels.'[15] Now I may be mistaken in believing that I am thinking (I may be dreaming, or some power, evil or benign, may be using my mind like a tape-recorder to play off its own thoughts), but this wide range of conscious awareness cannot be written off thus—if I have it, I have it and there can be no mistake about my having it.

There is a further objection that can be made to the *cogito*, namely that the 'I' of 'I think' is invalidly assumed; all that Descartes can rightly assert is 'think' or 'thinking'; the 'I' is an additional factor unjustifiably tacked on, a particularisation of thought by assigning it to a person. His answer to this would probably be that the 'I-ness' of thinking is something which is given in the very process of thought; thinking implies self-awareness: 'It is so obvious that it is I who doubt, understand and will, that no further explanation is required. And it is I who imagine . . . I who sense or perceive physical things through my senses. . . .'[16] The 'I' of *cogito* is not extraneous, therefore, but an essential part of it—thought *must* be particularised in a person thinking. In any case it seems likely that Descartes did not intend the *cogito* to be understood as a formal logical argument, syllogistic or otherwise; he was certainly aware that for its expression as a complete syllogism a major premise was necessary:

He who says, *I think, hence I am or exist*, does not deduce existence from thought by a syllogism, but by a simple act of mental vision he recognises it as if it were a thing which is known through itself. This is evident from the fact that, if it were deduced syllogistically, the major premise, *that everything which thinks is or exists*, would have to be known previously; but it has been learned rather from the individual's experience—that unless he exists he cannot think.[17]

In other words, I see intuitively in my own experience the necessary connection between 'I think' and 'I exist'; I do not so much argue it as perceive it, and then in the light of this intuitive perception I see that the wider truth of the major premise is also involved.

In this view of the 'I', the self, Descartes' modernity of outlook is again apparent. First, he directs attention to mind as *active*—its function

[15] *Discourse*, trans. Wollaston, p. 111.
[16] *Ibid.*, p. 112.
[17] *Replies to Objections*, 2, 3; quoted in Copleston, *History of Philosophy*, vol. iv (1958), p. 91.

is not to accept on authority nor merely to deduce the logical consequences of assumptions provided for it in advance, but to enquire, to deliberate, to venture forth imaginatively, to disagree, to decide for itself; and by the inclusion in the self of perception, feeling, judgment and other activities he greatly extends the range of what is to be classified as mental. Second, he emphasises the subjectivity of self, thus indicating a new world of inner experience available for exploration and preparing the way for the intensive study of mental phenomena which has since become the science of psychology.

To his own satisfaction, at least, Descartes has now established a secure starting-point for his philosophical system: the fact of one's own existence as a thinking, conscious self is unassailable even by the most searching scepticism. However, something more than a thinking self is required for a comprehensive system of philosophy; he must therefore enquire whether there is any other certainty to which the *cogito* points and which can be incorporated into his structure. There is indeed such a certainty, namely God, and his next step is to demonstrate this. Now apart from his purpose in constructing a philosophical system there were two further vital reasons why he must prove the existence of God. Despite his insistence on clear and distinct ideas as bearing on themselves the stamp of truth, Descartes well understood that human reason could produce no final argument against rejecting them; certainly the existence of the self is assured, but other ideas are not, for lurking in the background is always the shadow of the deceiving demon. He needed, therefore, an external guarantor of the truth of ideas, and what could this be but God? Moreover, the existence of a thinking self is no evidence for an external world of material objects; yet common sense and the consensus of experience demand that we suppose such a world to exist. Once again, he needed God as the guarantor that it does; for God, being perfect in all respects, would not allow us to be deceived in a belief so fundamental and so widely held. And so: 'I must consider at the first opportunity whether God exists and, if he does, whether he can be a deceiver; for without assurance on these two points I do not see how it is possible to be certain of anything.'[18]

His proofs are ontological, but they proceed along different lines from St Anselm's while employing the same concept of perfection (see pp. 74-5 above). The ideas in the human mind, he says, come partly from within itself and partly from outside; 'substance' is an example of the former, 'heat', 'cold', 'noise' of the latter. Among these ideas is that of the mind's own imperfection; for it is aware that it doubts, and to doubt is to fall short of knowledge and therefore of perfection; this in turn gives rise to the idea of perfection and so to the concept of God. By 'God', he explains,

[18] *Discourse*, trans. Wollaston, p. 119.

'I mean an infinite, eternal, immutable and independent substance, all-knowing and all-powerful.'[19] Now these ideas—infinite, eternal, etc.—cannot originate within myself, for I am finite, transient, etc., and it is impossible for the finite to conceive from its own resources the idea of the infinite, or the transient that of the eternal; nor can the imperfect conjure from itself the concept of perfection. Why so? Because—and here Descartes introduces an *a priori* principle from scholastic philosophy—

it is something manifest to the natural light of the mind that there must be at least as much reality in the efficient and total cause as in its effect. For whence does the effect draw its reality except from the cause? And how can the cause communicate this reality, unless it has it in itself? From this it follows that . . . the more perfect or more real cannot follow and depend upon the less perfect.[20]

Since, then, the finite cannot of itself conceive the infinite nor the transient the eternal nor the imperfect the perfect, it must be that the ideas of the infinite etc. come from outside the mind and that this source must be a God who actually exists.

A second argument uses the idea of perfection rather differently: if I were the cause of my own existence, I would be the cause of the idea of perfection which is in my mind; but the same scholastic principle requires that, in order to cause the idea of perfection, I should have to be perfect, i.e. God, and this is obviously not so. There must therefore be, external to myself, a cause both of my existence and of my idea of perfection, and this is God. These arguments suffer from much the same weaknesses as St Anselm's. Dependent on *a priori* principles concerning causation and perfection, they are analytic, not synthetic; they explicate what is contained in the assumptions they presuppose rather than establish existential facts.

However, Descartes himself believes that he has now established two certainties—the self, and God; but these are not enough, for we also seem to have experience of an external world; he must therefore go on to enquire into the reality of this experience—is it genuine or illusory? Can certainty be found here too? In this enquiry Descartes is confronted by a major difficulty: he has already shown that the essence of self is conscious awareness; the seat of this consciousness is the mind, which is non-material and therefore distinct in kind from the material body and in some sense independent of it. Mind is not only distinct from body; it is also distinct from the material world which provides the apparent objects of sensation. This distinction is reinforced by Descartes' use of the concept of substance, inherited via medieval thinkers from Aristotle. He defines substance

---

[19] *Discourse*, trans. Wollaston, p. 127.   [20] *Ibid.*, p. 123.

as 'a thing existing in such a manner that it has need of no other thing in order to exist';[21] strictly this can apply only to God, but he extends it to include also 'conscious substance' or mind and 'corporeal substance' or matter. The world of human experience is divided into these last two, mind and matter, each of which is characterised by a principal property or, as Descartes calls it, attribute; the attribute of mind is thought, of matter extension. Now if mind and matter thus belong to two different categories of existence, how is communication possible between them? How does mind make contact with things external to itself or even know that they exist at all? He has already agreed that, apart from the *cogito*, human reason has no final argument against scepticism; it could be, therefore, that our apparent experience of an external world is wholly illusory. For, although sensations have a peculiar vividness and immediacy which persuades us that they emanate from real objects external to us, yet the fact of optical and other sensory illusion gives cause to doubt the evidence of the senses. Moreover, it could even be that human nature is so constituted 'as to be deceived even when the truth seemed most obvious'.[22] To this Descartes has no answer nor any guarantee of the existence of an external world save faith in God's integrity—the perfection of his character cannot allow us to be deceived. We can therefore be certain that an external world exists, but only because we have already proved the existence of God.

Such, then, is Descartes' quest for certainty; starting from the, to him, indubitable experience of self-awareness and its implication of existence, he proceeds by means of the idea of perfection to demonstrate the existence of God, and in God's perfection of character he finds the justification for accepting as genuine our belief in an external world. What success can he claim? Despite the criticisms of the *cogito* already stated it does seem that here, in the elemental fact of consciousness, Descartes comes as near as may be to finding a point of certainty in human experience. To describe the nature or explain the origin of this consciousness may not be possible, either now or ever; and it can, of course, be distorted by disease or drugs and temporarily put into abeyance by anaesthetics; nor can we be sure that it is not a prolonged dream or the playing of some pre-recorded celestial tape. Yet there is, surely, something which we experience as conscious awareness of ourselves and our environment, and this presumes —perhaps is the same as—existence. At the very least it can be claimed that *something exists* or that there *is* existence—though what either of these expressions could mean is far from obvious (the meaning of 'existence' is evidently a matter which requires further investigation). Descartes is on

[21] *Rules . . .*, trans. Anscombe and Geach, p. 192.
[22] *Discourse*, trans. Wollaston, p. 157.

weaker ground in adding to this elemental certainty the particularisation of 'I', of selfhood; though here again, as he himself asserts, the overwhelming experience which most human beings have of their personal, particularised consciousness gives him some support.

Two further comments: first, whatever certainty the *cogito* possesses is psychological rather than logical; it depends not so much on inference as on intuition, 'a simple act of mental vision'. This raises the important question of the validity of intuition as a source of knowledge, but discussion of it must be postponed to the next chapter. Second, even if its certainty is granted, the *cogito* will not support the weight of the metaphysical edifice that Descartes erects on it. For reasons already advanced his second focus of certainty is by no means secure—God's existence cannot be demonstrated by analytical argument—and the same must be said of his third focus which depends on it. As will be seen in chapter 7, the existence of an external world, in the sense of a material universe existing objectively and independently of mind, cannot be taken for granted and can in all seriousness be denied.

Must it be assumed, then, that the quest for certainty is a futile exercise? Can any worthwhile certainty be found? In attempting an answer we must bear in mind the distinction already mentioned between psychological and logical certainty (p. 30). To the area of the former belongs the elemental self-awareness of the *cogito*—if indeed we grant its certainty. Some would also include immediate sensory awareness, for instance of colour or sound: when we are waiting at traffic-lights, we do not doubt that red is red or green green, and when the telephone rings at our elbow, we do not normally doubt our hearing; in either case we accept as certain the immediate impression of our senses. Yet on reflection we are bound to admit that sensation is fallible; drugs or mental disturbance can cause us to 'see' and 'hear' what makes no impression on others with us. It might be argued that even so there is no doubt of my actually having a sensation which to me at that moment is green or shrill, whether or not it corresponds to anything actually occurring; but certainty of such a kind is hardly worth much; it is not *cognitive* certainty, the secure and considered knowledge that such and such is indisputably the case. Certainty is sometimes claimed for memory—though not by philosophers when they are philosophising: 'I know that Jane's telephone number is 22448'; but memory is notoriously fallible and it is common experience to find on checking that the number is 22488. Psychological certainty abounds in religious utterance and in poetry: 'I know that my Redeemer liveth'; 'Beauty is truth, truth beauty'. Certainty of the last kind can be of enormous value in human life, inducing effort and sacrifice which would otherwise be inconceivable; but it is often superficial and transitory—like knowing one is in love—sometimes even dangerous—like the assurance of an uninformed conscience.

Logical certainty, on the other hand, is indeed indubitable; the conclusions of valid deductive inference are necessarily so; they cannot be otherwise. But—and here is the rub—their value in the quest for certainty depends on their premises: if these are *a priori* definitions or axioms agreed for the purpose of argument or 'truths of reason', the conclusions, being analytic or, as some would say, tautologous, give us no information beyond what is already contained in the premises; they tell us nothing new about the world. If the premises are empirical, generalised from experience, they share the logical weakness of all empirical generalisations, the possibility of refutation; and this weakness is, of course, passed on to the conclusions (see below, pp. 177-9). Logical certainty, then, though available, is of dubious value. What Descartes was seeking, and what most of those who have any interest in the problem are seeking, is *existential* certainty, certainty about the universe and man's place in it. Unhappily, from what has already been said the indications are that this is unattainable; the human situation is such, so it would seem, that epistemological certainty of the cosmic kind eludes our grasp. 'Faith', says the writer of the *Letter to the Hebrews*, 'makes us certain of realities we do not see'; but those for whom faith is unacceptable must be content to live, at the best, with probability.[23]

Is scepticism, then, the proper attitude in the man for whom religious faith has no appeal? This is far too big a question for more than the briefest comment. A degree of scepticism, reasoned and courteous, is proper to any serious thinker, whether he be philosopher, scientist or theologian—Descartes has a lesson for us here. Conclusions are tentative until the evidence justifies acceptance, and even then they remain open to further scrutiny and testing. Total scepticism, however, is a *practical* if not an intellectual impossibility, for no man can remain uncommitted—the exigencies of living preclude it. This at any rate is the conclusion Hume reaches at the end of his sceptical enquiries. The total sceptic

must acknowledge, if he will acknowledge anything, that all human life must perish, were his principles universally and steadily to prevail. All

---

[23] It might be different if it were possible to prove the existence of *a priori* propositions that were *synthetic*, not analytic; from which, that is, there could be deduced in advance of experience new information about the world. This was Kant's problem in his *Critique of Pure Reason*; but though he concluded that there are such propositions, he denied that they have any validity beyond the range of experience—they cannot form the starting-point for metaphysical systems which try to picture what lies beyond experience. See chapter 9.

discourse, all action would immediately cease and men remain in a total lethargy till the necessities of nature, unsatisfied, put an end to their miserable existence.[24]

A 'mitigated scepticism' he approves, but excess of it, though it 'may flourish and triumph in the schools, where it is indeed difficult, if not impossible to refute',[25] is dissipated by the hard light of day.

In conclusion something more must be said on Descartes' distinction between mind and matter, for it raises acute difficulties of which he was himself at least partially aware. The dualism was by no means new in Descartes, for it had already appeared in Plato's contrast between the world of Forms, intellectually apprehended, and the, for him, unreal world of physical objects; a similar dichotomy is found in Aristotle between the pure intellectuality of the 'unmoved mover' (and of *nous* in man) and the inferior 'being' of the sensory world. In Descartes the contrast is heightened by his account of matter: its basic feature is three-dimensional extension; to this he adds the ingredient of motion, without which matter would be static. The material world therefore consists of matter spatially extended in different shapes and sizes, and in constant motion; it is a mechanistic, quantitative world whose phenomena are adequately explained by efficient, as distinct from final, causes. But the basic feature of mind is thought, and between this and the mechanism of the physical world there seems no possibility of communication; they belong to different orders of reality.

There are two facets to the problem, the mind/body relationship and that between mind and the so-called external world. Since the body is material and the mind non-material, how can they cooperate? Clearly they do, for the mind perceives through bodily senses and controls the movement of limbs and other bodily functions. How then does this occur? At what point do mind and body meet in the act of sense perception and of initiating movement? Descartes supposed the place of this interaction to be a small gland within the brain; we now know that he was wrong and that there is no precise locus of confrontation where mind and body merge into each other. In recent times a notable attack has been made on this aspect of the problem by the Oxford philosopher, Professor Gilbert Ryle:[26] the dualism, which he refers to as 'Descartes' myth' and 'the dogma of the Ghost in the Machine', is entirely fictitious; it arises from regarding mind and matter as belonging to the same logical type or category when in fact

[24] *Enquiry concerning Human Understanding*, XII, ii, 128; ed. L. A. Selby-Bigge (Oxford, Clarendon Press, 1902), p. 160.
[25] *Ibid.*, XII, ii, 126; ed. Selby-Bigge, p. 159.
[26] *The Concept of Mind* (Hutchinson, 1949), esp. ch. 1, 'Descartes' myth'.

they do not—like saying 'she arrived home in a flood of tears and a sedan-chair'; because they belong to different categories, there is no dichotomy and it is pointless to contrast them.

The other facet of the problem has proved equally intractable. If mind and matter are as different as Descartes alleged, what contact can there ever be between mind and the supposedly external world? What happens in the act of perception?—does the mind actually perceive external objects or (as Descartes believed) does it only perceive images within itself which somehow 'represent' the objects outside? If this is so, if the mind perceives only its own contents, how can we be sure that the images are accurate representations of external objects or even that the latter exist at all? Again, how can the mind have knowledge of something whose nature is entirely alien to its own—by what means and in what sense can pure thought know extended physical objects? From consideration of these and other questions there have emerged two contrasting positions, idealism and materialism;[27] there are many versions of these, but broadly speaking the former regards matter as dependent on and subordinate to mind, existing only in so far as it is the object of thought, whether an individual's or God's; the latter regards matter as the basic constituent of the universe, and mind as a byproduct, manifestation or epiphenomenon, like the bloom on a ripe plum.[28] More will be found on these two positions and generally on the relation between the mind and external objects in the chapters on Locke, Berkeley and Kant.

[27] 'Idealism' in its philosophical meanings must be distinguished from the popular use to denote altruism, the possession of ideals; similarly 'materialism' does not here mean being committed to 'materialistic' values.

[28] The imagery is Aristotle's, who uses it in *Ethics* X, 1174b in his account of pleasure; this, he says, is the crowning perfection of an activity, 'like the bloom on ripe fruit'.

Further study

Descartes

The following books will assist entry into Descartes' philosophy, but none of them is a simple introduction: s. v. KEELING, *Descartes* (Benn, 1934); N. KEMP SMITH, *Studies in the Cartesian Philosophy* (Macmillan, 1902) and *New Studies in the Philosophy of Descartes* (Macmillan, 1952). Reference should also be made to the general histories and *The Encyclopedia of Philosophy* mentioned on pp. 37-8.

Descartes' *Discourse* and *Meditations* (which should be read in full) are printed in the Penguin translation by A. WOLLASTON (1960); the Everyman's Library edition (trans. J. VEITCH, Dent, 1912) has these and the *Principles of Philosophy*. Another selection is that of E. ANSCOMBE and

P. T. GEACH, *Descartes: Philosophical Writings* (Nelson, 1954), which has the *Discourse* and *Meditations*, parts of the *Principles* and much else.

The quest for certainty

It would be helpful to read again the section in chapter 1 above on rationalism and empiricism and to supplement this with W. H. WALSH, *Reason and Experience* (Oxford, Clarendon Press, 1947), especially chapters 2, 3, 4, 5.

On the general question of certainty in knowledge there are helpful chapters in A. J. AYER, *The Problem of Knowledge* (Penguin, 1956; ch. 2); HOSPERS' *Introduction to Philosophical Analysis* (chs 2, 3); and, for a strongly anti-rationalist view, REICHENBACH's *Rise of Scientific Philosophy* (ch. 3). Further discussion of it can be found in J. DEWEY, *The Quest for Certainty* (Allen & Unwin, 1930), chs 1, 2; N. MALCOLM, *Knowledge and Certainty* (Englewood Cliffs, Prentice-Hall, 1963); and, with specific reference to Descartes, A. G. A. BALZ, *Descartes and the Modern Mind*, Part II: *The Quest for Certainty* (Yale University Press, 1952). There are also several articles in W. DONEY, *Descartes* (Macmillan's 'Modern Studies in Philosophy') and many more listed in the bibliography. There is much of value, too, in Hume's *Enquiry concerning Human Understanding*, especially sections 4, 5 and 12; in Locke's *Essay*, Book IV, chs 1–4 and 15–17; and in Mill's *Logic*, Book II, chs 5–7, and III, ch 1. See also chs 6, 8, 10 below.

On mind and matter and the Cartesian duality G. RYLE, *The Concept of Mind* (Hutchinson, 1949; Penguin, 1963) is essential reading, certainly the first chapter, 'Descartes' myth'; and see the chapter, 'Professor Ryle's attack on dualism' by A. C. EWING, in *Clarity is not Enough*, ed. H. D. LEWIS (Allen & Unwin, 1963). EWING's *Fundamental Questions of Philosophy*, chs 4, 5, 6, and RUSSELL's *Problems of Philosophy*, chs 1, 2, 3, 4, offer helpful surveys; more difficult is J. LAIRD, *Our Minds and Matter* (Cambridge University Press, 1934); and there is a stimulating essay by G. E. MOORE, 'Material things', in *Some Main Problems of Philosophy* (Allen & Unwin, 1953), and another, 'Proof of an external world', in J. N. FINDLAY, ed., *Studies in Philosophy* (Oxford University Press, 1966). R. J. HIRST, ed., *Perception and the External World* (New York, Macmillan, 1965) is a valuable collection of articles relevant to this issue.

6 Locke

The origin and nature of knowledge

Biographical note

Locke's philosophical work was in a sense only a byproduct of a life which was mostly busy in other fields. For although Locke was always a student (in the broader meaning), he spent only the first ten years after graduation in professional academic studies. He was born near Bristol in 1632, was sent to Westminster School and from there won a scholarship to Christ Church, Oxford; here, after graduating M.A. in 1658, he was elected to a senior studentship and later to a lectureship in Greek. Meanwhile he had become keenly interested in experimental science, partly, no doubt, for reasons of temperament, partly in reaction against the arid logical training to which students were subjected at that time. He associates himself with a group of Oxford men who were exploring a very different approach to knowledge, based on observation and experiment; they included Robert Boyle, famous for his 'law' on the volume of gases. Within this interest in science Locke developed a particular attachment to medicine, and eventually he was granted both the degree of Bachelor of Medicine and a faculty to practise as a physician. In 1668 he was elected a Fellow of the newly founded Royal Society. Another major interest which grew during these Oxford years was in politics and civil affairs; this led to his appointment in 1665 to a brief diplomatic mission to the Elector of Brandenburg. In the following year he was introduced to Lord Ashley, later the Earl of Shaftesbury, who recognised his ability and made him his private physician and secretary; through him Locke became involved in the stormy politics of this revolutionary period, and when Shaftesbury was forced to flee to Holland to escape the wrath of Charles II, Locke followed him and spent six years in voluntary exile. The revolution of 1688 (which ousted James II) enabled him to return without fear to England; the rest of his life, until his death in 1704, he gave partly to study and writing, partly to various official appointments which kept him in close touch with the government.

Locke's empirical philosophy is expounded in An Essay concerning Human Understanding, *a book which he wrote over a period of twenty years, finished during his stay in Holland and published in 1690.*[1] *He wrote three preparatory drafts and made many revisions in later editions; even so the book is excessively long and lacks the coherence and consistency one expects of a major philosophical work. Yet this, strangely, is one of its virtues; for the ambiguities and inconsistencies which Locke failed either to notice or resolve spurred subsequent thinkers to look for a more adequate account of empiricism. In addition to the* Essay *he wrote on politics, religion and education; his* Two Treatises of Government *is an important contribution to political theory, and* Some Thoughts concerning Education *is a delightful and readable statement of the education he thought desirable for a young gentleman of his time. In all his writings, and in his life as well, Locke shows himself a wise, humane and civilised person, strongly biased towards prudence and common sense and passionately attached to the truth—'I never write for anything but truth,' he says in a letter to a friend, 'and never publish anything to others which I am not fully persuaded of myself.'*[2] *Despite his great learning and practical gifts he remained modest and unpretentious; even in the* Essay *he saw himself only as 'an under-labourer . . . clearing the ground a little and removing some of the rubbish that lies in the way to knowledge'.*[3]

The nature of knowledge and the sources from which it is derived had exercised philosophers for long before Locke's time. We have seen how Plato distinguished between knowledge and belief and sought to establish the former on the permanence and immutability of the Forms; knowledge is recollection and is acquired (or re-acquired) by the resolute rejection of sensory experience and the practice of pure thought. Aristotle likewise was concerned to find a secure basis for knowledge, and though

[1] Locke has described the process of its composition in his introductory 'Epistle to the Reader': '. . . having been thus begun by chance, was continued by entreaty, written by incoherent parcels, and after long intervals of neglect resumed again as my humour or occasions permitted; and at last, in retirement when an attendance on my health gave me leisure, it was brought into that order thou now seest it.' He is aware of the excessive length of the book and its repetitiousness, 'but to confess the truth, I am now too lazy, or too busy, to make it shorter'—an avowal which is both commendable for its honesty and in keeping with his character.

[2] R. I. Aaron, *John Locke* (Oxford University Press, 2nd edn, 1955), p. 46.

[3] 'Epistle to the Reader', in *An Essay concerning Human Understanding*, ed. A. S. Pringle-Pattison (Oxford University Press, 1924), p. 7. (Further references will be to this edition.)

Locke

he dismissed the Theory of Forms as untenable, he was nevertheless obliged to find a substitute in his own theory of the essential form embodied in each individual substance; this, the universal in the particular, is that which can be known. In St Thomas we have noted the crucial distinction between revealed and natural knowledge, the former bestowed on man by divine grace, the latter developed from sense perception by the formation of intellectual concepts. As for Descartes, the pursuit of indubitable knowledge was the starting-point of his whole philosophical endeavour; without the *cogito* his metaphysical system would have neither basis nor justification.

The importance for a philosopher of establishing some theory of knowledge is clear from these few examples—which could be multiplied time and again; it has also been shown in chapter I, where an attempt was made to describe epistemology and to indicate some of the intriguing questions which it seeks to examine. It is not, however, simply a matter of intellectual fascination, the attraction of perplexity; the philosopher needs assurance that his enterprise is viable. For this he must lay the spectre of scepticism and demonstrate, to his own satisfaction at least, that knowledge is both meaningful and within his grasp—that there is something to be known and means of knowing it, that he may have faith in his own intellectual processes and rely on rational communication with other minds. Moreover, theories of knowledge have far-reaching implications—they are convertible into metaphysical systems and ideals of life (as in Plato, for instance); and the concept of knowledge is indissociable from other important concepts, such as truth, science and experience, indeed from the whole intellectual and cultural tradition of the human race.

In chapter I attention was drawn to the existence of two different approaches to philosophy involving distinct views on the nature of knowledge and carrying important implications for metaphysics; these are rationalism and empiricism. The former, it was said, regards human reason as an independent source of knowledge enjoying access to *a priori* truths which it apprehends without reference to experience. Empiricism, on the other hand, asserts that all knowledge derives from observation and experience; reason contributes indispensably to the creation of knowledge but cannot of itself originate it—*nihil in intellectu quod prius non fuerit in sensu*. From the fourth century B.C. to the seventeenth A.D. rationalism was predominant; this was due mainly to the influence of Plato and Aristotle, the latter reinforced in the thirteenth century by St Thomas. Yet the history of empiricism, as has already been noted, reaches back to the pre-Socratics; the appeal to experience is strong in Aristotle, though overshadowed by the rationalism of his master; St Thomas bases natural knowledge firmly on sense perception, and in the same century the rebel

Franciscan, Roger Bacon, proclaimed the importance of experimental science as an indispensable means to truth—'without experience nothing can be known sufficiently'.[4] William of Ockham, another rebellious Franciscan, shared the same movement of thought, as also did Francis Bacon in the age of Elizabeth. By Locke's time empiricism had increased its hold; experimental science was well established and led to notable advances in scientific knowledge during the seventeenth century.[5] Nevertheless, though William of Ockham, the two Bacons and other experimentalists contributed greatly to the formation of scientific method and the techniques of research, they made no systematic attempt to analyse and justify the claim that knowledge derives ultimately from experience. They did not think to question either the competence of the human mind to acquire knowledge from this source or the limits of its power to do so; nor did they enquire into the means by which knowledge is created from the raw materials of sense perception. Moreover the decadent rationalism which persisted in the Oxford of Locke's day was incapable of accommodating the new methods and discoveries of empirical science: reason was regarded as essentially deductive and the final justification of new knowledge lay, not in experimental evidence, but in *a priori* principles which were held to be self-evident. It seemed, therefore, to Locke that a new examination of knowledge and of the process of its acquisition was long overdue. The proper starting-point for philosophical enquiry, he insisted, is the nature and capacities of the human mind itself—what can it know and how does it acquire the knowledge it has? of what can it be certain and how distinguish between knowledge and mere belief? His claim to greatness rests partly on this, partly on the fact that, in attempting to present an empirical account of knowledge, he raised numerous problems which have exercised philosophers from that day to this. It is not without justice (yet it should not be without qualification) that Locke is commonly referred to as the founder of empiricism; furthermore, to him more than to any other is due the epistemological slant which has long been characteristic of British philosophy.

The origin of his own investigations he describes in the 'Epistle to the Reader' which introduces the *Essay*:

Were it fit to trouble thee with the history of this *Essay*, I should tell thee that five or six friends, meeting at my chamber and discoursing on a subject very remote from this, found themselves quickly at a stand by the difficulties that rose on every side. After we had awhile puzzled our-

---

[4] R. McKeon, ed., *Selections from Medieval Philosophers*, vol ii (London, Scribner's, 1931), p. 72.

[5] Galileo, Kepler, Boyle and Harvey are among the great names of this century.

selves without coming any nearer a resolution of those doubts which perplexed us, it came into my thoughts that we took a wrong course; and
that before we set ourselves upon enquiries of that nature, it was necessary
to examine our own abilities and see what objects our understandings
were, or were not, fitted to deal with.[6]

The purpose of the book, he later explains, is 'to enquire into the original,
certainty and extent of human knowledge, together with the grounds and
degrees of belief, opinion and assent'.[7] Its central thesis is that all our
knowledge derives ultimately from experience. At birth the mind is like
an empty cabinet or a blank sheet of paper, 'void of all characters, without
any ideas'; it has no innate ideas or principles 'which the soul receives in
its very first being and brings into the world with it'.[8] Whence, then, Locke
asks, does it acquire 'that vast store which the busy and boundless fancy
of man has painted on it with an almost endless variety? Whence has it
all the materials of reason and knowledge?' He continues: 'To this I
answer, in one word, from EXPERIENCE; in that all our knowledge is
founded and from that it ultimately derives itself.'[9] This is not to deny
that the mind has innate potentialities or that heredity is a determining
factor in human attainment; in *Thoughts concerning Education* Locke
affirms repeatedly the power of natural endowment to predispose children's
behaviour—'the bias will always hang on that side nature first placed it';[10]
and he was too keen an observer to overlook the obvious fact of inequality
in their capacities. What he does deny is that the mind brings with it into
the world any epistemological *content*, or that knowledge is a reminiscence, as Plato suggested, of something learnt in a previous existence.

What, then, are the materials of knowledge? We are all aware, Locke
says, that we think, and what the 'mind is applied about whilst thinking'
is 'the ideas that are there'.[11] 'Ideas' come from two sources within
experience, sensation and reflection:

First, our senses conversant about particular sensible objects, do convey into
the mind several distinct perceptions of things, according to those various
ways wherein those objects do affect them. And thus we come by those
ideas we have of *yellow, white, heat, cold, soft, hard, bitter, sweet,* and
all those which we call sensible qualities. . . . Secondly, the other fountain
from which experience furnisheth the understanding with ideas is the
perception of the operations of our own minds within us, as it is employed
about the ideas it has got. . . . And such are *perception, thinking, doubting,*

---

[6] p. 4.
[7] *Essay* I, 1, 2; p. 9.
[8] *Essay* I, ii, 15; p. 22; II, i, 2; p. 42; I, ii, 1; p. 16.
[9] *Essay* II, i, 2; p. 42.
[10] *Thoughts . . .*, para. 102; ed. F. W. Garforth (Heinemann, 1964), p. 59.
[11] *Essay* II, i, 1; p. 42.

believing, reasoning, knowing, willing, and all the different actings of our own minds.[12]

From these two sources comes 'our whole stock of ideas; . . . we have nothing in our minds which did not come in one of these two ways'.[13] The basic ingredients of knowledge, then, are 'ideas' of the external world supplied by sense perception and 'ideas' of the inner world of thought and feeling of which we are aware through introspection. 'Ideas', Locke continues, whether of sense or reflection, are both simple and complex. Simple 'ideas' present themselves readymade, and so long as sense and thought are active they cannot be rejected; nor can they be altered, but, as the raw materials of knowledge, they must be accepted as they are. Nevertheless, although the mind is passive in the initial receiving of them, it has the power to combine them to form complex 'ideas'; in so doing it adds to the range and content of its own reflection. It can also relate 'ideas' to one another and abstract from them to form general truths.

At the level of common sense this may seem a plausible enough statement of the origins of knowledge, but, as will be seen later, it contains numerous difficulties which Locke left unresolved. Moreover, he confuses the issue by giving different accounts, at different points in the *Essay*, of what he understands by both simple and complex 'ideas'. At one time he stresses the uniform character of what he regards as simple 'ideas' of sensation, for instance, the coldness of ice or the whiteness of a lily; at another he emphasises the passivity of the mind in receiving them; elsewhere he thinks of them as the smallest units of sensory experience. His account of simple 'ideas' of reflection is equally vague—it can be seen at a glance that in the list quoted in the passage above Locke is combining under the same heading mental experiences which are widely different in character. Of complex 'ideas' he gives different accounts in the first and fourth editions of the *Essay*; the latter was added without deleting the earlier or attempting to reconcile them. However, it is unnecessary to follow him further into the intricacies and (it must be admitted) confusions of his doctrine of 'ideas'; it is enough to remark at this point that, although Locke's description of the origin of knowledge corresponds broadly with the manner in which it seems to be constructed from simple elements given in experience, he evidently gave insufficient thought to what precisely he conceived these simple elements to be and what the nature of the complex structures built out of them.

After describing its origin in experience Locke proceeds to examine the

[12] *Essay* II, i, 3, 4; pp. 43-4.
[13] *Essay* II, i, 5; p. 45. Some 'ideas', however, are the joint product of sense and reflection; Locke instances pleasure, pain, existence, unity, power, succession (II, vii).

nature of knowledge itself: 'Since the mind, in all its thoughts and reasonings, hath no other immediate object but its own ideas . . . , it is evident that our knowledge is only conversant about them.' In what, then, does it consist? It is, he says, 'the perception of the connexion and agreement or disagreement and repugnancy of any of our ideas'.[14] When we have the assurance that certain 'ideas' 'agree' or 'disagree', then we have knowledge. He instances the perception that white is not black and that the sum of the internal angles of a triangle is equal to two right angles; this he elaborates by indicating four kinds of agreement and disagreement —identity or diversity, relation, coexistence or necessary connection, and real existence. There are occasions when we perceive infallibly that something is itself and not another thing—that white is white, not red, and that round is round, not square; these are instances of identity and diversity, and when clearly grasped, they constitute knowledge. Examples of relation are cited earlier in the *Essay* and include comparison (larger and smaller, like and unlike), affinity (father and son), cause, implication (king implies subject, husband implies wife).[15] By coexistence Locke means the inevitable conjunction of *a* with *b*, for instance, gold with yellow, weight and malleability—qualities with which it is invariably associated. Of real existence the only example he gives is God, the 'idea' of whom (so he believed) can be proved to correspond to an actually existing being. All this is far from clear, but what Locke seems to be claiming is that knowledge consists in the perception of necessary implication between 'ideas'; its criteria are coherence and certainty. This suggests an ideal of knowledge which, despite his empirical pretensions, still leans heavily on the rationalist tradition.

Locke proceeds to divide knowledge into three types or, as he calls them, 'degrees'; these are: intuitive, demonstrative and 'sensitive'. Intuitive knowledge is apprehended immediately without any process of reasoning: 'In this the mind is at no pains of proving or examining, but perceives the truth as the eye doth light, only by being directed towards it. Thus the mind perceives that white is not black, that a circle is not a triangle.'[16] Demonstrative knowledge, which for various reasons he regards as inferior to intuitive, is reached by inference through one or more 'intermediate ideas' from premise to conclusion; an obvious example is the deductive reasoning of mathematics. These two degrees of knowledge both offer certainty; one can be sure of their validity. The third and lowest degree is what Locke calls 'sensitive' knowledge, by which he means an apprehension of the objects of the external world by means of our senses. This is not properly knowledge, as Locke understands it, since it does not offer certainty, but 'going beyond bare probability, and yet not reaching perfectly

[14] *Essay* IV, i, 1, 2; p. 255. [15] *Essay* II, xxv, 2. [16] *Essay* IV, ii, 1; p. 261.

to either of the foregoing degrees of certainty, passes under the name of knowledge'.[17] In demonstrative knowledge a single train of valid reasoning is sufficient to prove certainty in the conclusion; sensitive knowledge, however, requires numerous trains to establish the conclusion with sufficient probability to command assent.

What is this sensitive knowledge, and why does Locke find it necessary to add it to the other two? Knowledge is of the agreement and disagreement of 'ideas', and 'ideas' are in our minds. 'But,' he goes on: 'whether there be anything more than barely that idea in our minds, whether we can thence certainly infer the existence of anything without us, which corresponds to that idea, is that whereof some men think there may be a question made'[18]—as does Locke himself (p. 109 below). How *can* one be certain that an 'idea' in the mind represents a real object outside it, the 'idea' of a rose the actual flower? How be certain of the existence of particular objects round about us? There is no such certainty, but one may have at least a reasonable assurance 'that deserves the name of knowledge'.[19] Locke is in something of a dilemma here: his definition of knowledge excludes this awareness of external objects, yet there can be no doubt to his mind that these exist: between an actual taste or smell and the same sensation remembered or imagined there is a plain difference which suggests that the former has a reality which the latter lacks; our senses corroborate one another—one can feel as well as see a fire—and this again suggests the existence of an objective reality as the common source of each sensation; moreover, by our manipulation of external objects (as, for practical purposes, we take them to be) we contrive for ourselves pleasure and pain—and these feelings are not renewed when the objects are merely remembered and not directly sensed; finally, to doubt the existence of objects external to us implies a degree of scepticism which Locke cannot credit in any reasonable man. For all these reasons and despite his earlier definition in terms of intuition and demonstration Locke felt bound to admit the immediate sensory perception of objects within the category of knowledge, albeit reluctantly and as the lowest of the three degrees. Sensitive knowledge extends, however, no further than the immediate testimony of our senses, when we are actually hearing, seeing, feeling, and so on; if an object is out of sight, there is no guarantee of its continued existence; though the probability of this may be high, it has neither the certainty of genuine knowledge nor even a reasonable assurance.

Although Locke is to some extent contradicting himself, his account of sensitive knowledge is not without importance: it points to a distinction between two quite different kinds of knowledge, mathematical and

[17] *Essay* IV, ii, 14; p. 265; cf. xi; pp. 321 ff.
[18] *Ibid.*, p. 266.   [19] *Essay* IV, xi, 3; p. 322.

scientific (in the modern sense).[20] The former is hypothetical and deductive; the mathematician makes assumptions and deduces from them conclusions which, if the inference is valid, are indubitably certain; but the conclusions do not necessarily correspond to anything in the actual world. For knowledge of actual existence we must look beyond reason to observation; herein lies the role of science. Now the scientist, though he uses mathematical techniques and deductive inference in the course of his work, relies basically on induction, whose conclusions are never more than probable; here, then, the certainty of mathematics is unattainable. Yet we cannot reasonably reject the conclusions of science from the category of knowledge: for practical purposes they are acceptable, they are seen to work, they present us with a coherent picture of the world. We must therefore submit to the distinction between certainty and probability and modify our concept of knowledge accordingly. In Locke much of this is only latent, yet he is clearly feeling his way towards it. There is, he says, 'no science of bodies. . . . Certainty and demonstration are things we must not in these matters pretend to.'[21] Moreover, he gives considerable attention to probability, whose task is 'to supply the defects of our knowledge and to guide us where that fails';[22] he suggests rules to be observed and pitfalls to be avoided in the formation of probable judgments, and distinguishes degrees of probability according to the available evidence. It is here, even more perhaps than in his claim to derive all knowledge from experience, that Locke is shifting away from the rationalist position towards a genuine empiricism.

Locke's attempt to construct an empirical epistemology based on 'ideas' of sense and reflection raises a number of difficult problems; some of these he recognised and attempted to answer, others he left to later thinkers. One, clearly, is the relationship between the mind and what we call the external world. The mind, Locke tells us, knows only its own 'ideas'; if this is so, how can it know either that there is an external world at all (since it has no direct perception of one) or, assuming that there is one, that 'ideas' faithfully represent it? Locke is aware of this difficulty, as is evident from the passage quoted above in the discussion of sensitive knowledge (p. 108); elsewhere he writes:

Our knowledge, therefore, is real only so far as there is conformity between our ideas and the reality of things. But what shall be here the criterion?

---

[20] See above, pp. 12–13 and below, pp. 206–7.

[21] *Essay* IV, iii, 26; p. 283. By 'science' Locke means a coherent, demonstrably certain system of knowledge, whether empirical or non-empirical or both. He does not mean the dominantly empirical process of observation, hypothesis and experiment which is what 'science' suggests to us.   [22]*Essay* IV, xv, 4; p. 335.

How shall the mind, when it perceives nothing but its own ideas, know that they agree with things themselves?[23]

His answer to it is partial and unsatisfactory. There are some 'ideas', he says, which assuredly correspond to an external reality; among them are simple 'ideas'

which since the mind . . . can by no means make to itself, must necessarily be the product of things operating on the mind in a natural way, and producing therein those perceptions which by the wisdom and will of our Maker they are ordained and adapted to. From whence it follows that simple ideas are not fictions of our fancies, but the natural and regular productions of things without us, really operating upon us.[24]

As examples he gives the 'ideas' of whiteness and bitterness. But this is no solution. The argument depends on the assertion that the mind is incapable of producing simple 'ideas' out of itself independently of perception, as apparently happens in hallucination; and Locke has not shown in his account of 'ideas' that it cannot happen in ordinary experience. In effect he resorts, as did Descartes (p. 95), to reliance on the trustworthiness of God, by whose wisdom and will 'things operating on the mind' produce there 'those perceptions which . . . they are ordained and adapted to'.[25]

Moreover, he is left with an account of the mind which resembles the dualism of Descartes and has become known as 'representationalism': the mind does not know external realities directly but requires an intermediary between itself and the objects it apprehends; what it knows is not objects themselves but the intermediary—call it 'idea' or what you will—which 'represents' the external object and is the medium by which the object is known. Now it can be agreed that in a sense our experience of the external world is in fact representational; we never actually *see* a table but only a certain aspect of it which indicates to our minds the whole object; nor do we *see* colours but only wavelengths which are transmuted by retina and brain into the visual experience of colour. Strict representationalism, however, is full of difficulties and cannot be accepted as an adequate account of the mind's relationship with external objects. Any such account must depend in turn on an adequate theory of perception, and Locke never thought this out; instead he shelved the whole question as insoluble:

Impressions made on the retina by rays of light I think I understand, and motions from thence continued to the brain may be conceived; and that

---

[23] *Essay* IV, iv, 3; p. 288.
[24] *Essay* IV, iv, 4; p. 288.
[25] *Ibid.*

these produce ideas in our minds I am persuaded, but in a manner to me incomprehensible. This I can resolve only into the good pleasure of God, whose ways are past finding out.[26]

This may perhaps be sound religion, but it is not sound empiricism.

Another problem implicit in Locke's empiricism is that of causation. The source of knowledge, he tells us, is 'ideas'; we have 'ideas' of innumerable physical objects which are observed to act and interact upon one another; hence arise complex 'ideas' which express relations of different kinds that hold between them. Such are 'ideas' of comparative size, spatial position, temporal sequence and cause–effect. The 'idea' of cause–effect arises from two sources: one is experience of change and succession in the natural world—we see that wax melts when fire is applied, that a ball is set in motion when another strikes it, and thus we come to the 'idea' of cause–effect; the other is our experience of our own volition in which, Locke says, we have a direct awareness of a cause (an act of will) producing an effect (the result of the act). As an explanation of the empirical origin of the 'idea' of cause–effect this is perhaps acceptable, but it does not explain the notion, which we undoubtedly have, of necessary connection between cause and effect which is expressed in the *a priori* 'law' that every effect must have a cause. A thoroughgoing empiricism must show that this concept of necessary connection is also derivable from experience and is neither innate nor a truth of reason apprehended non-empirically. In fact Locke does not do this; nor does he give any satisfactory analysis of the causal relation; rather, he seems to assume that 'every effect must have a cause' is a truth grasped intuitively and therefore indubitable. It was left to Hume, as will be seen, to devise an empirical solution to this problem.

Yet another problem is that of personal identity. How, by means of 'ideas', do we come to the knowledge of ourselves as persons, the *same* persons at different times and places? How are these separate units of experience woven into a single fabric that we call the self? The rationalist may affirm as a truth of reason and the theologian as a truth divinely revealed that man has or is a soul and that the existence of his soul is the guarantee of his selfhood and of his identity as the same person. The empiricist cannot do this; he must explain how the concept of self and personal identity arises from experience—in Locke's case, from the 'ideas' of sense and reflection which are the sole source of knowledge. Locke's solution, briefly, is that the notion of personal identity depends partly on bodily continuity—we call a person the same if his body is identifiably

[26] *Examination of Malebranche*, 10; *Works of John Locke* (London, 1824), vol. viii, p. 217.

the same at different times and places—partly on continuity of consciousness:

As far as any intelligent being can repeat the idea of any past action with the same consciousness it had of it at first, and with the same consciousness it has of any present action, so far it is the same personal self. For it is by the consciousness it has of its present thoughts and actions that it is *self to itself* now, and so will be the same self as far as the same consciousness can extend to actions past or to come.[27]

But this does not make clear how the unity of the self as a coherent person is known from the separate 'ideas' given in experience, and one suspects that Locke, if pressed, would again fall back on intuition as the real source of our knowledge of self.[28] This was another problem which was left to Hume to explore more thoroughly.

A special difficulty in which Locke found himself as a result of his doctrine of 'ideas' was that of explaining the notion of substance. In one form or another this had been an accepted part of rationalist thinking from the time of Aristotle,[29] and Locke, for all his empiricism, was not disposed to abandon it. He distinguishes between particular substances, like 'man', 'gold', 'water', 'horse', and the general concept of substance as an underlying substratum in which various qualities inhere. The former are complex 'ideas' formed 'by collecting such combinations of simple ideas as are, by experience and observation of men's senses, taken notice of to exist together, and are therefore supposed to flow from the particular internal constitution or unknown essence of that substance'.[30] Thus, the 'ideas' of yellowness, fusibility, solubility in *aqua regia*,[31] etc., give us the complex 'idea' of the particular substance we call gold. Nevertheless, Locke continues, the mind is not satisfied with this conjunction of simple 'ideas': 'Not imagining how these simple "ideas" can subsist by themselves, we accustom ourselves to suppose some *substratum* wherein they do subsist

[27] *Essay* II, xxvii, 10; p. 189.
[28] He does in fact say: 'We have the knowledge of *our own existence* by intuition' (*Essay* IV, ix, 2; p. 309).
[29] There are three distinguishable meanings of 'substance' in the rationalist tradition:

    1. that which can be subject, but not predicate, of a logical proposition;
    2. that which is capable of independent existence;
    3. the substratum in which qualities inhere.

Locke is chiefly concerned with the last of these; he mentions the second (*Essay* IV, vi, 11), but does not pursue it. See above on Aristotle, pp. 59–60, in whom all three can be found; and on Descartes, pp. 94–5, in whom the second is dominant.
[30] *Essay* II, xxiii, 3; p. 156.
[31] A mixture of nitric and hydrochloric acids.

and from which they do result, which therefore we call *substance*.'[32] In other words, there is a constraint upon the mind to infer the general concept of substance as a support or receptacle for the simple 'ideas' or qualities of particular things.

Now on Locke's empirical principles a complex 'idea', like 'man' or 'gold', can be validly explained as composed of simple 'ideas'; but the general notion of substance as a substrate or support of qualities cannot be explained in this way, as he himself was aware. The 'idea' to which we give the general name of substance is 'nothing but the supposed, but unknown, support of those qualities we find existing, which we imagine cannot exist *sine re substante*, without something to support them'.[33] Of this support, however, we have no clear or distinct 'idea'; rather

we talk like children, who, being questioned what such a thing is which they know not, readily give this satisfactory answer, that it is *something*; which in truth signifies no more, when so used either by children or men, but that they know not what, and that the thing they pretend to know and talk of is what they have no distinct idea of at all, and so are perfectly ignorant of it and in the dark.[34]

Earlier in the *Essay* Locke had affirmed that the 'idea' of substance 'would be of general use for mankind to have';[35] yet here too he had denied that such an 'idea' was the product of either sensation or reflection. Nevertheless, he calls it an 'idea', and if it is not the product of sensation or reflection, how does it arise? It seems to be something quite foreign to his empirical premises, an alien entity which the mind creates by inference to serve its own purposes. Clearly Locke is in a dilemma here: the concept of substance was so much a part of the furniture of thought in his time that it was impossible to dispense with it; yet he could find no justification for it in his own empiricism—if all our knowledge comes from 'ideas' of sensation and reflection, then the concept of substance eludes explanation. Though Locke himself was unable to find a solution, his doubts initiated a process of criticism which led to the gradual discrediting of 'substance' as a philosophical concept; outside the tradition of St Thomas it plays little part in twentieth-century philosophy.

A more fundamental criticism, already hinted at, is that of unclarity in the use of his central concept 'idea'. Sense perception, we are told, gives us 'ideas', and so does reflection; but 'yellow', 'white', 'heat', etc. are totally unlike 'perception', 'thinking', etc., and to call them by the same name is at best confusing, at worst incompetent. (No wonder Professor

[32] *Essay* II, xxiii, 1; p. 155.
[33] *Essay* II, xxiii, 2; p. 156.
[34] *Ibid.*, pp. 155–6.
[35] *Essay* I, iv, 19; p. 39.

Ryle calls it 'this Pandora's box of a word' and classes it among 'the folk-
lore of philosophy'.)[36] Indeed, the range of 'ideas' is so wide—'space',
'motion', 'solidity', 'existence', 'unity', etc.—that their inclusion within
a single category under the name of 'idea' is evidently hazardous unless
preceded by a careful analysis of each 'idea'—and after that it might well
seem impossible. Nor is it by any means obvious that the 'ideas' which he
instances as 'simple' are possessed of that 'uncompounded . . . uniform
appearance'[37] which he attributes to them: awareness of something as
'white' or 'solid' would seem to involve, over and above the mere sense
impression, comparison with similar 'ideas', reference to a context of
language and convention, and hence a measure of interpretation. Certainly,
Locke should have given more thought to his 'ideas'; the brief explanation
of his use of the word, which he offers early in the *Essay*, is altogether too
hasty and facile.[38] Yet it can be said in mitigation that, as he was blazing
a trail, it was impossible for him to smooth out every tangle in his path,
and that, since his aim was to present in general terms an empirical account
of knowledge, he was more concerned, as Professor Woozley says, to use
the notion of 'ideas' than to talk about it.[39] Even so, since Locke claimed to
be constructing knowledge from its simplest elements in experience, he
might have been expected to investigate more closely the precise nature of
these 'atomic' constituents and the manner of the mind's apprehension of
them. It can be objected further that in his account of 'ideas' he uses
metaphorical expressions whose meaning is far from clear: the mind is
like a 'blank sheet' at birth—but does this preclude an *a priori* structure
by which, as Kant was to suggest, the mind imposes its own pattern or
interpretation on phenomena? 'Ideas' are said to be 'in' the mind—but
in what sense is anything *in* the mind? Sensible objects are said to be
'external' to the mind and 'ideas' of reflection 'internal'—again, in what
sense can the mind be said to have an outside and an inside? These
questions are not as trivial as they may seem, and an empiricist who uses
such expressions must face their implications squarely.

There are yet further criticisms that can be made of Locke's empirical
epistemology. Despite his claim to establish knowledge exclusively on

[36] C. B. Martin and D. M. Armstrong, eds, *Locke and Berkeley* (Macmillan, 1968), pp. 17, 23.

[37] *Essay* II, ii, 1; p. 53.

[38] *Essay* I, i, 8; pp. 15–16: 'It being that term which, I think, seems best
to stand for whatsoever is the object of the understanding when a man
thinks, I have used it to express whatever is meant by *phantasm, notion,
species or whatever it is which the mind can be employed about in thinking.*' (Cf. IV, xxi, 4.)

[39] A. D. Woozley, ed., *John Locke: An Essay concerning Human Understanding* (Collins, 1964), p. 30.

experience there remain in his thought strong traces of the traditional rationalism which still dominated the schools and universities. Such, for instance, are his demand that knowledge must be certain and his use of terms like 'substance' and 'essence', which were part of the stock-in-trade of scholastic thought but had little to contribute to the new empiricism. Yet the charge should not be too heavily pressed, for no innovator can extricate himself completely from the mode of thought he is trying to displace. It may also be objected that he confused philosophy with psychology, that he attempted by reason alone to answer questions about the operation of the mind which only the fullest and most patient research was capable of answering; in particular he should have given more attention to the mechanism of sense perception and the means by which sensory data are transmuted into mental content. But in the seventeenth century philosophy and psychology were not differentiated (nor were they for another two hundred years), and the idea that the mind itself can be subjected, like other natural phenomena, to observation and experiment was still in process of gestation. It can be further argued that, partly as a result of this, Locke's account of mind is too mechanical—as though it were indeed an 'empty cabinet' to be stored with content or a 'blank sheet' waiting for the pen, instead of (in the more appropriate imagery of William James) a 'stream of consciousness'. Again, the criticism is just but should not be over-pressed; no man can think two centuries ahead of his time or anticipate conclusions which are the fruit of long processes of investigation and intellectual growth.

What, then, was Locke's positive achievement, what his success in enquiring into 'the original, certainty and extent of human knowledge'? He did not, it must be admitted, succeed in establishing a coherent empirical epistemology; this is clear from the criticisms already noted—and not altogether surprising. For the creation of knowledge from the date of experience is a process far more complex than Locke conceived, involving physiological and psychological factors beyond the reach of seventeenth-century research; and his task was made more difficult by the absence of conceptual distinctions which are now taken for granted—hence in part his confused and confusing use of 'idea'. Yet in an odd sense his failure was in itself a positive contribution to epistemology by reason of the unresolved problems it left for later philosophers—the external world and its relation to mental experience, perception, causation, the knowledge of self and many others. Thus, albeit indirectly, he prepared the way for further advance, fulfilling thereby his own description of himself as an 'under-labourer . . . clearing the ground a little and removing some of the rubbish that lies in the way to knowledge'.[40]

[40] 'Epistle to the Reader', p. 7.

But there is more to it than this; for the distinction he makes between the different degrees of knowledge—intuitive, demonstrative and sensitive—can help us to a clearer understanding of what it means to know. Following the rationalist ideal Locke claims certainty for knowledge: 'What we once know, we are certain is so; and we may be secure that there are no latent proofs undiscovered which may overturn our knowledge or bring it into doubt.'[41] Yet he sees that the ideal is not always attainable: sensory knowledge of the external world amounts to no more than a reasonable assurance, which is enough, however, for practical purposes. This in itself (as was noted above) is a significant step towards a scientific conception of knowledge. But Locke also seems to be moving towards the view that to say one knows is to claim that one's assertion is supported by evidence and is rationally justifiable. On this view the criterion of knowledge is not so much certainty as a conviction securely based on reasoned argument and established by means which are open to inspection and are acceptable to expert opinion; knowledge is not immune from refutation, but yields to stronger evidence and more convincing reasons. Locke does not say all this, but such would seem to be the bearing of his distinction between the different degrees of knowledge. An important consequence for the epistemologist, if he accepts this account of knowledge, is that he will concern himself less with the questions, 'What is knowledge?' and 'How can I achieve certainty?' and more with seeking legitimate grounds both for assurance and for the sceptical doubts which undermine it.

Where one would be most likely to disagree with him is in his hankering after certainty and his claim that intuition provides it. Like Descartes he holds to a mathematical ideal of knowledge and has the same faith in the immediate insights of the human mind; their 'clear light', he says, is irresistible, 'like bright sunshine'. But intuition, as Professor Ayer suggests,[42] may simply be a screen for disguising the fact that no reasonable ground for an assertion has yet been found—a kind of epistemological 'God of the gaps' to fill the blanks in the sequence of explanation. This may be less than fair, for methods exist of testing intuition and sorting out the less from the more reliable: for instance, we can ask whether a particular intuition is consistent with beliefs already widely held, whether it 'works' in practice and in predicting events, whether similar intuitions occur in similar circumstances. Nevertheless, since intuitions can and often do conflict, many judge it safer not to place too much trust in them—though they might still agree with Locke that intuition is an indispensable part of the process of inference which gives us demonstrative knowledge,

[41] *Essay* IV, xvi, 3; p. 337.
[42] *The Problem of Knowledge* (Penguin, 1956), p. 33.

necessary in all the connexions of the intermediate ideas, without which we cannot attain knowledge and certainty'.[43]

Locke was a pioneer. He was educated in one view of knowledge, saw its weaknesses, and tried to establish another. His attempt was impeded by the human impossibility of shedding totally the habits of thought and terminology to which one has become inured; rationalism clung too closely to him to be discarded for a complete change of garment. He did not solve the problems he posed, but as a bridge-builder, forging a passage from the old to the new, he accomplished work of great value. For he had the merit of asking the right questions and of suggesting others equally fruitful—what does it mean to 'know'? how can the claim to know be justified? is knowledge absolute or susceptible of degree? how far does language confuse our epistemological enquiries?[44] In philosophy this is often more important than finding answers.

[43] *Essay* IV, ii, 1; p. 262.
[44] *Essay* III, x, xi, 'Of the Abuse of Words', 'Of the Remedies of the foregoing etc. These chapters are omitted from Pringle-Pattison's edition; see Woozley, pp. 306 ff.

Further study

Locke

D. J. O'CONNOR, *John Locke* (Penguin, 1952) and R. I. AARON, *John Locke* (Oxford University Press, 2nd edn, 1955) are good general introductions to Locke's philosophy. For his life (which is of great interest in itself) M. CRANSTON, *John Locke* (Longmans, 1957) is now the best.

There are two abridged and edited versions of the *Essay concerning Human Understanding*: A. S. PRINGLE-PATTISON (Oxford University Press, 1924) and A. D. WOOZLEY (Collins, 1964). There is no need initially to read the whole even of the abridged editions; the reader can easily find what he needs for the present chapter by referring to the index and table of contents. In addition he might read parts of Book III (chs 1–3 and 9–11) which is of considerable interest in view of contemporary philosophical emphasis on language.

Of the Conduct of the Understanding, published posthumously in 1706, was intended by Locke to be an additional chapter to the *Essay*; it can be read as such or as a fascinating early manual of clear thinking. His *Some Thoughts concerning Education* is a wise, humane and readable practical treatise on education. The present writer has edited both of these, the former published by Teachers College Press, New York (1966), and the latter by Heinemann Educational Books (1964).

Knowledge

C. R. MORRIS, *Locke, Berkeley, Hume* (Oxford University Press, 1931) is a helpful introduction to Locke's account of knowledge and to the British empirical tradition. J. W. YOLTON, *John Locke and the Way of Ideas* (Oxford University Press, 1956) should also be consulted, as well as his more recent book, *Locke and the Compass of Human Understanding* (Cambridge University Press, 1970).

Introductions to general theory of knowledge include WOOZLEY's *Theory of Knowledge* (p. 54 above); J. HARTLAND-SWANN, *An Analysis of Knowing* (Allen & Unwin, 1958); and R. M. CHISHOLM, *Theory of Knowledge* (Prentice-Hall, 1966). There are chapters in HOSPERS, *Introduction to Philosophical Analysis* (chs 2, 3) and in EWING, *Fundamental Questions of Philosophy* (ch. 2), which elucidate the rationalist/empiricist distinction; and for a more extensive survey W. H. WALSH, *Reason and Experience* (Oxford University Press, 1947) is invaluable. Most of RUSSELL's *Problems of Philosophy* is epistemological in bearing; AYER's *The Problem of Knowledge* examines the issues from an empirical standpoint. JOHN DEWEY also writes as a confirmed empiricist and from the particular angle of pragmatism; for instance the first three chapters in R. J. BERNSTEIN, ed., *John Dewey on Experience, Nature and Freedom* (New York, Liberal Arts Press, 1960). C. LANDESMAN, ed., *The Foundations of Knowledge* (Prentice-Hall, 1970), is a collection of readings in the philosophy of knowledge, most of them modern but including also Descartes, Locke and Berkeley.

Articles include: D. ODEGARD, 'Locke as an empiricist', *Philosophy*, 40 (1965); H. E. ALLISON, 'Locke on personal identity', *Journal of the History of Ideas*, 27 (1966); and K. R. POPPER, 'On the Sources of knowledge and ignorance', in *Studies in Philosophy*, ed. J. N. FINDLAY (Oxford University Press, 1966). There are many others in the volume in the Macmillan series, *Locke and Berkeley*, ed. C. B. MARTIN and C. M. ARMSTRONG. (It will be assumed henceforth that the reader is aware of this series, and no further reference will be made to it.)

7 Berkeley

The external world

Biographical note

George Berkeley, an Englishman by descent, was born near Kilkenny, in southern Ireland, in 1685. At the age of fifteen he went to Trinity College, Dublin, where he studied mathematics, languages, logic and philosophy; he graduated B.A. in 1704 and three years later was made a Fellow of the College; shortly afterwards, as required by the statutes, he was ordained into the Anglican Church. He held various academic posts until 1724, when he became Dean of Derry; in 1734 he was made Bishop of Cloyne, in the extreme south of Ireland. He was married in 1728 and had several children, not all of whom survived infancy. Towards the end of his life he retired to Oxford, where his son, George was an undergraduate; he died suddenly in 1753.

This bald chronological sketch tells nothing of the man himself; yet of Berkeley, more than of most philosophers, it is true to say that his character is the key to his work and that an understanding of the latter requires a knowledge of the former. Although in his later years he lived quietly, occupied mainly with the work of his diocese, the upbringing of his family and the pursuit of his studies, he was far from ignorant of the world or careless of its condition. Between 1713 and 1721 he not only travelled widely in France and Italy, but also spent a number of years in London; here he became intimate with men of letters, like Swift, Addison, Steele and Pope, as well as with members of the Court and Parliament. Not that he was a place-seeker or interested only in the intelligent and well-to-do; in his travels abroad he noted the ways of life of tradesmen and ordinary folk, and in his native Ireland he strove to rouse the public conscience against the poverty, starvation and disease that were rife at that time. Indeed, he was a man possessed by a reforming zeal which expressed itself both in his writings, philosophical and otherwise, and in his activities.

The most ambitious practical manifestation of this zeal was his project for the founding of a college in Bermuda for the sons of planters and Indians from the mainland. After receiving a general education with a strong religious bias they would return to spread Christianity and culture among their own people. Berkeley advocated his scheme with such fervour and persistence that he secured not only the promise of a considerable sum from private subscription but even Parliamentary approval for a government grant of £20,000. Relying on these he set sail for Rhode Island in 1728 and set up his headquarters; once there, he realised that Bermuda was too far from the mainland and planned to establish his college on Rhode Island instead. However, the government grant never materialised and Berkeley returned to London with his mission unaccomplished. Again and again he took up his pen to write on the social and economic problems of his time; in 1721 he had published, in answer to the calamities caused by the South Sea Bubble, An Essay towards preventing the Ruin of Great Britain, *in which he advocated a return to religion, industry and public service; to the Catholic clergy of Ireland he wrote* A Word to the Wise, *urging their support for better social and economic conditions; he wrote, too, on political obedience, on economic problems and on the medicinal properties of tar-water which, so he hoped, might afford some relief to the appalling suffering he saw about him.*

His enthusiasm extended also to his philosophical writings, in all of which, in one way or another, he is pleading a case. The most important are: Essay Towards a New Theory of Vision *(1709),* Treatise concerning the Principles of Human Knowledge *(1710),* Three Dialogues between Hylas and Philonous *(1713),* De Motu *(1721), and* Alciphron or the Minute Philosopher *(1732); the last is a piece of Christian apologetic and of less philosophical interest than the rest. In these Berkeley reveals himself not only as an able philosopher with a subtle and penetrating mind, but also as a master both of English style and of the philosophical dialogue; his writing is fluent, lucid, precise, logical and, on occasions, salted with telling wit; and behind all this lies a 'sensitive mind that donned with ease so fine a verbal vesture'.*[1]

      To most of us the external world presents no obvious problems beyond those which arise from living in it. We move about on it and in it and through it; we plough it for crops and carve it up into plots we call our own; we make cars and aeroplanes and houses out of it; we ingest it in food and drink; our bodies are composed of it—*are* it, in fact, or part of it—and at death are incorporated with the rest of it. In all this we take

[1] T. E. Jessop, *George Berkeley* (Longmans, 1959, Writers and their Work), p. 8.

the external world for granted—sometimes hostile, sometimes benign, more often indifferent, but at least law-governed and predictable. Certainly it never occurs to us to question its existence, to doubt that there is *something*, other than and outside ourselves, with which we must learn to have dealings. Nor, in the ordinary course of events, do we stop to consider the nature of our awareness of and relationship with it; these too, unless prompted, perhaps, by some failure in our mental or sensory performance, we simply accept as given. Why, then, should the external world be a source of perplexity for philosophers?

As early as the fifth century, Greek thinkers had made the distinction between appearance and reality, between the world as our senses apprehend it and the world as it actually is. Knowledge, they argued, is certain; its objects, therefore, must be permanent, immutable; because the external world is characterised by change, it cannot be known in any strict sense; since knowledge requires an object, there must, then, be a reality which transcends the external sensory world; the former is authentic, genuine, the latter a mere appearance, specious, deceptive, unreal. This is an *a priori* argument based on assumptions about knowledge which are not generally acceptable; but it receives some support from the facts of daily experience. For instance, we know that our senses deceive us, that things are not always what they seem; optical illusion provides examples enough of this. It is evident, too, that part at least of the appearance of things is due to our sense organs: grass is not in itself green; it reflects light waves of a frequency which registers on retina and brain a colour experience we call by that name; eyes other than human may not (and some clearly do not) see it so. What, then, is grass like *in itself*? We do not and cannot know, but must be content instead to distinguish between the object as it *is* and as it *appears* (normally to human beings)—hence again the contrast of reality with mere appearance. Whether or not one is persuaded by such arguments, there is sufficient force in them to suggest the need for second thoughts about the external world—is it what it purports to be in sensory experience? Or is it a façade concealing a reality perhaps totally inapprehensible?

Further disturbing questions, some of them already mentioned in the chapters on Descartes and Locke, are suggested by a consideration of perception. When we see a book or hear a bell, visual and auditory impressions (Locke's 'ideas') occur in the brain—we see shape and colour, we hear a sound; but what we see and hear is very different from the actual book or tolling of the bell: sensory impressions are mental, light and sound waves are not; the former are somehow 'inside' the mind, the latter 'outside'. Hence comes the dualism of Descartes and the gulf between Locke's 'ideas' and the objects they represent. Now there can be no serious doubt of the existence of sensory impressions occurring 'in the mind'; we are directly aware of them as an integral part of our consciousness; they may, of course, be due to drugs or disease, but surely they *exist*. What we cannot be certain of, however, is that they correspond with or represent anything 'outside' the mind, actual physical objects or events. There is no guarantee, so it appears, that such objects and events exist at all, though in the ordinary affairs of life—and for that matter in the far-from-ordinary activities of science and technology—it is assumed they do. Now if there can be no certain knowledge of the external world or of its existence; if it is an un-knowable something, transcending human knowledge but assumed to exist simply to provide tidy causal explanation of mental occurrences; if we can manage, as for all practical purposes we apparently do, without insisting that impressions 'in the mind' represent realities 'outside' it—is not the external world altogether unnecessary both as concept and as fact? Would it not be even tidier, and more economic, to dispense with it and make do with 'ideas', or whatever we choose to call them, 'in the mind'? In other words, why require two worlds, when one is enough? By this argument the existence of an external world is not only beyond all possibility of proof, it is also superfluous. This position, known as 'idealism' or, more specifically, 'subjective idealism', is the one taken by Berkeley.

There are two points to note before examining his arguments: first, it was stated earlier in this book that, as far as human nature allows, philosophy is a disinterested activity which studies problems for their own sake, because they fascinate and perplex; Berkeley is a partial exception to this rule, for although his reasoning is scrupulously fair and honest, the motive behind it is an urgent desire to defend Christianity against certain dangers by which he thought it was threatened. This is apparent in the subtitles of his two main philosophical works[2] and is clearly stated in the last sentence of the *Principles*:

For, after all, what deserves the first place in our studies is the consideration of God and our duty; which to promote, as it was the main drift and design of my labours, so shall I esteem them altogether useless and ineffectual if, by what I have said, I cannot inspire my readers with a pious sense of the presence of God; and, having shown the falseness or vanity of those barren speculations which make the chief employment of learned men, the better

---

[2] *Principles*: Wherein the chief causes of error and difficulty in the sciences, with the grounds of scepticism, atheism and irreligion are enquired into.

Three Dialogues: The design of which is plainly to demonstrate the reality and perfection of human knowledge, the incorporeal nature of the soul, and the immediate providence of a Deity: in opposition to sceptics and atheists. Also to open a method for rendering the sciences more easy, useful and compendious.

dispose them to reverence and embrace the salutary truths of the Gospel, which to know and to practise is the highest perfection of human nature.

The second point, which follows from this, is that Berkeley's work—as indeed all philosophy—belongs to a historical context; the dangers he sought to avert were neither imaginary nor contrived for the purpose of argument, but belonged to the circumstances of his time.

The less serious of these dangers came from a group of men who styled themselves 'free-thinkers' and exercised a powerful influence in contemporary London society; they impugned the religious and moral teaching of Christianity, claimed emancipation from social conventions, and adopted an attitude to life which was worldly and (in the modern, loose sense of the word) materialistic. It is against these that Berkeley directs his *Alciphron*; he dubs them 'minute philosophers', 'libertines in thought, who can no more endure the restraints of logic than those of religion or government';[3] but of their intellectual pretensions he thought little.

Far more formidable opponents were the seventeenth-century scientists and philosophers, men of indisputable intellectual standing, who had fashioned new ways of investigating the natural world, new kinds of thinking about its structure and processes. Among them were Descartes, Newton and Locke. It was not simply that there had been a revolution in method, from the formulation of *a priori* theories about nature to direct observation—this in itself was innocuous, indeed positively good. Observation was now wedded to mathematics and took the form of measurement; mathematics made accurate prediction possible and led to the formulation of precise laws for the explanation and prediction of phenomena (Newton's work on gravitation and motion is an obvious example of this).

This was not all; the scientists and philosophers had invented new concepts like 'force', 'attraction', 'space', 'matter', and treated them not simply as convenient fictions to assist them in explaining and predicting, but as things actually existing in their own right. They had, so it seemed, created a world which ran itself by unalterable rules and needed no God for its support; it was a mathematico-mechanical world, determined, predictable, self-contained, and depersonalised. For those who accepted such a world it was an easy step to atheism; not only to atheism, however, but to scepticism: so long as the concepts of 'force' etc. are recognised as human fictions devised for a specific purpose, there is no difficulty; the problem arises when they come to be regarded as entities, things which actually exist. We do not see, hear, touch, or otherwise observe 'force', 'attraction', 'space'; how, then, can we know what they are like? or that they exist at all? Are not the scientist and the philosopher creating a world of incomprehensibles—which they claim to be the *real* world, the actual

[3] Quoted in Jessop, p. 13.

nature of things—a world which eludes the grasp of man's enquiring mind and where knowledge evaporates into uncertainty? This, at any rate, is how it seemed to Berkeley.

Although he mounts a prolonged attack on 'abstract ideas' in general, the brunt of it is directed against 'matter' as it was then understood by contemporary philosophers. For he thought that all the evils of his time, by which he was deeply troubled, were due to a decline in religious faith and this in turn to the atheistic implications of a universe conceived in terms of matter and mechanism:

> As we have shown the doctrine of matter or corporeal substance to have been the main pillar and support of scepticism, so likewise upon the same foundation have been raised all the impious schemes of atheism and irreligion. . . . How great a friend *material substance* has been to atheists in all ages were needless to relate. All their monstrous systems have so visible and necessary a dependence on it that, when this corner-stone is once removed, the whole fabric cannot choose but fall to the ground. . . . The existence of matter, or bodies unperceived, has not only been the main support of atheists and fatalists, but on the same principle doth idolatry likewise in all its various forms depend.[4]

What, in fact, was he attacking? What did he understand by 'matter', 'corporeal substance', 'material substance' and 'bodies unperceived'? In order to answer this, a distinction must first be made between two possible meanings of 'matter'. In common parlance, then as now, it means the things we see, touch, taste etc. in the world around us; it is the external world of more or less solid objects—the ground we tread on, the walls of our houses, our very bodies, the air they breathe and the food they consume. Such is the popular, commonsense account of matter. However, there was also current in the seventeenth and eighteenth centuries a special, philosophical meaning; it was this that Berkeley was attacking, and to avoid misunderstanding we must examine closely what it was.

The best approach is through Locke, who was the chief exponent of the philosophical implications of the new science and the most eminent of recent British philosophers; moreover, the account of matter in his *Essay* is both the source and the principal target of Berkeley's critical assault. Locke accepted the view, implicit in the work of Descartes, Newton and others, that the natural world is mechanical in structure and operation; he also accepted the view, then generally held, that matter, the stuff of the world, is atomic or 'corpuscular'. He further held, as was seen above (pp. 107, 109), that the mind knows directly only its own 'ideas' and has no

---

[4] *Principles*, paras. 92, 94; ed. G. J. Warnock, *George Berkeley: The Principles of Human Knowledge, Three Dialogues between Hylas and Philonous* (Collins, 1962), pp. 111–12. (In the following notes on these two publications all page references are to this edition.)

direct contact with external objects. As for matter itself, or 'material sub-stance', he affirmed, following Descartes, that it has primary and secondary qualities, of which the former (shape, size, motion, etc.) belong to it essentially, while the latter (colour, taste, temperature, etc.) are due in part to the response of the human mind. The seeds of scepticism are already apparent here: if the mind knows only its own 'ideas', how can it know that there is an external world at all or, if there is one, what it is like and whether 'ideas' truly represent it? And what is this 'material substance', which Locke assumes as the receptacle or substratum of qualities? Locke himself has no answer to this; the mind has no 'idea' of it and its nature is therefore unknowable; he refers to it as 'something I know not what'.

To Berkeley these doctrines seemed dangerous both in their sceptical tendency and in their suggestion that the world is a machine which runs itself without God. They also seemed nonsensical philosophically. First, they resulted in a dualism of mind and matter which it was impossible to bridge; this criticism has already been developed in discussing Descartes (pp. 94–5, 98–9). Second, the distinction between primary and secondary qualities was untenable; for the former, he argued, are just as susceptible as the latter to modification by the human mind and cannot therefore be said to belong unalterably to matter itself.[5] Third, there was an inherent contra-diction in Locke's 'material substance'; somehow it contained, or was capable of giving rise to, qualities which Locke supposed to be at least partly mental, while it was itself entirely non-mental, non-thinking and non-sensory. Fourth, 'material substance' was incapable of giving an adequate account of causation; for it implied a mechanical concept of cause whereby one event precedes and another follows, but without any sug-gestion of will, agency or purpose; a true cause, Berkeley argued, *originates* something, *makes* something happen, and matter cannot do this (see below, pp. 132–3). Finally, it seemed preposterous that 'the visible beauty of creation', which derives largely from so-called secondary qualities, should not belong to things themselves but be reduced to 'a false imaginary glare'.[6]

Now if matter, in the philosophical sense, involves such contradictions and absurdities, would it not be a great deal simpler to dispense with it altogether? Not only is it unintelligible, it is also *unnecessary*; for experience can be explained perfectly well without it. This is the step that

[5] *Ibid.*, para.14; 'Now, why may we not as well argue that figure and extension are not patterns or resemblances of qualities existing in matter, because to the same eye at different stations, or eyes of a different texture at the same station, they appear various, and cannot therefore be the images of anything settled and determinate without [i.e. outside] the mind?' In other words, shape, size, etc., just as much as colour, etc., are 'in the eye of the beholder'.

[6] *Three Dialogues*, p. 197.

Berkeley now takes. Following Locke, he asserts that what the mind knows is 'ideas'; but he departs from Locke in declaring that there is nothing else to be known—no shadowy realm of unknowables that mind somehow mirrors, no hypothetical 'material substance' in which sensible qualities inhere:

It is evident to anyone who takes a survey of the objects of human knowledge, that they are either *ideas* actually imprinted on the senses; or else such as are perceived by attending to the passions and operations of the mind; or lastly, *ideas* formed by help of memory and imagination—either compounding, dividing or barely representing those originally perceived in the aforesaid ways. . . . And as several of these are observed to accompany each other, they come to be marked by one name, and so to be reputed as one THING.[7]

What we call the material or corporeal world is the sum of the 'ideas' received into the mind via the senses; and each particular material object is the sum of the 'ideas' associated with it:

Thus, for example, a certain colour, taste, smell, figure and consistence having been observed to go together, are accounted one distinct thing, signified by the name *apple*; other collections of ideas constitute a stone, a tree, a book, and the like sensible things.[8]

There is nothing extra-mental, nothing non-mental; everything that can be said to exist is an 'idea' or sum of 'ideas' in the mind,[9] and only in so far as it is an 'idea' can it be said to exist at all; as Berkeley puts it, its *esse* is *percipi*—its existence consists in its being perceived:

That neither our thoughts, nor passions, nor ideas formed by the imagination, exist without the mind, is what everybody will allow. And to me it is no less evident that the various SENSATIONS or *ideas implanted on the sense*, however blended or combined together (that is, whatever *objects* they compose), cannot exist otherwise than in a mind perceiving them. . . . The table I write on I say exists, that is, I see and feel it; and if I were out of my study I should say it existed—meaning thereby that if I was in my study I might perceive it, or that some other spirit actually does perceive it. There was an odour, that is, it was smelt; there was a sound, that is, it was heard; a colour or figure, and it was perceived by sight or touch. That is all that I can understand by these and the like expressions. For as to what is said of the absolute existence of unthinking things without any relation to their being perceived, that is to me perfectly unintelligible. Their *esse* is *percipi*, nor is it possible they should have any existence out of the minds or thinking things which perceive them.[10]

---

[7] *Principles*, para. 1; p. 65.
[8] *Ibid.*
[9] Though not necessarily the *human* mind, as will be seen.
[10] *Principles*, para. 3; p. 66.

And again:

Some truths there are so near and obvious to the mind that a man need only open his eyes to see them. Such I take this important one to be, viz., that all the choir of heaven and furniture of earth, in a word, all those bodies which compose the mighty frame of the world, have not any subsistence without a mind—that their *being* is *to be perceived or known*; that consequently so long as they are not actually perceived by me, or do not exist in my mind or that of any other created spirit, they must either have no existence at all, or else subsist in the mind of some Eternal Spirit— it being perfectly unintelligible . . . to attribute to any single part of them an existence independent of a spirit. To be convinced of which, the reader need only reflect, and try to separate in his own thoughts the *being* of a sensible thing from its *being perceived*.[11]

There are, thus, two kinds of things, two kinds of reality in the universe —minds (or spirits, as Berkeley prefers to call them) and 'ideas'; apart from these nothing whatever exists. Spirit is the fundamental reality, the only 'substance'; it alone is active, capable of knowing and willing, of apprehending 'ideas'; it cannot itself be an 'idea', for 'ideas' are passive, dependent, and the passive cannot represent the active:

A spirit is one simple, undivided, active being—as it *perceives* ideas it is called the *Understanding*, and as it *produces* or otherwise *operates* about them it is called the *Will*. Hence there can be no *idea* formed of a soul or spirit; for all ideas whatever, being passive and inert, cannot represent unto us, by way of image or likeness, that which acts.[12]

The *esse* of spirit is *percipere*, that of 'ideas' is *percipi*; the whole meaning of existence, therefore, is given in the full phrase, *esse* is *percipere* or *percipi*. This is the doctrine which Berkeley himself called 'immaterialism'[13] and which is also known as 'idealism'—that the basic stuff of the universe is mental or spiritual, that there is no 'material substance' and that everything that is not itself mind or spirit must in some way be apprehended by or contained in mind:

THING or BEING is the most general name of all: it comprehends under it two kinds entirely distinct and heterogeneous and which have nothing common but the name, viz., SPIRITS and IDEAS. The former are active, indivisible substances; the latter are inert, fleeting or dependent beings, which subsist not by themselves, but are supported by, or exist in minds or spiritual substances.[14]

Within the category of spirit there is a division into finite (human) and infinite (divine); every 'idea', therefore, is perceived 'if not by created mind, yet certainly by the infinite mind of God'. The existence of an infinite mind

[11] *Ibid.*, para. 6; pp. 67–8. [12] *Ibid.*, para. 27; p. 77.
[13] e.g. in *Three Dialogues*, pp. 254–5. [14] *Principles*, para. 89; p. 109.

is demonstrated, so Berkeley argues, by the very nature of experience: we are conscious of a world external to us, and what we perceive in it is given, not chosen—in other words, the world is what it is and for the most part must be accepted as such; this points to the existence of a spirit other than ourselves from whom our 'ideas' of the world derive; this spirit must surely, by reason of the limitless number and variety of 'ideas' presented to us, himself be infinite; and his goodness and his providence are amply shown by the orderliness and reliability of natural law:

> The ideas of Sense are more strong, lively and distinct than those of the Imagination; they have likewise a steadiness, order and coherence, and are not excited at random, as those which are the effects of human wills often are, but in a regular train or series—the admirable connexion whereof sufficiently testifies the wisdom and benevolence of its Author. Now the set rules or established methods wherein the Mind we depend on excites in us the ideas of sense, are called the *laws* of *nature*, and these we learn by experience.[15]

It is obvious that in his account of immaterialism Berkeley uses the word 'idea' in a special way; failure to grasp this has frequently resulted in a misunderstanding of his thought. In the first section of *Principles* he distinguishes three kinds of 'idea': those 'actually imprinted on the senses'; 'such as are perceived by attending to the passions and operations of the mind'; and 'ideas formed by help of memory and imagination', which he later calls 'images'. So far he follows Locke; he fundamentally departs from Locke, of course, in denying that 'ideas' mirror external objects—there are *no* external objects, only 'ideas'. Principally, however, he means by 'ideas' our sensations and perceptions of the external world—colours, smells, sounds, etc., and the objects, such as apples, trees and houses, which sensations present to us when they are combined; these he carefully distinguishes from 'images' which the mind composes out of remembered 'ideas' and which are unreal in so far as they are not directly given in experience. He also distinguishes them from 'notions', whose meaning approximates to the modern use of 'idea' in the sense of 'thought', 'concept'.

Now Berkeley denies the existence of 'matter' and of 'external objects', but he does not deny the existence of things which constitute what, in ordinary parlance, we call the external world. The external world is the sum of our 'ideas'; and every object in it is the sum of the 'ideas' which compose that object. In fact, his use of 'idea' comes very close to the popular use of 'matter', 'thing', 'external object'. What he is saying is this: when I say, 'I see an object', what I really mean is, 'I have visual sensations (i.e. "ideas") of a certain kind', *not*, 'there is some object external to

[15] *Ibid.*, para. 30; pp. 78-9.

me which my sensations represent'. The whole conception of an object is superfluous; all I need to explain this visual experience is 'ideas'; these *are* the so-called external object: 'There was an odour, that is, it was smelt; there was a sound, that is, it was heard; a colour or figure, and it was perceived by sight or touch. That is all that I can understand by these and the like expressions.'[16] He is asking us to adopt a different use of language —the language of 'ideas', which are mental, instead of the language of 'external objects', which are non-mental. Berkeley does, indeed, suggest that he might equally well have used 'thing' instead of 'idea';[17] he chose not to do so because 'thing' has a wider range of meaning (and might therefore more easily mislead), and also, in common usage, suggests 'external object', which is precisely what he wants to avoid.

Two objections have been commonly made to Berkeley's immaterialism; both of them are readily countered. What, it has been asked, becomes of 'external objects', like tables and houses, when neither I nor any other human being is perceiving them? Do they simply cease to exist. No, of course not, Berkeley would reply: the existence of 'external objects' does not depend solely on human perception; God also perceives them, and their continued existence is therefore guaranteed.[18] The second objection is weightier, but Berkeley's answer is clear and cogent: does not immaterialism reduce experience to the status of dream or fancy? If 'external objects' are nothing but 'ideas' in our minds, are they not deprived of reality and rendered vacuous and insubstantial? Dr Johnson, so Boswell tells us, 'striking his foot with mighty force against a stone' exclaimed, 'I refute it *thus.*' And William Cowper had Berkeley in mind when, in his poem, *Anti-Thelyphthora*, he described the fair maid Hypothesis as teaching:

That substances and modes of every kind
Are mere impressions on the passive mind;

---

[16] *Ibid.*, para. 3; p. 66.
[17] *Ibid.*, para. 39; p. 83.
[18] This objection and Berkeley's answer are wittily expressed in the two limericks:

There was once a man who said, 'God
Must think it exceedingly odd
    If he finds that this tree
    Continues to be
When there's no one about in the Quad.'

Dear Sir, Your astonishment's odd:
I am always about in the Quad;
    And that's why the tree
    Will continue to be,
Since observed by Yours faithfully, God.

Oxford Dictionary of Quotations (2nd edn, rev. 1956), p. 305; 5.

> And he that splits his cranium, splits at most
> A fancied head against a fancied post.[19]

But this is to misunderstand immaterialism.

Berkeley did not deny the reality of 'external objects', and he took great pains to say so clearly and unequivocally:

It will be objected that by the foregoing principles all that is real and substantial in nature is banished out of the world, and instead thereof a chimerical scheme of *ideas* takes place. All things that exist exist only in the mind, that is they are purely notional. What therefore becomes of the sun, moon and stars? What must we think of houses, rivers, mountains, trees, stones; nay, even of our own bodies? Are all these but so many chimeras and illusions on the fancy?—To all which, and whatever else of the same sort may be objected, I answer that by the principles premised we are not deprived of any one thing in nature. Whatever we see, feel, hear, or any wise conceive or understand, remains as secure as ever, and is as real as ever. There is a *rerum natura*, and the distinction between realities and chimeras retains its full force. . . . I do not argue against the existence of any one thing that we can apprehend either by sense or reflection. That the things I see with my eyes and touch with my hands do exist, really exist, I make not the least question. The only thing whose existence we deny is that which *Philosophers* call matter or corporeal substance. . . . And if any man thinks this detracts from the existence or reality of things, he is very far from understanding what hath been premised in the plainest terms I could think of.[20]

The objects around us are no less solid by reason of immaterialism; for solidity is an 'idea' perceived by sight and touch and its reality is therefore beyond dispute. What Berkeley *is* denying is the existence of what philosophers called 'material substance', which, as has been shown, he thought both unintelligible and unnecessary.

Certainly, at first reading immaterialism may seem paradoxical and contrary to common sense; but Berkeley himself took entirely the opposite view; indeed he believed that he was upholding common sense against the metaphysical absurdities of philosophers who invented superfluous entities in their attempt to explain experience. In his *Philosophical Commentaries*, a collection of observations and comments jotted down in notebooks, he writes: 'Mem: To be eternally banishing metaphysics etc., and recalling men to common sense.'[21] In the *Three Dialogues*, speaking through Philonous, he writes of the 'fantastical conceits' of philosophers and explains that, since he abandoned them for 'the plain dictates of nature and common sense', he finds his 'understanding strangely enlightened' and that he can 'now easily comprehend a great many things which before were

[19] Jessop, p. 24.   [20] *Principles*, paras. 34–6; pp. 80–1.
[21] A. A. Luce and T. E. Jessop, eds, *The Works of George Berkeley, Bishop of Cloyne* (Nelson, 1948–57), vol. i, p. 91, 751.

all mystery and riddle'.[22] It should be obvious from these quotations that part of Berkeley's aim was deliberately to avoid paradox and mystification.

In Berkeley's view it was Locke, and the scientists and philosophers for whom he spoke, who were guilty of mystification. For they duplicated the world by assuming both matter *and* mind, material substance *and* 'ideas'— two separate and irreconcilable orders of existence which yet in some odd way must be supposed to interact. They were also, he thought, guilty of misusing language, or at least of failing to understand it; and he thought it an essential part of his task to show what is meant by terms like 'matter' and 'existence'. 'Matter' in the sense of something external to mind or of some receptacle for qualities is otiose and meaningless; experience is explicable more easily and more economically by means of mind and 'ideas', and these, therefore, are the words that should be used to describe it. So too with 'existence'; Berkeley aims to clarify the meaning of the word by showing that it does not presuppose or include 'matter', but need refer only to 'ideas' in the mind. 'Let it not be said that I take away existence', he writes; 'I only declare the meaning of the word so far as I can comprehend it.'[23] Again: 'The chief thing I do or pretend to do is only to remove the mist or veil of words.'[24] Our philosophical difficulties are, in fact, largely of our own making: 'We have first raised a dust and then complain we cannot see.'[25] Berkeley is very well aware of the snares of language, as was Locke and, indeed, most of the great philosophers—and in this he strikingly anticipates contemporary English philosophy. He desires 'that men would think before they speak and settle the meaning of their words';[26] he is aware that language has functions other than communication, for instance, to persuade, to indoctrinate and to evoke emotion. 'Most parts of our knowledge', he writes in *Principles*, 'have been strangely perplexed and darkened by the *abuse* of words and general ways of speech wherein they are delivered.'[27] It is interesting to compare these views with those of Ludwig Wittgenstein in chapter 12.

Yet for all Berkeley's eloquence and subtlety of argument there remains a lingering suspicion that all is not well; his account of 'matter' and 'existence' has not quite the self-evident cogency which he thought it had. Common sense, confirmed by the general consensus of opinion, holds stubbornly to the view that there exists externally to the human mind a *something*—call it 'matter', 'ideas', 'things', 'external objects' or what you

[22] *Three Dialogues*, p. 150.
[23] *Philosophical Commentaries*, Luce and Jessop, vol. i, p. 74, 593.
[24] *Ibid.*, i, p. 78, 642.
[25] *Principles*, introd., para. 3; p. 46.
[26] *Phil. Comm.*, p. 69, 553.
[27] *Principles*, introd., para. 21; p. 61.

The Scope of Philosophy

will—which is independent of human experiencing; something which existed before there were human beings to perceive and will continue to exist after the human race has disappeared. It is this that the scientist calls the 'physical universe', this that is governed by 'natural law' and is therefore predictable in its operations, this from which organic life has sprung. Now Berkeley accepts this externality; he does not deny the reality of 'material objects', nor (if he had known of evolution) would he have denied the existence of a universe before the emergence of the human race and after its ultimate demise; but all this, he asserts, consists of 'ideas' which are always in the mind of God and sometimes in the minds of men.[28] A universe independent of human perceiving can exist only as 'ideas' in the mind of God, without whom it would vanish away. Berkeley's immaterialism therefore needs God for its support; like Descartes and even Locke he requires for his doctrine a divine guarantee.[29] This can hardly be acceptable to those who do not share his theistic beliefs. The universe, it seems, can be described in the language either of 'matter' or 'ideas', science or religion; inevitably Berkeley chose the latter alternatives, but the former are not thereby necessarily invalidated.

The external world of so-called material objects appears to be governed by causal laws and uniformities; Berkeley felt bound, therefore, to concern himself with the problem of causation, but his solution is no more satisfactory than Locke's, though for a different reason. In the phenomenal world of 'ideas' there is no causation in the sense that a makes b to happen; experience warrants no more than the assumption that a regularly precedes b and that b regularly follows a; a is not the cause of b (in the popular sense) but only a sign that b will follow: 'The connexion of ideas does not imply the relation of *cause* and *effect*, but only a *mark* or *sign* with the *thing signified*. The fire which I see is not the cause of the pain I suffer upon my approaching it, but the mark that forewarns me of it.'[30]

This is an empirical account of causation in line, so far, with Locke's and (as will be seen) with Hume's. But Berkeley goes on to say that there *is* genuine causation in the activity of spirits; God *makes* things happen, and so do human beings. In this way he restores causation to the phenomenal world: where no human agency is involved, every 'idea' is caused by God and it is correct to say, therefore, that b is caused, but by God, not by a. However, God is not the only causal agency; man, too, can make

[28] This suggests a further criticism, namely that Berkeley's universe involves a dualism, just as do those of Descartes and Locke: there are 'ideas' in human minds and 'ideas' in God's mind, and they appear to belong to two different orders of existence, since the former are transient and the latter permanent.

[29] pp. 95 and 110 above.

[30] *Principles*, para. 65; p. 97.

132

things happen—and hence comes evil, when he deviates from the will of God as expressed in the moral law. Thus Berkeley gives first an empirical account of cause, whereby effective causation is eliminated from the natural world; he then resorts to a religious or metaphysical account which re-admits it, as it were, by the back door.

Although Berkeley is usually included among empirical philosophers, he is only half an empiricist and even this, in a sense, by accident. His chief motive was the vindication of a religious view of life and experience against the 'materialistic' doctrines assumed, implied or actively preached by the scientists and philosophers of his time. To do this he found it neces-sary to formulate initially a very simple version of empiricism which com-pletely excluded 'matter' from the concept of existence; only that can be said to exist, he affirmed, which is either perceived or perceiving, 'ideas' and 'spirits'. This, however, is only one side of his philosophy; the other is a religious—some would call it a metaphysical—belief in God and in divine providence. He may be said, therefore, as Professor Copleston has put it, to have 'utilised empiricism in the service of a spiritualist meta-physical philosophy';[31] and although he attacks metaphysics as it appears in the 'fantastic conceits' of contemporary science, his real purpose is not to destroy metaphysics but to dissociate it from 'materialism'. Like Locke, he stands with a foot in either camp, empiricist and rationalist; but it can be said that both his empiricism and his rationalism are more coherent and more convincing than those of his predecessor. Moreover, there is in him a certain fascination which has powerfully attracted many who have studied him deeply; this lies partly in his style, partly in the integrity and conspicuous goodness of the man himself, but more especially in his thought. For by making God the ultimate basis of experience Berkeley *personalises* the universe; instead of the interplay of regular but aimless forces, he offers us the momently support of God whose control is not only orderly but purposeful and providential.

His attempt to clarify the relationship between the human mind and the external world, involving though it does the virtual disappearance of the latter and, seemingly, an affront to common sense, is nevertheless not implausible; nor is it self-contradictory and therefore logically unaccept-able. Admittedly, not all can share his Christian premises which ensure the continued existence of objects as 'ideas' in God's mind, even when they are not perceived by human beings. Yet there are kinds of idealism which are not dependent on Christian or theistic doctrine; such, for instance, is phenomenalism, one variant of which asserts that the existence of an object is to be equated, not with *being* perceived but with *perceiv-ability*, i.e. the potentiality of being perceived whenever it comes within

[31] *A History of Philosophy*, vol. v (Burns & Oates, 2nd impr., 1961), 258.

range of organs of perception. Thus, J. S. Mill suggests that the proper description of matter is 'the permanent possibility of sensation'. Later phenomenalists have argued that this involves awkward metaphysical assumptions: after all, what sort of a thing can a permanent possibility of sensation be? and how does its potential existence—its perceivability— differ from its objectified existence in perception? are there two grades of existence? We seem to have on our hands an occult, shadowy entity, like Locke's 'something I know not what' (p. 113), which somehow blossoms into existence as soon as it is perceived; this is a very odd notion, to say the least. Phenomenalists of this kind prefer to use the term 'sense data' in referring to our perceptual experiences, not thereby necessarily presupposing the existence of external objects as the origin or cause of sensations or perceptions, but indicating simply what we are *directly* aware of in perception—colour sensations (red, blue, etc.), touch sensations (rough, smooth, etc.), and so on. These sense data are the genuine raw material of knowledge, the only items in experience whose existence is indubitable; it is from these that we construct what we call external objects—chairs, trees and the rest of the perceived world—all of which, in one way or another, are interpretations of sense data. The arguments for and against phenomenalism are too complicated for brief summary, but there is one obvious objection that can be mentioned: how is it possible to explain the regularity and orderliness of sense data except on the assumption that there is something 'behind' them? For not only do we experience sense data of colour and shape which lead us to construct, for instance, the external object we call the moon, but we can also predict that these sense data will be of such and such a kind (or even totally absent during an eclipse) tomorrow, next week and a hundred years hence. How is such predictability possible if it does not originate from a source 'beyond' the sense data themselves?

The main alternative to idealism, whether in its Berkeleian form or as phenomenalism, is realism;[32] but this too lacks conclusive argument in its favour. The predictability of sense experience has been held to demonstrate its causal origin in actual objects (as in the previous paragraph); but this does not dispose of the theistic idealist who might retort that the predictability of our perceptions ('ideas' in Berkeley's language) is built into them by divine guarantee—there is thus no need for external objects. Moreover, if one accepts the view that a world of material objects exists external to the mind, it seems impossible to escape from a representational account of perception—'ideas' inside the mind reflecting objects outside it; but then, as we have seen in Locke, it becomes impossible to justify either the existence of external objects or resemblance between them and 'ideas'. The

[32] See pp. 51–2, and note.

strongest argument for realism in some form is the consensus of common sense, for in the ordinary affairs of life no normal person doubts the separate existence of objects external to the mind; but consensus is not proof, and the philosopher looks for arguments more convincing than this. It may well be that neither proof nor refutation will be forthcoming and that here, as in other enquiries, we must be content with Locke's 'assurance that deserves the name of knowledge' (p. 108). It may also be—and this is quite a different thought—that in asking whether an external world exists we are posing the wrong question; instead, perhaps, we should ask what we *mean* when we use the terms 'external world', 'external object'—an approach to the problem which is not far removed from Berkeley himself (pp. 128–9 and 131). If we adopt this view, it will be necessary to subject such terms to close analysis in order to determine their meaning in actual use; this is a task especially suited to the techniques of modern linguistic philosophy, on which more will be found in chapter 12. Finally, it can be said with some certainty that progress towards a solution of the problem will depend on further developments in psychology, in the physiology of the nervous system and in physics; from these sciences we may hope for new insight into the nature of perception and of matter, and thus into their interrelationship. Empirical and philosophical enquiry must here go hand in hand.

Further study

Berkeley

G. J. WARNOCK, *Berkeley* (Penguin, 1953) is a good general introduction; to this may be added G. D. HICKS, *Berkeley* (Benn, 1932) and the biography by A. A. LUCE, *The Life of George Berkeley Bishop of Cloyne* (Nelson, 1949). Later studies include A. D. RITCHIE, *George Berkeley: a Reappraisal* (Manchester University Press, 1967) and W. E. STEINKRAUS, ed., *New Studies in Berkeley's Philosophy* (Holt, Rinehart & Winston, 1966). J. O. WISDOM, *The Unconscious Origin of Berkeley's Philosophy* (Hogarth Press and Institute of Psycho-Analysis, 1953) is an interesting study from a particular angle.

The standard edition of Berkeley's works is A. A. LUCE and T. E. JESSOP, eds., *The Works of George Berkeley, Bishop of Cloyne* (9 vols, Nelson, 1948–57); but there are many selections, including G. J. WARNOCK, *Principles* and *Three Dialogues* (Collins, Fontana Library, 1962); A. D. LINDSAY, *Principles, Three Dialogues, New Theory of Vision* (Dent, Everyman's Library, 1910, repr. 1963); and T. E. JESSOP (Nelson, Philosophical Texts, 1952), which includes these and other works.

Berkeley has a grace and lucidity of style which make him a delight to read; the works most relevant to the present chapter are, of course,

Principles and *Three Dialogues*, to which might be added *An Essay towards a New Theory of Vision*.

The external world

See the suggested reading for ch. 5 (last para.); also D. LOCKE, *Perception and our Knowledge of the External World* (Allen & Unwin, 1967).

HOSPERS, *Philosophical Analysis*, provides a useful introduction to the comparative claims of realism, idealism and phenomenalism; WHITELEY, *Introduction to Metaphysics* (p. 68 above), also has something on this. For more advanced study of idealism there are A. C. EWING, *Idealism* (Methuen, 3rd edn, 1961) and *The Idealist Tradition from Berkeley to Blanshard* (The Free Press, Glencoe, 1957), a selection of readings; and N. KEMP SMITH, *Prolegomena to an Idealist Theory of Knowledge* (Macmillan, 1924). Specifically on Berkeley's idealism there are C. R. MORRIS, *Locke, Berkeley, Hume* (Oxford University Press, 1931); A. A. LUCE, *Berkeley's Immaterialism* (Nelson, 1945; a commentary on *Principles*), *Sense without Matter* (Nelson, 1954), and *The Dialectic of Immaterialism* (Hodder & Stoughton, 1963).

For a realist account of perception see D. M. ARMSTRONG, *Perception and the Physical World* (Routledge, 1961), and for a phenomenalist approach, BERTRAND RUSSELL, *Our Knowledge of the External World* (Allen & Unwin, rev. edn 1926), and A. J. AYER, *The Foundations of Empirical Knowledge* (Macmillan, 1940).

For articles refer to the following: G. E. MOORE, 'The refutation of idealism', *Philosophical Studies* (Routledge, 1922), ch. 1; W. T. STACE, 'The refutation of realism', *Mind*, 43 (1934); A. A. LUCE, 'Berkeley's existence in the Mind', *Mind*, 50 (1941), and 'The Berkeleyan idea of sense', *Aristotelian Society Supplement*, 27 (1953); C. D. BROAD, 'Berkeley's denial of material substance', *Philosophical Review*, 63 (1954); and A. C. EWING, R. I. AARON and D. G. C. MACNABB, 'The causal argument for physical objects', *Aristotelian Society Supplement*, 19 (1945).

8 Hume

The concept of cause

Biographical note

*David Hume was a Scotsman, born in Edinburgh in 1711
of a family whose home was in Berwickshire. He entered the university
of Edinburgh in 1723 and left it, without a degree, before he was sixteen.
His family intended him for a career in law, but he had no taste for this
nor for business, which he also tried for a time. In his brief autobiography,
posthumously published, Hume declares that he had 'a passion for
literature . . . and an insurmountable aversion to everything but the pur-
suits of philosophy and general learning;*[1] *it is not surprising, therefore,
that he should leave for France, where he could live frugally on a small
inheritance and devote himself to writing. Here, in the years 1734–37, he
wrote* A Treatise of Human Nature, *a work which he had projected at
university and for which he had high hopes; however, in his own words,
'it fell dead-born from the press'. Returning to Scotland, he continued his
writing undeterred and in 1741–42 published* Essays, Moral and Political,
*a work whose favourable reception encouraged him to revise and republish
his* Treatise.

The first two Parts of this were published in 1748 as Philosophical Essays
concerning Human Understanding; *three years later a second edition
appeared under the present title,* An Enquiry concerning Human Understanding; *in the same year as the latter there was also published the revised
Part III of the original* Treatise, *entitled* An Enquiry concerning the
Principles of Morals. *In the revised form, known briefly as the* Enquiries,
the Treatise *was more kindly received.* Political Discourses *was published
in 1752, and in the same year Hume was appointed librarian to the Faculty
of Advocates in Edinburgh. With the resources of the library at his disposal he now devoted himself to historical writing with such vigour that
he was able, between 1754 and 1761, to publish several volumes of a*

[1] R. Wollheim, ed., *Hume on Religion* (Collins, 1963), p. 271.

comprehensive history of England from the invasions of Julius Caesar to the revolution of 1688.

In 1763 Hume went to Paris as secretary to the British Embassy; for a time, during the absence of the Ambassador, he was chargé d'affaires. It was during this period in France that he met and befriended Rousseau, whom he took back to Britain with him when he returned in 1766; however, the friendship was shortlived, for Rousseau's suspicious nature convinced him that Hume was plotting against him; the result was a protracted quarrel followed eventually by Rousseau's return to France. For two years Hume served as Under-Secretary of State in London; he then returned to Edinburgh, where he spent the rest of his life. He died in 1776 after a long illness borne with patience and dignity. Apart from his writings on philosophy, morals and politics Hume also wrote on religion; his main works in this field were The Natural History of Religion *and* Dialogues concerning Natural Religion.[2] *Here, as in philosophy, his position is sceptical and antidogmatic; so much so that he acquired a reputation for atheism which barred him from the Chair of Ethics at Edinburgh and of Logic at Glasgow, for both of which he applied. It also ensured that his writings were placed on the* Index librorum prohibitorum *of the Roman Church.*

Though more closely devoted to scholarship than Locke, he was equally a man of the world who could serve his country willingly and ably in affairs of state. He writes of himself:

I was a man of mild dispositions, of command of temper, of an open, social, and cheerful humour, capable of attachment, but little susceptible of enmity, and of great moderation in all my passions. Even my love of literary fame, my ruling passion, never soured my temper, notwithstanding my frequent disappointments. My company was not unacceptable to the young and careless, as well as to the studious and literary; and as I took a particular pleasure in the company of modest women, I had no reason to be displeased with the reception I met with from them.[3]

Happily, this account of himself is confirmed by the testimony of his friends.

The concept of cause has played a prominent part in the history of philosophy. We have seen how Plato used the Forms as causal agents to explain the presence in particular objects of qualities like size, colour and beauty—'it is by Beauty that beautiful things are beautiful' (p. 47), and it is the Form of Good that 'gives the objects of knowledge

---

[2] The latter was written before 1761 but published posthumously in 1779.
[3] Wollheim, pp. 278–9.

their truth and the mind the power of knowing. It is the cause of knowledge and truth' (p. 47). Aristotle, rejecting as he did the Theory of Forms, was bound also to reject the account of causation associated with it; instead he supposed there to be four distinct causal factors involved in anything becoming or being what it is—material, formal, final and efficient (p. 63). The concept of cause plays some part in all five of Aquinas's arguments for the existence of God, more especially in the second and fourth; and Descartes also finds it indispensable in his rendering of the ontological argument—'there must be at least as much reality in the efficient and total cause as in the effect' (p. 94). Finally, in Berkeley it can be said that God is the cause of the continued existence of objects when they are no longer perceived by human senses.

The importance of the concept is no less in science and daily life. In his investigation of the natural world the scientist finds that its events are not entirely random nor its objects wholly unconnected: when x occurs, y is normally observed to follow, and an object a is regularly found in association with another object b. The existence of such uniformities has often been described by using the word 'cause': x is said to be the cause of y; a and b are said to be causally connected. For instance, if blue litmus paper is dropped in acid, it turns red; the acidity is the cause (it may be said) of the change of colour. Again, the volume of a given quantity of gas is found to vary with its pressure—increase the one and the other is diminished; the two are therefore said to be causally related. The significance of this is twofold: the concept of cause enables the scientist not only to explain the uniformities he observes, but also to *predict*; since x and y are causally related, he assumes that whenever x occurs, y will follow, or that wherever a, so also b. Without prediction based on causal uniformities science could hardly exist—at least it would be little more than a compilation of observed data; an advanced technology would be altogether impossible. What is true of science is true also of daily life: in the ordinary course of things we agree that fire causes burns, germs cause disease, and over-eating was the cause of Johnny's biliousness; and equally with the scientist we assume that once a causal linkage is established, it can be used to predict what will happen in the future—hence fireguards, inoculation and a prescribed limit to the consumption of sweets.

Hume was well aware of the importance of the causal concept:

All reasonings concerning matter of fact seem to be founded on the relation of *Cause and Effect*. By means of that relation alone we can go beyond the evidence of our memory and senses. If you were to ask a man why he believes any matter of fact which is absent—for instance that his friend is in the country or in France—he would give you a reason; and this reason would be some other fact, as a letter received from him, or the knowledge of his former resolutions and promises. A man finding a watch or any other machine in a desert island would conclude that there had once been men in that island. All our reasonings concerning fact are of the same nature. And here it is constantly supposed that there is a connexion between the present fact and that which is inferred from it. Were there nothing to bind them together, the inference would be entirely precarious.[4]

Without this concept to link them, facts would be individual, isolated; it would be impossible to reason from one to another or to argue that the future would bear any resemblance to the past. Yet it had not, Hume thought, been submitted to the close examination that its importance deserved: philosophers and scientists had assumed without critical analysis that they knew what they meant when they talked about cause and effect; they had too readily assumed the existence of a universal causal principle that every object and event is causally linked to other objects and events; from which it would follow that whenever there was realised a certain set of conditions or circumstances, C, there would follow a certain event, E; and vice versa, whenever E occurred, the prior existence of C could be presumed. Hume was especially troubled about a particular extension of the causal principle which was characteristic of rationalist philosophy, namely, that there is some intrinsic power or quality in a cause which *produces* the effect; in other words, an effect does not just happen, it is *made* to happen, it *must* happen whenever there exists the appropriate cause or set of causal conditions. This, the entailment theory of causation as it is sometimes called, we shall look at more closely later.

First, however, we must attempt a more general survey of Hume's philosophical position and purpose. It was an essential part of that purpose to develop and improve the empirical account of knowledge already partially explored by Locke and Berkeley. For neither of these had escaped inconsistency, Locke because of rationalist presuppositions about the nature of knowledge, Berkeley because of theological doctrines to which, as a Christian bishop, he was unavoidably committed. It was Hume who first showed in what direction the human mind is led by an uncompromising adherence to the view that all mental content is the product of experience; he pressed to its limits the effort to create a consistent empiricism—and in doing so he raised incidentally a number of issues which are still very much alive today. Yet he had a wider purpose even than this, for he aimed not merely to give a consistent empirical account of knowledge, but also to apply the methods of physical science to man himself and thus establish a science of human nature:

There is no question of importance whose decision is not comprised in the science of man; and there is none which can be decided with any certainty

---

[4] *Enquiries*, ed. L. A. Selby-Bigge (Oxford, Clarendon Press, 2nd edn, 1902), IV, i, 22; pp. 26-7. (Further references will be to this edition.)

before we become acquainted with that science. From this station we may extend our conquests over all those sciences which more intimately concern human life.[5]

He continues, emphasising his empirical intentions: 'And as the science of man is the only solid foundation for the other sciences, so the only solid foundation we can give to this science itself must be laid on experience and observation.' He is aware, of course, that in exploring *human* nature experiment is either impossible or severely restricted; but by careful observation, including introspection, it should be possible to construct a science 'which will not be inferior in certainty, and will be much superior in utility, to any other in human comprehension'.[6] The investigation will include not only epistemology and psychology, but also man's moral nature; this last is examined at length in Book III of the *Treatise* and in the *Enquiry concerning the Principles of Morals*.

Colouring these intentions, and reciprocally both a product of and a stimulus to his empirical enquiries, was Hume's belief that the search for an absolute or final knowledge which would explain the whole complicated universe of things was illusory and doomed to failure, that the rationalist claim for certainty in knowledge was untenable and that the probing of ultimate causes was a task beyond the reach of human intellect. He writes:

The utmost effort of human reason is to reduce the principles productive of natural phenomena to a greater simplicity and to resolve the many particular effects into a few general causes by means of reasonings from analogy, experience and observation. But as to the causes of these general causes, we should in vain attempt their discovery. . . . These ultimate springs and principles are totally shut up from human curiosity and enquiry.[7]

The human mind is 'by no means fitted for such remote and abstruse subjects' and must be confined within the limits proper to its capacities, namely the consideration of what is presented to it by observation and experience. Hume, as has already been noted, was not favourably disposed to metaphysics of the speculative kind.

He develops his empirical account of the mind along the same general lines as Locke but he takes it further and is more consistent. All the contents of our minds are ultimately derived from the data of our senses, both the 'outer' senses of sight, touch, etc., and so-called 'inner' senses, like pleasure and pain. Though the mind in its imaginative flights may seem

[5] *Treatise*, ed. L. A. Selby-Bigge (Oxford, Clarendon Press, 1888), introd., p. xx. (Further references will be to this edition.)
[6] *Ibid.*, p. xxiii.
[7] *Enquiries*, IV, i, 26; p. 30.

to overleap the bounds of sense and nature, yet in fact, Hume asserts, 'all this creative power of the mind amounts to no more than the faculty of compounding, transposing, augmenting or diminishing the materials afforded us by the senses and experience'.[8] He gives to the mind's contents the general name of 'perceptions', but divides them into two distinct categories, 'impressions' and 'ideas'. (It is clear that he is using all three words in a sense peculiar to himself, and the reader must be alive to this.) 'Impressions' are the immediate data of experience given to us in sensation—what we see, hear or touch as colour, sound or cold—or in our 'inner' awareness of emotions like love and hate and of willing. 'Ideas' are the copies of 'impressions', 'the faint images of these in thinking and reasoning'.[9] Except in certain abnormal circumstances, such as nightmare or hallucination, 'impressions' are always the more vivid of the two. Hume further divides these two classes of 'perception' into simple and complex; for instance, our 'impression' of an apple is complex, consisting of a number of simple 'impressions' of colour, shape, texture and taste; and similarly with our 'idea' of an apple.

It follows that every 'idea' has an 'impression' corresponding to it; or at least we can say that it is built from 'impressions'. Simple 'ideas' correspond to simple 'impressions'—'all our simple ideas in their first appearance are derived from simple impressions, which are correspondent to them and which they exactly represent'.[10] Thus our 'idea' of the blue sky corresponds to the visual 'impression' of blueness. Complex 'ideas', on the other hand, may have no exactly corresponding 'impression', for (as Hume himself remarks) we have no 'impression' corresponding to such an 'idea' as the Golden City or New Jerusalem; but any complex 'idea' must be constructed from 'impressions' and is therefore derived, if indirectly, from experience. It follows that 'impressions' precede 'ideas' and that experience is prior to thinking about experience. There is another item in Hume's empiricism which he is at pains to emphasise and which is especially important for his analysis of causation; it is that every 'impression' is a distinct and separate entity: 'Every distinct perception which enters into the composition of the human mind is a distinct existence and is different and distinguishable and separable from every other perception, either contemporary or successive.'[11] There is no intrinsic relatedness between our perceptions of the external world or between the occurrences

[8] *Enquiries*, II, 13; p. 19.
[9] *Treatise*, I, i, 1; p. 1.
[10] *Ibid.*, I, i, 1; p. 4.
[11] *Ibid.*, I, iv, 6; p. 259; cf. Appendix, p. 636: 'There are two principles which I cannot render consistent; nor is it in my power to renounce either of them, viz., *that all our distinct perceptions are distinct existences*, and *that the mind never perceives any real connexion among distinct existences.*'

of love and hate and acts of will which we are aware of within ourselves;
each is distinct from every other, in itself an isolated, detached event.

How, then, is it possible to account for the order, pattern and relatedness which our minds do in fact impose on their contents? This cannot,
surely, be the result of pure chance? Hume finds his solution to this
problem in a psychological theory of association. Locke had already
pointed out that certain 'ideas' 'have a *natural* correspondence and connexion one with another' and that it is the mind's function to 'hold them
together in that union and correspondence which is founded in their
peculiar beings'.[12] Other 'ideas', he thought, have no natural connection,
but are linked in the mind solely as a result of association through custom
or habit. Apart from affirming that association of those 'ideas' which are
not naturally connected can lead to serious intellectual and moral error,
Locke goes no further. Hume, however, makes association the basic
principle of the mind's operation, capable of explaining not only the casual
musing of idle reflection, but also the disciplined reasoning of science.
'Impressions', he argues, can appear in the mind as 'ideas' either of memory
or of imagination; memory preserves in general the order and position of
the original 'impressions'; imagination is not restricted in this way, but
can separate, combine and rearrange 'ideas' to please itself. Nevertheless,
imagination is not entirely free, for it tends to follow certain paths which
link 'ideas' together: 'Were ideas entirely loose and unconnected, chance
alone would join them, and 'tis impossible the same simple ideas should
fall regularly into complex ones (as they commonly do) without some bond
of union among them.'[13]

This associative link between 'ideas' is not an intrinsic bond encapsulated in their nature (as Locke seems to have thought), nor is its operation
inevitable—for in that case imagination would not be free; it is rather 'a
gentle force which commonly prevails . . ., nature in a manner pointing
out to everyone those simple ideas which are most proper to be united
into a complex one'.[14] (This, it may be remarked in passing, is the language
of metaphor and even of metaphysics, and is curiously out of character
with Hume's matter-of-fact empiricism.) It depends on certain features of
the 'ideas' themselves as they are presented in experience, namely, resemblance, contiguity in time or place, and the relationship of cause–effect.[15]
Similarity between 'ideas' disposes the mind to associate them and so, for

[12] *Essay* II, xxxiii, 5; ed. A. S. Pringle-Pattison, p. 217.

[13] *Treatise*, I, i, 4; p. 10.

[14] *Ibid.*, pp. 10–11.

[15] These are not necessarily the only features that promote association:
'These principles I allow to be neither the *infallible* nor the *sole* causes of
an union among ideas,' *Treatise*, I, iii, 6; p. 92 (and see below, p. 146 and
note). But cf. *Enquiries*, V, ii, 41; p. 50.

instance, to classify them under a single heading, like trees or dogs; or where two 'ideas' occur in close proximity, spatial or temporal, the same 'gentle force' prompts the mind to link them—lightning and thunder, wind and waves. As for cause–effect, 'there is no relation which produces a stronger connexion in the fancy and makes one idea more readily recall another than the relation of cause and effect betwixt objects'.[16] Hume compares association with the principle of universal attraction in physics; like that, it manifests itself everywhere in manifold ways and must be accepted simply as fact without prying into the reasons for it.

Before going on to examine Hume's positive account of the concept of cause it will be helpful first to adopt a negative approach and establish what he rejects. It was an assumption of rationalist philosophy, as it is also of common parlance, that to say that *a* causes *b* is to imply that there exists in *a* some causal power, some essential efficatory force, which necessitates or entails the occurrence of *b*—hence the 'entailment' theory of causation. Thus, when we say that lightning causes thunder or that increased pressure causes a reduction in the volume of a gas, what we are assuming (though without acknowledgement) is that there is some intimate connection between the two events in either pair such that the one is productive of the other—it *makes* it happen. This view of causation Hume resolutely denies; he repudiates any account of it which involves the notions of 'efficacy, agency, power, force, energy, necessity, connexion and productive quality' as operating between events and necessarily binding them to one another.[17] There are two related lines of thought which lead him to this conclusion: first, he insists, as we have seen, that every event is 'a distinct existence', an isolated item of experience. This is in part a presupposition of his empiricism, an *a priori* principle which he assumes rather than demonstrates, but it is supported by the second train of argument which is based on his doctrine of 'impressions' and 'ideas'. Every 'idea' in the mind is the result of some prior 'impression', some perception of inner or outer sense; now we never, Hume affirms, have any 'impression' of a link or connection binding one event to another—this is something we simply do not perceive or observe; and if there is no 'impression' of a link between events, there can be no 'idea' of it either; causal entailment corresponds to nothing in experience and is unacceptable, therefore, to an empirical philosophy. This is no less true of inner experience than of external events: though it may be argued that in volition, in the deliberate willing of some action, we are conscious of a power operating from will to deed, yet this is not so; we are aware only of the act of will and the ensuing deed, *not* of any link between them. Nor is there any plausibility in the argument that all events are effected by a divine intelligence which, operating by its own

[16] *Treatise*, I, i, 4; p. 11.   [17] *Ibid.*, I, iii, 14; p. 157.

laws, ensures that any event is followed by its proper consequent; in this 'we are got into fairyland', 'our line is too short to fathom such immense abysses' and all we can be sure of is 'our profound ignorance'.[18]

He concludes, then:

It appears that, in single instances of the operation of bodies, we never can by our utmost scrutiny discover anything but one event following another, without being able to comprehend any force or power by which the cause operates or any connexion between it and its supposed effect. The same difficulty occurs in contemplating the operations of mind on body—where we observe the motion of the latter to follow upon the volition of the former but are not able to observe or conceive the tie which binds together the motion and volition or the energy by which the mind produces this effect. . . . So that, upon the whole, there appears not throughout all nature any one instance of connexion which is conceivable by us. All events seem entirely loose and separate. One event follows another; but we never can observe any tie between them. They seem *conjoined*, but never *connected*. And as we can have no idea of any thing which never appeared to our outward sense or inward sentiment, the necessary conclusion *seems* to be that we have no idea of connexion or power at all and that these words are absolutely without any meaning, when employed either in philosophical reasonings or common life.[19]

This is not the whole of the story, however, for despite Hume's denial that any link between events is given in experience, the fact remains that we do assume such linkage and that necessary connection is commonly accepted as part of the concept of cause. Whence does this notion arise if not from observing it displayed in events? How otherwise can it be explained? These are questions for which he was bound, as a consistent empiricist, to offer an answer; but first we must turn to his own account of the causal concept.

If there is no basis in experience for assuming a necessary bond between one event and any other, no justification for believing in causal efficacy or entailment, what can legitimately be included in the concept of cause? What can we properly mean when we speak of *a* as 'causing' or 'the cause of' *b*? Hume's answer is clear and uncompromising: he insists, once again, on the distinctness, the isolated particularity of facts and events; further, any of them could, without logical contradiction, be different from, indeed quite contrary to, what it is—'*That the sun will not rise tomorrow* is no less intelligible a proposition and implies no more contradiction than the affirmation *that it will rise*';[20] there can therefore be no logical inference from one to another. Yet we do predict from one fact or event to another; we do infer from *a* to *b* as if there were a logical bond between them. Are we wrong in so doing? *Philosophically*, yes, says Hume; *psychologically*,

---

[18] *Enquiries*, VII, i, 57; pp. 72-3.
[19] *Ibid.*, VII, ii, 58; pp. 73-4.   [20] *Ibid.*, IV, i, 21; pp. 25-6.

no. Such inferences 'are *not* founded on reasoning or any process of the understanding';[21] their justification is psychological, not logical, and arises from the principle of association of ideas.

Hume has already affirmed three associative factors in experience—resemblance, contiguity and the cause–effect relation, of which the last is itself the product of association. When we survey the world around us, we find that certain facts, features and events are contiguous in space, time or both—lightning and thunder, wind and waves, flower and scent, fire and heat. We also find that certain events follow each other in temporal succession—frost is followed by burst pipes, a nail in a tyre by a puncture, heating a metal rod by expansion, running by breathlessness, over-eating by stomach-pains. Moreover, these instances of contiguity and succession occur not once or twice but again and again: thunder is a *regular* concomitant of lightning, as are waves of wind; in certain conditions frost is *regularly* followed by burst pipes, breathlessness is a *regular* consequent of running, and stomach-ache of over-eating. The concept of cause, Hume says, arises from the observation that certain features of experience are *constantly* associated in these two ways, and we have no right (consistently with empiricism) to include in the concept any more than this—the constant conjunction of facts and events in the relations of contiguity and temporal succession. This is all we can mean when we speak of *a* as the cause of *b*, that wherever we find *a*, there we also constantly find *b*, that whenever *a* occurs, *b* is constantly found to follow. If we go further and assume the existence of some bond of entailment between them, we are exceeding the observed facts of experience and incorporating in the concept something which has no place in it:

When we look about us towards external objects and consider the operation of causes, we are never able in a single instance to discover any power or necessary connexion, any quality which binds the effect to the cause and renders the one an infallible consequence of the other. We only find that the one does actually, in fact, follow the other.[22]

Hence follows Hume's conclusion, already noted, that inference from cause to effect, including predictive inference into the future, is not a rational process justifiable by logic, but, as he goes on to show, a psychological mechanism based on habit or custom.[23]

All this, as Hume remarks, is 'pretty remote from the common theories of philosophy', and he is at pains to make his position unmistakably clear.

[21] *Enquiries*, IV, ii, 28; p. 32.
[22] *Ibid.*, VII, i, 50; p. 63 (cf. p. 143 above). Hume would not, I think, deny that there *may* be some bond of entailment between events, but he would reject emphatically any suggestion that this is a datum of experience.
[23] *Ibid.*, V, i, 38; p. 46.

All inference concerning matters of observed fact, whether it is causal or otherwise, whether it refers to present or future, must be regarded, not as a rational process, but as a kind of psychological determination:

Having found in many instances that any two kinds of objects—flame and heat, snow and cold—have always been conjoined together, if flame or snow be presented anew to the senses, the mind is carried by custom to expect heat or cold and to *believe* that such a quality does exist and will discover itself upon a nearer approach. This belief is the necessary result of placing the mind in such circumstances. It is an operation of the soul, when we are so situated, as unavoidable as to feel the passion of love when we receive benefits, or hatred when we meet with injuries. All these operations are a species of natural instincts, which no reasoning or process of the thought and understanding is able either to produce or to prevent.[24]

Again:

All inferences from experience . . . are effects of custom, not of reasoning. Custom, then, is the great guide of human life. It is that principle alone which renders our experience useful to us and makes us expect for the future a similar train of events with those which have appeared in the past.[25]

This includes, of course, inductive inference, whereby we generalise from particular experiences and use our generalisations to predict into the future (pp. 12–13). Hitherto I have always found bread nourishing; I therefore infer that it will always be so. But, Hume protests, there is no logical connection between these two propositions: 'If you insist that the inference is made by a chain of reasoning, I desire you to produce that reasoning'[26] —and this cannot be done. The basis of induction is the assumption that what has not been experienced is or will be similar to what has, and it *is* an assumption, no more, prompted by the constitution of our minds, which leads us to expect in the future what we have been accustomed to in the past. As for the causal principle that every effect must have a cause and every cause an effect, this too has no other justification than a psychological propensity to project into the future what has been regularly experienced in the past—an expectation of similarity, a presumption of uniformity. *Rational* justification it has none.

Before moving on to the final stage of Hume's account of causation—his explanation of the assumed element of necessity in the causal link—we must pause to comment on what has just been said. First, it may be questioned whether causal and inductive inferences are wholly a matter of association and habit, as Hume would have us believe; this may well be

[24] *Ibid.*
[25] *Ibid.*, V, i, 36; pp. 43–4; cf. *Treatise*, I, iii, 13; p. 147.
[26] *Enquiries*, IV, ii, 29; p. 34.

acceptable as explaining the basic psychological mechanism which initially prompted human beings to infer from the known to the unknown—an instinctive survival factor enabling them to achieve security in a world full of dangers; but civilisation has refined this primitive mechanism into a nice calculation of probabilities which enables us to choose, if not with certainty, at least with reasonable assurance, between alternatives. It is, of course, quite impossible to *prove* (in the sense of certain demonstration) that the sun will rise tomorrow, bread nourish instead of poisoning, or Arsenal beat Manchester United; but the odds can be calculated, often with great accuracy, and a conclusion drawn which is reasoned and logical, highly probable if not entirely certain. 'All probable reasoning', Hume wrote, 'is nothing but a species of sensation',[27] that is, the pressure of habit inclining decision in a direction suggested by past experience. But in the hands of a mathematician probability has become a precision tool whose operation is both logically defensible and also of great practical value.

Second, it may further be questioned whether Hume's account of causality is preferable to that which he rejects. He will not include within the concept any suggestion of a causal bond or entailment which *makes b* follow *a*; this would be to go beyond the facts of experience, to read into them what cannot be discovered by observation, to abandon therefore the empirical position and trespass into metaphysics. Yet his own view contains elements which are hard to justify from experience alone: as a result of habitual experience the mind is 'determined' to infer from cause to effect by 'a natural transition' which is the 'necessary result' of the circumstances in which it is placed; this propensity of the mind is 'a species of natural instincts', 'a gentle force which commonly prevails'.[28] But does this genuinely advance our understanding of the matter? It seems that Hume has transferred the notion of causal entailment from the material world to the mental, from what we perceive to what happens in our minds; the problem is now psychological instead of metaphysical, but it remains a problem; mystery cannot be dispelled by changing its location. For he can offer no explanation, any more than could Locke (p. 111), for the compulsive power of association; he writes of it as 'a kind of pre-established harmony' effected by custom 'between the course of nature and the succession of our ideas' (and even suggests that its practical utility is such that 'those who delight in the discovery and contemplation of *final causes* have here ample subject to employ their wonder and admiration' !).[29] Moreover, it seems impossible to justify it from his own premises—no 'ideas'

[27] *Treatise*, I, iii, 8; p. 103.
[28] *Ibid.*, I, iii, 11; p. 128, and I, iii, 13; p. 147; *Enquiries*, V, i, 38; p. 46, and pp. 46-7; *Treatise*, I, i, 4; p. 10.
[29] *Enquiries*, V, ii, 44; pp. 54-5.

without 'impressions', and every event a 'distinct existence'; for we have no 'impression' of a bond between associated 'ideas', any more than we have between will and deed (p. 144), and no right, therefore, to assume a 'force', 'instinct' or anything else which links them.

However, there is a point of interest here which perhaps gives a clue to what we shall find in Kant. Without the operation of association our mental powers would be severely inhibited—'all our knowledge must have been limited to the narrow sphere of our memory and senses; and we should never have been able to adjust means to ends or employ our natural powers either to the producing of good or avoiding of evil'.[30] And even if its existence cannot be proved from empirical premises, it must nevertheless be *assumed* in order to explain and to justify our intellectual processes; it must be accepted as something built into our mental constitution, a presupposition of rationality and of knowledge. If this is what Hume had in mind, it is not so far removed from Kant's position in his *Critique of Pure Reason.*

The final stage of Hume's account of causation, his explanation of the notion of necessity in the relation of cause and effect, can be dealt with briefly, for his answer must now be clear. He has denied that any bond of entailment exists between events as they are experienced; *a* does not cause *b* in the sense of producing *b* or making it happen—it does just happen, and that is all we can say of it. The notion of causality arises simply from the observation of *a* and *b* in constant conjunction: they are repeatedly experienced together and successively. Causal argument has no philosophical *justification*, but only a psychological *explanation* based on association. The element of necessity which we read into the causal situation is purely mental; it is an expression of the feeling we have when our minds are impelled by the force of association to link one 'idea' with another:

After a repetition of similar instances the mind is carried by habit, upon the appearance of one event, to expect its usual attendant and to believe that it will exist. This connexion, therefore, that we *feel* in the mind, this customary transition of the imagination from one object to its usual attendant, is the sentiment or impression from which we form the idea of power or necessary connexion.[31]

In the *Treatise* Hume concludes his account of causation with two definitions, one of which presents cause–effect as a 'philosophical', the other as a 'natural' relation. The first is stated in terms simply of contiguity, succession and constant conjunction: 'We may define a CAUSE to be "An object precedent and contiguous to another, and where all the objects

[30] *Ibid.,* p. 55.
[31] *Ibid.,* VII, ii, 59; p. 75.

resembling the former are placed in like relations of precedency and contiguity to those objects that resemble the latter." ' The second incorporates his psychological explanation of causal inference: 'A CAUSE is an object precedent and contiguous to another and so united with it that the idea of the one determines the mind to form the idea of the other. . . .'[32] What Hume seems to be saying in offering these two definitions is this: a philosophical analysis of the concept of cause, if it adheres to strictly empirical premises, reveals no more than the three factors, contiguity, succession and constant conjunction; this is *all* the meaning that can properly be included in the concept, all that the facts of observation yield. In such analysis there is no justification of causal inference, no explanation, only the bare facts; without resort to metaphysics—which Hume, of course, eschews—philosophy cannot *justify* causal inference, and it is not its function to *explain*. For explanation one must turn to psychology and the principle of association—and some may also find here a partial justification, for causal inference *works* in enabling mankind to achieve rationality and practical adjustment to environment.

Readers of Hume who come to him expecting a metaphysical account of causation along rationalist lines or who bring with them the preconceptions embodied in the popular use of 'cause', will be disappointed with what they find in the *Treatise* and the first *Enquiry*. The bald picture presented by his philosophical definition—contiguity, succession, uniformity—may seem to trivialise the concept by robbing it of its essential content. But is this really so? The answer depends on what one expects of philosophy—ultimate explanation by transcendental metaphysical principles or clarification of thought—and on the presuppositions, rationalist or empiricist, with which one comes to it.

Hume's position is quite clear, and it can be argued in his defence that for science the concept of cause, though useful perhaps as a manner of speaking, is by no means indispensable. In investigating the actual world, whether his purpose is simply to advance knowledge or whether it includes also its application in promoting human welfare, the scientist can manage without the notion of causal entailment. It is enough for his purpose if he can establish statistical correlations between the facts he observes and make his hypotheses and predictions on the assumption that what has frequently happened in the past is likely to recur in the future—the principle of the uniformity of nature. If he is looking for 'the cause' of lung cancer, he needs only to show that the disease is constantly associated with, say, environmental factors, smoking habits or body-chemistry; from this he can proceed to the hypothesis that the factor or factors operative to produce it are x, y, z, alone or in combination; finally, he can predict that it will

[32] *Treatise*, I, iii, 14; p. 170.

decrease or disappear to the extent that these factors are eliminated. In so far as he sticks to science and statistics and avoids straying into theology or metaphysics, the possible existence of a causal bond or necessary connection between lung cancer and x, y, z is irrelevant. It is equally irrelevant to the practical task of eliminating the associative factors which in ordinary parlance we call 'causes'—except, perhaps, in so far as the word 'cause' has greater persuasive power for propaganda than such emotion-free terms as 'statistical correlation'.

There is a further point which is worth a brief notice: in common speech we regularly talk about '*the* cause' of so and so—'What is *the* cause of road accidents?' 'What was *the* cause of the French Revolution or the Second World War?', 'What was *the* cause of A's breakdown or B's miscarriage?'—as if in each case there were only *one* cause. However, it requires little thought to reveal that for any event there are several, perhaps a multitude of causal factors, all of which add up to produce the final result. Thus, it is not cigarettes alone that cause lung cancer, but also, perhaps, the way they are smoked, the way they are made or the tobacco grown, the desire of the manufacturer to increase his profits, the genetic make-up of the smoker, the degree of atmospheric pollution in the town he lives in, and so on. If we avoid thinking of cause in terms of entailment, we are more likely to appreciate the complexity of causal problems.

No one before Hume had seriously questioned the causal principle that every event must have a cause (at least in regard to events outside human volition, since this latter could be presumed to be non-determined) and that this could be assumed *a priori* as a necessary postulate of enquiry. Acceptance of the principle had usually involved also the entailment view of causation—the existence of a necessary bond between cause and effect. Hume's critical analysis presents us with an alternative: observation gives us no more than the constant conjunction of events in certain relations; the causal principle is only a psychological propensity to expect the future to resemble the past, and causal entailment a metaphysical myth without rational justification. These are the two main positions; each has its difficulties, which can only be hinted at here. Entailment is difficult to square with belief in free will, which, on moral as well as on common-sense grounds, most of us are reluctant to reject; moreover, as Hume has shown, there seems to be no justification for it in what we actually *observe*. Against Hume, on the other hand, it can be argued that the uniformities we find in events and the predictions we make from them are altogether too regular, too reliable, to be the result of coincidence; there must, surely, be some intrinsic connection between events, something which belongs to the very constitution of the universe and *disposes* certain things to follow each other in regular sequence. And Hume himself is not so far from

F

such a view when he writes of 'a kind of pre-established harmony between the course of nature and the succession of our ideas' (p. 148 above).[33] After all, to say that thunder just *does* follow lightning, that the volume of a gas just *happens* to be inversely proportional to its pressure, or that the mind just *happens* to associate *a* with *b* because it has observed them together in the past still leaves a gap in explanation, a question-mark which is irritating to human reason.

[33] *Enquiries*, V, ii, 44; p. 54.

Further study

Hume

General accounts of Hume's philosophy can be found in A. H. BASSON, *David Hume* (Penguin, 1958, and Dover Publications, 1968); D. G. C. MACNABB, *David Hume: his Theory of Knowledge and Morality* (Blackwell, 2nd edn, 1966); B. M. LAING, *David Hume* (Benn, 1932); and N. KEMP SMITH, *The Philosophy of David Hume* (Macmillan, 1941). More specific in their approach are A. G. N. FLEW, *Hume's Philosophy of Belief: a Study of his First Inquiry* (Routledge, 1961); H. H. PRICE, *Hume's Theory of the External World* (Oxford, Clarendon Press, 1940); and J. PASSMORE, *Hume's Intentions* (Cambridge University Press, 1952). J. Y. T. GREIG, *David Hume* (Cape, 1931) is a readable life.

Hume's style has the attraction of a frosty day—cold, clear and bracing. The student could well make his way through the *Enquiry concerning Human Understanding*, supplementing it (for the purpose of the present chapter) with relevant sections of the *Treatise*. There are editions of both of these, by L. A. SELBY-BIGGE (Oxford, Clarendon Press, respectively 1902, 2nd edn, and 1888). D. C. YALDEN-THOMSON, *Hume: Theory of Knowledge* (Nelson, 1951) has the first *Enquiry* in full and selections from *Treatise*, Book I. It would also be well worth while to dip into the *Enquiry concerning the Principles of Morals*, which, like its twin, is a philosophical classic. Hume's writings on religion are also of great interest—*The Natural History of Religion* and *Dialogues concerning Natural Religion*; these, with other writings are in R. WOLLHEIM, *Hume on Religion* (Collins 1963).

Causation

The relevant passages in Hume are: *Treatise*, Book I, Part I, Sections 1–4; Part III, 2–9, 12–15; *Enquiry concerning Human Understanding*, Sections 2–7. With these can be compared J. S. MILL, *Logic*, Book III, 4–6, and VI, 2; and THOMAS REID, *Essays on the Active Powers of the Human Mind*, Essay 4, 'Of the Liberty of Moral Agents'.

There are chapters on causation in the following: A. J. AYER, *Foundations of Empirical Knowledge* (ch. 4); EWING, *Fundamental Questions* (chs 8, 9) and *Idealism* (ch. 4, para. 3); HOSPERS, *Philosophical Analysis* (ch. 4);

J. M. E. MCTAGGART, *Philosophical Studies* (Arnold, 1934), ch. 7; REICHEN-BACH, *Rise of Scientific Philosophy* (ch. 10); S. STEBBING, *Philosophy and the Physicists* (Methuen, 1937), Part 3; and A. E. TAYLOR, *Elements of Metaphysics* (Methuen, 1903), Book II, ch. 5. These are not all written from the same point of view. When the reader has digested some of these, he may feel ready for M. BUNGE, *Causality* (Harvard University Press, 1959) or H. L. A. HART and A. M. HONORÉ, *Causation in the Law* (Oxford, Clarendon Press, 1959).

Among numerous articles are the following: A. C. EWING, 'A defence of causality', *Aristotelian Society Proceedings*, 33 (1933); BERTRAND RUSSELL, 'On the notion of cause', in *Mysticism and Logic* (Longmans, 1917); G. J. WARNOCK, 'Every event has a cause', in A. G. N. FLEW, ed., *Logic and Language* (2nd series, Blackwell, 1959); and R. TAYLOR, 'Causation', *Monist*, 47 (1963). On a particularly fascinating aspect of causation there are: M. A. E. DUMMETT and A. G. N FLEW, 'Can an effect precede its cause?', *Aristotelian Society Supplement*, 28 (1954); R. M. CHISHOLM and R. TAYLOR, 'Making things to have happened', *Analysis*, 20 (1960); and M. A. E. DUMMETT, 'Bringing about the past', *Philosophical Review*, 73 (1964).

9 Kant

(a) The vindication of knowledge
(b) The ethic of duty

Biographical note

Immanuel Kant was born at Königsberg in 1724. His grandfather, so he tells us, was a Scot, one of many who emigrated to northern Europe at the end of the seventeenth century; it is possible that Kant was mistaken about his ancestry, but it is an interesting thought that he may have shared Scottish blood with David Hume, who supplied the initial stimulus and motive for his philosophical achievement. His parents were poor, respectable and deeply religious; Kant writes with great respect of their simple piety which found its expression more in sincerity of life and conduct than in formal practices. From school, where he gained a thorough knowledge of Latin and a smattering of Greek, he passed to the University of Königsberg. Here his attention was devoted chiefly to mathematics and science, though he was also introduced to metaphysics, which later became and remained the focus of his philosophical interests. At the end of his university studies Kant could find no academic post and was compelled to spend the next seven or eight years as a private tutor in various German families. In 1755 he was given authority to lecture privately at his own university, receiving no salary but only the fees paid by his students. Eventually, in 1770, he was appointed to the Chair of Logic and Metaphysics at Königsberg, and this he held until ill health forced him to stop lecturing. He died in 1804. His physique was poor; this and the demands of his work necessitated from middle life a strict personal regime for which he became noted—his neighbours, so it was said, set their clocks by him as he set off daily at precisely the same hour for his afternoon walk. Yet he was no recluse. He enjoyed social life, had numerous friends and in his younger days evidently led something of a gay life; even in later years he regularly invited several friends to his midday meal and spent the afternoon in conversation with them. More-over, although the character of his major works scarcely suggests it, he was a popular lecturer who took pains to interest his students and to encourage them in independence of thought. Among his many and wide-ranging interests was educational reform—the result of reading Rousseau's Emile, *which so enthralled him as to cause him to miss his afternoon walk; his thoughts on education were published just before his death in a short book,* On Pedagogy. *He was also interested in science, for although Kant was fundamentally a rationalist, he did not, like Plato, despise the phenomenal world as an obstacle to knowledge. On the contrary, he was well acquainted with the scientific knowledge of his time, including Newtonian physics, and was firmly convinced of the competence of science within its own sphere; indeed he wrote a number of treatises on scientific matters, including one on a subject still of topical interest,* On Volcanoes on the Moon.

The vindication of knowledge

Kant's career can be divided into two distinct periods, commonly known as the 'pre-critical' and the 'critical'; the meaning of these words derives from the work of the second period and will become clear later. In the first he wrote and lectured on metaphysics, science and other subjects, showing no great originality or eminence of thought, but adhering in the main to the metaphysical position of the rationalist philosopher Leibniz as interpreted by his follower, Christian von Wolff. It did not occur to him at this time to question either the validity of metaphysics or the ability of human reason to describe reality. This period of Kant's work continued until, in the late 1760s, he read the philosophical writings of Hume, who, in Kant's own words, 'interrupted my dogmatic slumber and gave a completely different direction to my enquiries in the field of speculative philosophy'.[1]

What was it in Hume that jerked Kant out of his complacent acceptance of Leibnizian metaphysics into a new philosophical orientation? In developing his empiricism Hume arrived at a position of complete scepticism about the validity of knowledge; reference has already been made to this in chapters 1 and 5. He divides propositions or statements into two kinds, those expressing fact and those expressing relation; the former belong to science, the latter to mathematics and logic. About statements of fact, he argues, certainty is impossible, for it is always possible, at least logically, to conceive them to be false. Statements of relation are arrived at by deductive argument and, if the inference is valid, are necessarily what they are; but since the human mind is fallible, there is no guarantee that it has inferred correctly; hence even here certainty is

[1] *Prolegomena to Any Future Metaphysics*, ed. P. G. Lucas (Manchester University Press, 1953), p. 9. (Further references are to this edition.)

not assured. But surely, it may be objected, there are obvious certainties in nature, like the law of cause and effect, which can always be relied on because they are written, as it were, into the structure of the universe. Not at all, Hume replies; the law of causation, and others like it, are not part of the structure of the universe; they are merely dispositions of our own minds which, after repeated observation of (for example) effect following cause, is inclined to assume that effect *must* follow cause; the certainty is entirely illusory, a mere psychological state of expectation due to the association of ideas (p. 149).[2] What, then, of metaphysics? This is dismissed on several counts: first, metaphysical statements express neither facts nor relations and are therefore excluded, on Hume's argument, from meaningful discourse; second, even if this were not so, metaphysics would still be invalidated by the sceptical arguments which dispose of science and mathematics; third, it is doubtful whether the human mind is fitted for the kind of enquiry undertaken by metaphysicians—and it was part of Hume's purpose to show that it was not.

To Hume's argument from the fallibility of the human mind in reasoning there is no final answer; and it applies not only to the deductive inference of mathematics but to any inference, including that of science and metaphysics. However, a fundamental scepticism of this kind is untenable in practice, as Hume himself was aware, and can therefore be ignored. What, then, was the crux of Kant's problem in meeting Hume's sceptical challenge? Hume had analysed experience and as its ultimate constituents had found, so he thought, independent unrelated items of sensation which in some way are sorted out, classified and patterned in the mind. This ordering of the basic stuff of experience is, however, purely psychological, the product of custom, habit and association; it does not reflect any organisation of things as they are in themselves, nor does it carry any logical certainty. The knowledge it provides has no validity or authority; it does not possess that necessity which the rationalist regards as essential to knowledge; and the 'laws' which the scientist uses to explain experience are founded on nothing more than the habitual association of ideas in his own mind. It seems impossible, then, to start from unrelated sense data, as Hume had done, and arrive at knowledge in any acceptable sense.

Nevertheless, Kant argued, there *is* certainty in our knowledge; moreover it is a certainty which is independent of and prior to experience, enabling us to predict facts or events in advance of their discovery or occurrence. In mathematics, for instance, we know in advance of experience that $7 + 5$ necessarily $= 12$ and that the shortest distance between two

[2] *Prolegomena to Any Future Metaphysics*, ed. P. G. Lucas, pp. 5–6; the element of necessity in the concept of cause is 'a bastard of the imagination fathered by experience'.

points is necessarily a straight line; similarly in physics we know without experiment that any event will necessarily have a cause—if a metal rod has expanded there *must* have been a rise in temperature. Whence does this element of certainty and necessity enter into knowledge if, as Hume argued, it is not given in experience? Unless this question can be answered satisfactorily, neither mathematics nor physics (nor, by inference, any other science) has a reliable foundation. Metaphysics also claims to give us factual knowledge which is certain, necessary and independent of experience; it asserts, for instance, that God exists, that the human will is free, that the soul is immortal. How far is this claim justified? And if it cannot be justified, what place or function remains for metaphysics?

An attempt must now be made to state the problem in the technical language which Kant himself uses.[3] Like Hume, he distinguishes two kinds of proposition or statement; he calls them 'analytic' and 'synthetic', and they correspond to Hume's propositions of relation and fact. In an analytic proposition the idea of the predicate is contained in or implied by the idea of the subject and can be obtained from it by analysis; the example Kant offers is 'All bodies are extended', where 'extension' is part of the definition or concept of 'body' and is obviously, therefore, implied by it; another example (not Kant's) is 'Bachelors are unmarried', where again the predicate is clearly contained in the idea of 'bachelor'. Analytic propositions, Kant says, are 'explicative'—they explain without adding anything new to the original idea. Synthetic propositions, on the other hand, do add something new to the original idea; they are 'augmentative'; for example, 'All bodies are heavy', where 'heavy' is not implied by 'body', but is a new idea derived, not by analysis or 'explication', but from experience. Similarly, 'Water boils at 100°C at normal atmospheric pressure' and 'Distilled water is tasteless' provide new information about water which is discoverable only from experience, not from analysing the concept of water. Such propositions are 'synthetic' because they bring together (Greek, *syntithenai*) two ideas which are not necessarily related.

Kant makes a further distinction within the class of synthetic propositions. Some, he says, are derived entirely from experience; such, for instance, are factual statements based on observation—'Birds lay eggs', 'Ice is cold'; they are synthetic *a posteriori*, that is, they can be asserted only *after* experience. Others, he asserts, are synthetic *a priori*, that is, they can provide new factual information *before* experience and are not, therefore, derived from experience. Such, he claims, are the mathematical propositions $7 + 5 = 12$ and 'The shortest distance between two points is

[3] *Ibid.*, § 2, pp. 16 ff.; *Critique of Pure Reason* (henceforth referred to as *CPR*), introd. IV; trans. J. M. D. Meiklejohn, ed. A. D. Lindsay (Dent, 1934), pp. 30–4. (Further references are to this edition.)

a straight line'; or those of physics, such as 'In all corporeal change the quantity of matter remains the same' and the law of cause and effect.[4] Now analytic propositions are necessary and certain, because the predicate is logically implied by the subject; synthetic *a posteriori* propositions are neither certain nor necessary, for it is always logically possible for facts of experience to be otherwise than they are; synthetic *a priori* propositions, however, do have these qualities, so Kant claims—they enable us to predict with certainty and logical necessity in advance of actual experience. It is Kant's belief that the validity, indeed the possibility, of genuine knowledge, whether in mathematics or in science, depends on these synthetic *a priori* propositions; for they alone provide a knowledge which is certain, necessary and at the same time more fruitful than the merely explicative information of analytic propositions. His problem, therefore, is to show how such propositions are possible; if he succeeds, he will at the same time validate knowledge against Hume's attack.

It took Kant eleven years to work out his answer to the problem, from the time of his appointment to the Chair at Königsberg until the publication of the *Critique of Pure Reason* in 1781. During this period he laboured to construct what he called a 'transcendental philosophy', namely, a study of the origin, nature and function of the *a priori* elements in knowledge; 'transcendental', because its subject-matter was independent of and transcended experience.[5] His first exposition of it was in the *Critique* just mentioned,[6] whose title signifies in no way an attack on reason, but a critical analysis of its contribution to knowledge and incidentally of its limitations; and by 'pure' he means reason in so far as it is independent of and prior to experience—'pure reason is the faculty which contains the principles of cognizing anything absolutely *a priori*'.[7] There followed in 1788 the *Critique of Practical Reason*, which is concerned with moral experience, and in 1790 the *Critique of Judgement*, in which he examines aesthetic experience and the idea of purpose in nature. These, with other

---

[4] For Kant's argument see *Prolegomena*, pp. 19 ff.; many modern philosophers believe that Kant was mistaken here and that there are no *a priori* propositions which are also synthetic.

[5] *CPR*, pp. 38–40: 'I apply the term *transcendental* to all knowledge which is not so much occupied with objects as with the mode of cognition of these objects, so far as this mode of cognition is possible *a priori*. A system of such conceptions would be called *Transcendental Philosophy*.... It is the system of all the principles of pure reason ... a philosophy of the pure and merely speculative reason.'

[6] Owing to its difficulty the first edition of the *Critique* was not well received; to facilitate understanding Kant wrote the *Prolegomena* (1783) as a kind of reader's guide. The second edition of the *Critique*, incorporating material from the *Prolegomena*, was published in 1787.

[7] *CPR*, p. 38.

works within the same theme, are known as the 'critical philosophy'; hence come the names of the two periods of Kant's work. Kant regarded his transcendental philosophy as entirely novel—'a wholly new science which no one had previously even thought of, even the mere idea of which was unknown'.[8] It was designed to be, not a doctrine, 'but only a transcendental critique, because it aims, not at the enlargement, but at the correction and guidance of our knowledge, and is to serve as a touch-stone of the worth or worthlessness of all our knowledge *a priori*'.[9]

Kant's solution to the problem of knowledge involved what he believed to be a revolution in philosophy:

We here propose to do just what Copernicus did in attempting to explain the celestial movements. When he found that he could make no progress by assuming that all the heavenly bodies revolved round the spectator, he reversed the process and tried the experiment of assuming that the spectator revolved, while the stars remained at rest. We may make the same experiment with regard to the intuition [i.e. perception] of objects. If the intuition must conform to the nature of the objects, I do not see how we can know anything of them *a priori*. If, on the other hand, the object conforms to the nature of our faculty of intuition, I can then easily conceive the possibility of such an *a priori* knowledge.[10]

What is true of perception is also true, Kant continues, of conception, that is, of the mind's arrangement into organised knowledge of the material supplied by perception:

Before objects are given to me, that is *a priori*, I must presuppose in myself laws of the understanding which are expressed in conceptions *a priori*. To these conceptions, then, all the objects of experience must necessarily conform.[11]

What Kant is saying is this: hitherto philosophers and metaphysicians have tried to explain experience by assuming that there is an external world entirely independent of human thought, and that, to understand and describe this world, the mind must conform to it, take on its shape and structure and thus reflect it like a mirror; on this view, the laws of thought, of mathematics, science and metaphysics, are laws of things, embodied in the universe and discovered and exhibited by the mind. This assumption has been made untenable, however, by Hume's empiricism, which has shown that sensation, which supplies the data of our knowledge, cannot also provide the principles of connection and order by which knowledge is built; things in themselves do not embody the structure and pattern, the certainty and necessity which are characteristic of knowledge. Yet the mind does produce a knowledge which possesses these qualities; whence,

[8] *Prolegomena*, p. 11.   [9] *CPR*, p. 38.
[10] *Ibid.*, p. 12.   [11] *Ibid.*

then, do they come? The only possible answer is that they come *from the mind itself*. Instead, therefore, of assuming that mind conforms to objects, we must change our ground and assume that objects—as we experience them—conform to mind; that the mind itself has, as it were, a structure which it imposes on the world around it in the very process of experiencing it. The mind, Kant argues, possesses certain *a priori* principles which it applies to the world in the act of experience; these principles are 'pure' in the sense that they are empty of content until they are so applied. In itself the mind has no knowledge, nor does it create knowledge; but it supplies the conditions without which nothing can be either experienced or known. It is as if the mind surveys the world through spectacles which give all experience a certain shape and colour; everything it sees conforms inevitably to that shape and colour, since nothing is experienceable which does not.

It has been said that Kant, despite the basic rationalism of his position, moves more than half way towards empiricism. He recognises frankly in the opening words of his *Critique of Pure Reason* that 'all our knowledge begins with experience', adding, however, that 'it by no means follows that all arises out of experience'.[12] The former proposition he readily grants, since prior to experience the mind's structure has no content; knowledge is occasioned by the mind's contact via sensation with the world around it and by its introspection of its own activity; to this extent Kant is an empiricist. But knowledge incorporates elements supplied by the mind itself, and without these it cannot even begin to be knowledge; knowledge *arises*, therefore, by adding to the data of sensation mind's peculiar contribution. Since the very possibility of knowledge, or indeed of the most rudimentary experience, depends on this contribution, Kant may be said to be fundamentally a rationalist. It follows, of course, that the human mind can never know things as they are in themselves; it can only know things as patterned by its own inherent structure—through its own spectacles. If things are x and the mind y, then knowledge is $x + y$; the mind can know y (its own *a priori* principles) and it can know $x + y$; but x is completely unknowable, since it is a condition of being known at all that y must be added. Things in themselves Kant referred to as 'noumena'; things as we know them he called 'phenomena';[13] more will be said later of the important distinction between them.

What is it that mind contributes to experience and knowledge? In answering this question Kant distinguishes between perception and

[12] *Ibid.*, p. 25.

[13] Literally 'things thought' (Greek *noein*; pres. pass. partic., *nooumenos*) and 'things that appear' (Greek *phainesthai*; pres. partic., *phainomenos*); but 'noumena' are thinkable only in the sense that we can conceive their existence and perhaps imagine their nature; they cannot be *known*.

thought, between the mind's involvement in sensory experience and its operation on the results of sensory experience to produce organised knowledge; both are necessary:

Without the sensuous faculty no object would be given to us, and without the understanding no object would be thought. Thoughts without content are void; intuitions [perceptions] without conceptions blind. . . . Neither of these faculties can exchange its proper function.[14]

To the former, that is to perception, the mind contributes the elements of space and time; in the world as we experience it objects are related according to their position in three-dimensional space; they are also related in time (this is equally true of 'inner' experience, our consciousness of feelings, thoughts, reasonings and other mental events which occur 'inside' our minds). Kant does not mean that our senses are first aware of unordered sensations which are then fitted into a framework of space and time; he means that sensory experience is simply not possible for human beings save within this framework and that any act of sense perception involves, *a priori* and inevitably, these two elements. They are necessary conditions of sensory experience, so that everything our senses present to us is already positioned in space and time; but the positioning is not in things themselves, as had previously been supposed, but only in things as perceived by the human mind.

It is the same with thought, though here the situation is more complicated. In shaping the data of sense perception[15] into organised knowledge the mind applies certain principles which exist, not in the data, but in itself; they are *a priori* conditions of knowledge without which nothing can be thought or conceptually known. Like space and time they are—to revert to the previous metaphor—spectacles which give things an appearance which is not their own but is imposed on them by the very nature and constitution of the mind. These principles Kant calls 'categories', borrowing the word from the traditional vocabulary of logic; there are twelve of them, divided into four groups of three under the headings of quantity, quality, relation and modality.[16] The categories are not, it must be emphasised, part of the nature of things in themselves; what things are

[14] *CPR*, pp. 62–3.
[15] They are not *mere* data, i.e. purely given raw material, for the mind has already ordered them in space and time.
[16] They are:

quantity: unity, plurality, totality;
quality: reality, negation, limitation;
relation: substance–accident, cause–effect, agent–patient;
modality: possibility–impossibility, existence–non-existence, necessity–contingency.

like in themselves the human mind can never know, for everything it knows is known and *must* be known within the *a priori* framework determined by itself. Thus, the law of cause and effect describes, not the relation of things to each other, but a means by which the mind brings order and system into knowledge. What Kant is saying—and it may seem very strange to those who are unfamiliar with the idea—is that the mind has a conceptual structure of its own which it imposes on experience and by so doing gives to experience a pattern and intelligibility which it would not otherwise have.

The nature of Kant's reply to Hume is now clear. Hume had argued that sense perception gives us only isolated facts in which there is no principle of order and connection; such order as we seem to see in them is the result simply of custom or habit operating through the association of ideas. If this is correct, then there is no basis in experience for knowledge— not, at least, as knowledge was traditionally conceived in terms of certainty —nor any rational justification for prediction. Yet, Kant maintained, we *do* have knowledge of this kind, and we *can* predict events prior to experiencing them; and if the justification for this is not in things, in the data of experience, then it must be in the mind. By contributing the framework of space and time to our perception of the external world and by imposing on sense experience the conceptual framework of the categories, the mind imposes knowability on experience; because experience and knowledge embody these contributions from the mind as conditions of their very existence and because without them there can be no experience, no knowledge at all, it follows not only that knowledge is possible but that it can be certain and necessary. For example, since we know that experience, to be experience, must embody the principle of cause and effect, we also know that the same principle applies to all possible experience and can be used, therefore, in advance of experience to predict that any effect must necessarily have a cause.

Knowledge in general, then, has been saved from Hume's sceptical conclusions; so in particular have mathematics and science:

Now space and time are the two intuitions on which pure mathematics grounds all its cognitions and judgements that present themselves as at once apodeictic and necessary. . . . Geometry is grounded on the pure intuition of space. Arithmetic forms its own concepts of numbers by successive addition of units in time; and pure mathematics especially can only form its concepts of motion by means of the representation of time.[17]

And since, as Kant has already shown, space and time are not the products simply of mental habit, but are part of the *a priori* structure of experience,

[17] *Prolegomena*, p. 39; apodeictic = demonstrative, carrying certain proof.

mathematics is neither an arbitrary construction of the human intellect nor a purely explicative exercise; it is genuinely objective in character, not explicative merely, but synthetic or augmentative. So too in science, where the law of cause and effect provides the essential basis for the continuity and coherence of nature; if causation is built into experience *a priori*, then it can be relied on as a principle of scientific explanation and prediction.

But what of metaphysics?—has this survived Hume's criticism? The answer is yes and no. Traditionally metaphysics had been concerned with describing 'reality'—not the 'reality' of the ordinary everyday world, but a suprasensible reality which, supposedly, transcended ordinary experience and was apprehensible only by reason; its aim had been to disclose the nature of things in themselves. This, Kant has shown to be impossible; things in themselves are unknowable for the simple reason that whatever is known inevitably incorporates, in its very being known, a mental contribution which makes it more than a thing in itself. A metaphysics, therefore, which claims to present an objective knowledge of a transcendent reality of things in themselves is excluded from Kant's philosophy; but metaphysics as a study of the *a priori* conditions of experience, as an enquiry into the conceptual structure of mind, is certainly possible, for this is precisely what Kant had undertaken in his *Critique*. However, Kant has more than this to say on metaphysics. He admits that the impulse to metaphysics of the suprasensible kind is innate in man—something which drives him to explore beyond the boundaries of sense experience. This impulse, though it cannot provide knowledge, is not without value: it supplies what Kant calls 'ideas of reason' whose function is 'regulative'. The principal 'ideas of reason' are: the soul, as a permanent thinking self; the world as the totality of all phenomena; and God, the supreme Being, the unity and ground of all that is. These 'ideas', though they are beyond experience and therefore beyond proof, guide and motivate the mind in its search for truth; they are, as it were, experimental hypotheses which, by an act of faith, are accepted *as if* they were true, in order that the human mind may be extended to the limits of its capacity.

In his preface to the first edition of the *Critique of Pure Reason* Kant writes: 'My chief aim in this work has been thoroughness; and I make bold to say that there is not a single metaphysical problem that does not find its solution, or at least the key to its solution, here.[18] This was too great a claim, as Kant himself recognised, for he goes on to anticipate the scornful rejoinders of his readers. Yet his achievement was nevertheless immense. Hume had 'atomised' experience, dividing it into discrete items without rational connection; they are linked only by the propensity of the human mind to associate what it has habitually observed to be conjoined. On this

[18] *CPR*, p. 3.

view natural laws are no more than psychological tendencies, the uniformity of nature merely an expectation that future events will repeat the pattern of the past, and knowledge a matter of sensation and mental habit. Moreover, there is no guarantee here of the *universality* of knowledge, that the patterns my mental dispositions read into experience are valid also for my fellows. Kant restored rationality to knowledge; he did so, not by combining rationalism and empiricism, as has sometimes been suggested, but by drawing on each to create a novel synthesis of his own. Neither experience alone nor reason alone was the source of knowledge; it was only from their union, the former supplying content to the structure inherent in the latter, that knowledge could arise. Because this structure was *a priori*, a *condition* of experiencing, and because it was a structure common to all human minds, knowledge thereby assumed a universality and an objectivity which Hume had apparently denied it.

There are, of course, weaknesses in Kant's account of knowledge. One is his list of categories, which were not devised specifically for his own purpose but were based on distinctions already existing in traditional logic between different kinds of judgment. Hence there is about them a certain air of contrivance, a formal neatness which was to prove too inflexible for the needs of a rapidly developing experimental science. Yet Kant's importance here lies not so much in the correctness of his list, as in the fact that he conceived at all of the possibility that the mind brings its own structure *to* experience rather than discovering a structure *within* experience.

Another difficulty is his division between phenomenal and noumenal worlds: this seems to leave us with an area of reality which, though its existence can be inferred or at least imagined, can never be *known*; it remains in a twilit background, an elusive support for the solid structure of phenomena. (Even more difficult is his distinction, referred to below, between the phenomenal and noumenal selves, the one bound by natural law, the other free.) Is this, one wonders, any better than Berkeley's resort to God in order to justify the continued existence of external objects when they are not perceived by human beings? But there is a more solid objection than this; for it can be held that Kant is inconsistent in assuming the existence of noumena: his argument depends on causal inference—noumena *must* exist as the causal basis of phenomena, whereas, on his own principles, causal inference is correctly applied only to the phenomenal world and cannot be used to argue from phenomena to anything beyond them. A possible answer to this is that the existence of noumena is not reached by causal inference but is the logical counterpart of the existence of phenomena, its necessary correlate without which it cannot be thought, like obverse and reverse of the same coin. Nevertheless, there remains an uneasy feeling that noumena are somehow superfluous; since they cannot be known or proved to exist, we may as well dispense with them and accept a straightforward phenomenalism (pp. 133–4).

The ethic of duty

A brief description of ethics was given in chapter 1, but so far there has been no illustration from the work of philosophers themselves. Yet all those who have appeared in earlier chapters wrote something on this subject; some, like Plato, Aristotle and Hume, made contributions of permanent importance to moral philosophy—the *Ethics* of Aristotle is a classic in this field, and so too, perhaps, is the second of Hume's *Enquiries* on *The Principles of Morals*. In this book we shall consider only two principal examples of ethical problems, taken from Kant and Mill; the number could easily be extended, but that would be to exceed our purpose, which is to illustrate the scope of philosophical thinking.

What makes a person or an action morally good? This is a question that has been asked a multitude of times in the history of philosophy; the answers have been various, sometimes conflicting; certainly, none has yet been given that is universally acceptable. Partly this is due to misunderstandings about the word 'good' and to differences in its interpretation; but there are others, and ethically more fundamental, reasons than these. One answer is that an action is morally good if it is prompted by the right motive; but what is a right motive?—is patriotism such, or social justice or self-defence? And even a 'right' motive can be used to justify almost any kind of action, however normally repellent, as for instance the most appalling atrocities have been defended in the name of patriotism or religion. Another answer is that an action is morally good if it makes the maximum contribution to human happiness or wellbeing—this is close to J. S. Mill's view, which will be considered in the next chapter; but this assumes that happiness is or should be the goal of human endeavour and, a further complication, that we know what happiness is; moreover it makes moral worth depend on consequences, and these in turn depend on circumstances which are not always within our control. Is an action less morally good if, with the best of motives but through unforeseeable circumstances, it fails in its purpose, than one which, with little or no or even wrongful intention, achieves accidentally what the other did not? Others, again, have argued that the test of moral goodness is the extent to which an action springs from habits deeply rooted in the agent's character as a result of long and careful self-discipline: the good man is one who has so habituated himself to goodness that he does the right thing readily and easily like an expert craftsman.

Kant's view is different from all of these; he expounds it principally in two books, the *Critique of Practical Reason* and *Groundwork of the Metaphysic of Morals*. The latter of these begins with the sentence: 'It is impossible to conceive anything at all in the world, or even out of it, which can be taken as good without qualification except a good will.'[19] The proper criterion of goodness, Kant continues, is not motive or consequences; it is not intelligence, courage, resolution or any other quality of character, innate or habituate; still less is it power, wealth, honour or other external success. It is simply the good will 'estimable in itself and good apart from any further end':[20]

Even if, by some special disfavour of destiny or by the niggardly endowment of stepmotherly nature, this will is entirely lacking in power to carry out its intentions; if by its utmost effort it still accomplishes nothing . . . even then it would still shine like a jewel for its own sake as something which has its full value in itself.[21]

But what is a 'good will'? It is one which acts for the sake of duty—not simply *in accordance with duty*, which would admit motives of prudence and self-interest, or might come about by chance or in ignorance, but simply for duty's sake.

Suppose that I give a customer the correct weight of goods because I have been trained to do so or for fear of prosecution or to establish a reputation for honest dealing and thereby increase my profits; my action is not, in these circumstances, morally good. Certainly it is in accordance with duty, and right and commendable, but because it is not done for duty's sake it lacks moral worth. Again, I may be a person of benevolent temperament who happens to like helping other people; if I see a person in distress, I do not stop to argue the pros and cons of helping him nor to ask if this is my duty; I help because that is what comes naturally to me and gives me pleasure. But however *right* my action may be, it is not, on Kant's view, morally good, because it is done from inclination not for duty's sake.

Now one can agree fairly readily with Kant that actions performed from motives of prudence or self-interest are, if not totally lacking in moral worth, at least somehow deficient in it; and one can admit that persons who *are* naturally inclined to benevolence have a (perhaps unfair) moral advantage over those who are not. Yet it seems unnecessarily harsh to deny moral goodness, say, to the person who, as a result of deliberate self-discipline and self-habituation, has so disposed himself to kindliness that helping others comes to him like second nature, without inner conflict or

[19] *Groundwork of the Metaphysic of Morals*, trans. and ed. H. J. Paton (Hutchinson, 1947), p. 61.
[20] *Ibid.*, p. 64.   [21] *Ibid.*, p. 62.

any idea of doing his duty. Indeed, some might well argue that such a person is morally more mature than one who, torn between duty and desire, succeeds only after a struggle in obeying the former. A further objection to this concept of acting solely for duty's sake is that a man may be mistaken in his understanding of what his duty is; as a result he may do something which is morally wrong and which, had he followed inclination, instinct or common sense, he might have avoided. Suppose, for instance, that for religious reasons he disagrees with blood transfusion and allows his child to die for lack of it; he would surely say that he was doing his duty as he saw it in the light of his religious commitments; yet most of us would deplore his decision as wrong and contrary to his duty as a father and a human being. How does one decide in such a case what duty requires and who is right, who wrong? By what criteria does one determine one's moral obligations and where the course of duty lies? These questions take us to the next stage in Kant's argument.

'Duty', he says, 'is the necessity to act out of reverence for the law.'[22] By 'law' he means, of course, not man-made law, but the moral law; and by 'reverence' he means the subordination of all other motives to that of devotion to the commands of the moral law itself. The good will, therefore, is one which accepts and obeys in all circumstances the unconditional authority of the moral law or, in Kant's language, of the 'categorical imperative'. The meaning of this unfamiliar and somewhat forbidding expression is less obscure than the words suggest. An imperative is a command, and within the sphere of morals Kant distinguishes two contrasting types: a 'hypothetical imperative' is one to which qualifications are attached—'Work hard, *if* you want to succeed', 'Be honest, *if* you want to be respected'; such imperatives are prudential, they enjoin means to an end, they are conditional. By contrast, a categorical imperative has no strings attached; it is a plain, unconditional command which says simply, 'Do this'—not to achieve some further end or purpose, but for its own sake. But what *does* the categorical imperative command us to do? Kant believed that the distinguishing feature of human beings is reason, rationality, and this applies just as much in morals as in any other area of life. Now an obvious characteristic of reason is its universality; it is the same for all men everywhere and in all circumstances. The basic requirement of all moral action, therefore, is that the principle of choice ('maxim' is Kant's word) which governs it must be universalisable into a general moral law for all men; only thus can the action be justified as consistent with reason. Hence his first formulation of the categorical imperative is this: 'Act only on that maxim through which you can at the same time will that it should become a universal law.'[23]

[22] *Ibid.*, p. 68.   [23] *Ibid.*, p. 88.

The most persuasive of Kant's four practical illustrations is based on the requirement of honest dealing as a necessary presupposition of social life. A man who is in financial difficulties borrows money knowing that he will not be able to pay it back; in so doing he acts on the principle of personal advantage; universalise it and you see at once that it is self-contradictory and therefore inconsistent with reason:

> The universality of a law that everyone believing himself to be in need may make any promise he pleases with the intention not to keep it would make promising, and the very purpose of promising, itself impossible, since no one would believe he was being promised anything, but would laugh at utterances of this kind as empty shams.[24]

Trustworthy communication between persons, which is essential for the preservation of society and the enabling of civilised life within it, would become impossible, and the very concept of promising would be destroyed.

Kant offers several other formulations of the categorical imperative, each of which embodies in one way or another the element of universality while drawing attention at the same time to a particular aspect of moral choice: 'Act in such a way that you always treat humanity, whether in your own person or in the person of any other, never simply as a means, but always at the same time as an end.'[25] In other words, though it is often necessary to regard human beings as means to an end, for instance in war or economic production, yet the categorical imperative insists that, as rational creatures, they are of intrinsic value and therefore also ends in themselves.

A third formulation, though it resembles the first, draws attention to the human will as not merely obeying but by its decisions positively contributing to the moral law: 'So act that your will can regard itself at the same time as making universal law through its maxim.'[26] A fourth points to the importance of the autonomy of the will as central to a rational morality: 'Never to choose except in such a way that in the same volition the maxims of your choice are also present as universal law.'[27] Finally, he gives us the noble conception of an ideal 'kingdom of ends', such as would

[24] *Ibid.*, p. 90.

[25] *Ibid.*, p. 96.

[26] As quoted this is Paton's statement of the formula on p. 34 of his summary; the translation reads thus on pp. 98–9: 'From this there now follows our third practical principle for the will . . . namely, the Idea *of the will of every rational being as a will which makes universal law. . . .* The will is therefore not merely subject to the law, but is so subject that it must be considered as also *making the law* for itself and precisely on this account as first of all subject to the law.'

[27] *Ibid.*, p. 108.

exist if the maxims prescribed by the categorical imperative were universally obeyed: 'So act as if you were through your maxims a law-making
member of a kingdom of ends.'[28] Moral choice is not an individual matter
but an activity shared with other persons all of whom, equally with oneself,
are ends in themselves and contribute by their decisions to the moral law.

Just as the law of causation is a synthetic *a priori* principle in the sphere
of science, so too is the categorical imperative in that of morals. It is not
dependent on or inferred from moral experience, but prior to it; it derives
from the nature of reason itself in its practical activity and is embodied in
all moral experience whether or not we recognise its presence or obey it.
Kant's argument is too involved to reproduce in any detail, but it depends
essentially on the idea of freedom. Moral decision implies the freedom of
the will to choose; apart from this, morality is meaningless. But how is
freedom possible in a world governed by natural law where every effect
has its determining cause? It is possible, Kant argues, because man is a
creature of two worlds: as an organism he belongs to the natural or
'phenomenal' world and obeys its laws; but he is a member also of the
'noumenal' or intelligible world and as such is subject to the laws of
reason which require the freedom of the will in choosing; a free will is a
will directed by reason, and because, in Kant's view, rational decision is
also moral decision, such a will is a moral agent and subject *a priori* to the
demands of reason in the categorical imperative.

Kant goes on to argue the immortality of the soul and the existence of
God, basing his argument, not on theoretical grounds as previous philosophers had done, but on the demands of practical reason. It is impossible
to follow him into this, but one further important point should be noted:
Kant believed that he could prove by an examination of practical reason in
the sphere of morals what could not be proved by mathematics, science or
metaphysics. In other words, if there can be any insight at all for human
beings into a suprasensible reality, it comes through involvement in moral
choice in the space–time world of ordinary life; this involvement requires
as a practical necessity, a belief in freedom, immortality and God which
cannot be logically proved. Knowledge must therefore make way for faith
or, in Kant's own words: 'I must abolish *knowledge* to make room for
faith.'[29] Moral experience, with its requirement of believing where we
cannot prove, is thus a source of truth more potent and more profound
than the subtleties of intellectual discussion. This is a view with which
many later thinkers have found themselves in sympathy.

[28] Again, this is Paton's statement of the formula in his summary, p. 35;
see the text, pp. 100–3.
[29] *CPR*, p. 18 (where the translation is 'belief', not 'faith'; the German is
Glauben).

There is undoubtedly a certain attractiveness in Kant's ethic of duty; the dogged resolution of a man who sticks through thick and thin to a professed ideal of conduct—not for gain or advantage, but because he deems it his duty—appeals strongly to one side of our moral nature; we admire him for his loyalty to that 'stern Daughter of the Voice of God' that Wordsworth writes of in his *Ode to Duty*. At the same time one feels that Kant over-simplifies the issues: inclination, motive, common sense, habit, circumstances—these too are factors involved in moral choice, and to reject them out of hand as irrelevant to the judgment of moral worth seems unduly restrictive, if not perverse. Again, although universalisability is often a valuable criterion of ethical principles, it is not as conclusive as Kant supposed. 'Do unto others . . .' is a long-honoured and widely accepted test of obligation, and it is not only to be found in the Gospel of Jesus; but moral principles can in fact be universalised in such a way as to permit self-regarding action which excludes the advantage of others.[30] Moreover, the test of rational consistency—which is what universality amounts to—is applicable only to principles already existing or proposed; it does not tell us where to find our principles in the first place; at its best it is a sieve, not a source, of moral values. Finally, though Kant is absolutely right in insisting on the autonomy of the will in choosing, his distinction between the phenomenal and noumenal selves is far from convincing; a solution to the problem of freedom is not brought nearer by this dichotomy of human personality. It can be objected too that by attributing to man in his moral capacity an insight into noumena, things in themselves, Kant is dismissing metaphysics by one door to let it in at another, abandoning a metaphysics of knowledge for a metaphysics of faith (as he more or less admits in the sentence quoted above). He may well be right in making his ultimate stand on faith derived from moral experience, but one wonders how far this stand is the logically defensible position he claims, and how far an expression of his own profoundly religious mind.

[30] For instance: Do what you can to help others so long as you do not damage your own interests. There is no logical inconsistency involved in universalising this maxim; nor, as in Kant's example of promise-breaking, is any concept rendered meaningless or unreliable; but a society which rigidly adhered to this principle might not be very pleasant to live in!

Further study

Kant

General books on Kant include s. körner, *Kant* (Penguin, 1955); a. d. lindsay, *Kant* (Benn, 1934); and j. kemp, *The Philosophy of*

Kant (Oxford University Press, 1968); of these the first is perhaps the best to start with.

Kant is not easy to read even in the best of translations, and it will take the student all the time he can spare to master the texts which support the present chapter. However, his little book on education is well worth reading; there is a translation by Annette Churton in the Ann Arbor Paperbacks, University of Michigan Press.

Knowledge

Among the best editions of the *Critique of Pure Reason* is that of N. KEMP SMITH (Macmillan, rev. edn, 1933; abbreviated edn, 1934); with this there is his commentary (Macmillan, 2nd edn, 1923). Another good edition is J. M. D. MEIKLEJOHN's (Dent's Everyman's Library) with an introduction by A. D. Lindsay. Rather than start with the *Critique* itself it may be helpful to read first KANT's *Prolegomena to any Future Metaphysics*, trans. and ed. P. G. LUCAS (Manchester University Press, 1953); this was intended by Kant as a guide to the first edition of the *Critique* and to the changes in the second.

There are many books on Kant's theory of knowledge and experience, some of them very difficult; among the more manageable are: A. C. EWING, *A Short Commentary on Kant's Critique of Pure Reason* (2nd edn, Methuen, 1950); T. D. WELDON, *Introduction to Kant's Critique* (Oxford, Clarendon Press, 1st and shorter edn, 1945; 2nd edn, 1958). More advanced are: G. BIRD, *Kant's Theory of Knowledge* (Routledge, 1962); P. F. STRAWSON, *The Bounds of Sense* (Methuen, 1966); and R. P. WOLFF, *Kant's Theory of Mental Activity* (Harvard University Press, 1963). A. C. EWING, *Kant's Treatment of Causality* (Kegan Paul, 1924) is helpful; so are parts of Walsh's *Reason and Experience* mentioned above.

Ethics

Of Kant's ethical writings the *Groundwork of the Metaphysic of Morals*, ed. H. J. PATON (Hutchinson, 1947) is a better startingpoint than the *Critique of Practical Reason*; the former Paton calls 'one of the small books which are truly great', and he also has a commentary on it, *The Categorical Imperative* (Hutchinson, 1947). There is a brief and helpful commentary by W. D. ROSS, *Kant's Ethical Theory* (Oxford, Clarendon Press, 1954). For more general accounts of Kant's ethical theories there are: H. B. ACTON, *Kant's Moral Philosophy* (Macmillan, 1970) and J. G. MURPHY, *Kant: The Philosophy of Right* (Macmillan, 1970); and there are valuable chapters in A. E. TEALE, *Kantian Ethics* (Oxford University Press, 1951) and J. KEMP, *Reason, Action and Morality* (Routledge, 1964).

Of general books on ethics and problems of morality there is almost no end; an obvious extension of reading is into philosophers other than Kant and Mill who have contributed importantly to ethical thought, for instance,

Plato, Aristotle and Hume. The following are helpful introductions to ethics: A. C. EWING, *Ethics* (English Universities Press, 1953); W. K. FRANKENA, *Ethics* (Prentice-Hall, 1963); W. D. HUDSON, *Modern Moral Philosophy* (Macmillan, 1970); A. MONTEFIORE, *A Modern Introduction to Moral Philosophy* (Routledge, 1958); A. MACINTYRE, *A Short History of Ethics* (Routledge, 1967); and M. WARNOCK, *Ethics since 1900* (Oxford University Press, 1960). The Macmillan 'New Studies in Ethics' series already has introductions to many of the departments of ethical theory, including G. J. WARNOCK, *Contemporary Moral Philosophy* (1967).

Other useful books (among a great many) are: A. C. EWING, *The Definition of Good* (Routledge, 1947); J. FLETCHER, *Situation Ethics* (S.C.M., 1966), a limited but very interesting ethical position; A. C. GRAHAM, *The Problem of Value* (Hutchinson, 1961); W. D. ROSS, *The Right and the Good* (Oxford, Clarendon Press, 1930); and S. TOULMIN, *Reason in Ethics* (Cambridge University Press, 1950).

There are two interesting collections of articles in P. FOOT, *Theories of Ethics* (1967) and J. FEINBERG, *Moral Concepts* (1969), in the Oxford University Press 'Readings in Philosophy' series.

10   J. S. Mill

(a) The problem of induction
(b) The criterion of moral choice

Biographical note

John Stuart Mill's interest in philosophy was closely linked to practical motives; in this he is, like Berkeley, a partial exception to the description of philosophy as disinterested. His father, James Mill, was eminent in his time as a historian, philosopher and political reformer; he belonged to a group of men known as philosophical radicals, which was led by Jeremy Bentham and aimed at reforming the law, parliament, education, morality and the economic life of the nation according to the principles of utilitarianism. The education of John Stuart, his first child, born in 1806, was designed to imbue him with these principles and to inspire in him the same passion for reform; the account of it in John's Autobiography *is a classic of educational literature. Until the age of fourteen his only teachers were his father and himself; between the years of three and twelve he was put through a course of Greek and Latin reading wider and more exacting than is now expected of any schoolboy by the age of eighteen—or indeed of most undergraduates; in addition he learnt mathematics as far as the differential calculus and for his own interest read widely in history and science. 'Of children's books, any more than of playthings, I had scarcely any', though he admits to* Arabian Nights, Robinson Crusoe, Don Quixote *and a few others;*[1] *of poetry he read almost nothing save Pope's translation of the* Iliad, *which so delighted him that he read it twenty or thirty times. Religious teaching was rigorously excluded; James Mill was licensed as a preacher at the age of twenty-five but later abandoned Christianity and wished his son to have none of it.*

At twelve began a thorough drilling in logic which proved, he says, of lasting benefit; at the same time he extended further his reading of classical authors and helped his father correct the proofs of his History of India; *in the following year he was taken through 'a complete course of political*

---

[1] *Autobiography*, ed. H. J. Laski (Oxford University Press, 1924, repr. 1928 etc.), pp. 7–8. (Further page references are to this edition.)

*economy'.*² *At fourteen he went abroad for a year; thenceforth his father ceased to be directly his schoolmaster, though he remained in control of his education, and when John returned he was set to read a number of books which expounded the fundamentals of philosophical radicalism. By modern standards his education must appear seriously misguided; however, it is worth recording that Mill himself, looking back on it, was not altogether dissatisfied:*

*If I have accomplished anything, I owe it, among other fortunate circumstances, to the fact that through the early training bestowed on me by my father I started, I may fairly say, with an advantage of a quarter of a century over my contemporaries.*³

*Against this must be set the pathetic remark: 'I never was a boy; never played at cricket; it is better to let Nature have her way.'*⁴

In one respect, certainly, his education was successful; it gave him, as his father wished, an ardent zeal for political and social reform. At the age of seventeen, after a brief training in law, he was appointed a clerk to the East India Company and remained in its employment until it ceased to exist in 1858. He now indulged with all the energy of youth in propagating the principles he had been trained to embrace. In 1823 he founded the Utilitarian Society which met fortnightly for about three years at Bentham's house; between 1825 and 1830 he met regularly with a dozen other young men to read and discuss James Mill's Elements of Political Economy *and kindred books; during the same period he became a regular speaker at the London Debating Society which included a wide range of liberal thinkers in addition to the followers of Bentham. At the same time he was writing articles for* The Westminster Review, *founded by Bentham for the dissemination of his views. Among Mill's more audacious activities at this time was the distribution of pamphlets advocating birth control in order to limit population; for this, it seems, he was arrested and imprisoned, but the incident is not recorded in his* Autobiography.

In 1826 Mill suffered a severe nervous crisis which reduced him to a state of mental dejection; no doubt it sprang in part from the strains imposed by an education which overdeveloped his intellectual powers at the price of emotional atrophy. Release from his depression came especially from the poems of Wordsworth, whose love of mountains found a responsive echo in his own experience. However,

What made Wordsworth's poems a medicine for my state of mind was that they expressed, not mere outward beauty, but states of feeling and of

---

² *Autobiography*, ed. H. J. Laski, p. 23.
³ *Ibid*., p. 26.
⁴ Quoted in K. Britton, *John Stuart Mill* (Penguin, 1953), p. 13.

thought coloured by feeling under the excitement of beauty. They seemed to be the very culture of the feelings which I was in quest of.[5]

The crisis left Mill still committed to philosophical radicalism and its policy of reform, but his opinions were modified in two important respects. First, though he never abandoned Bentham's utilitarian principle that happiness is the end of life, he now saw that it must be sought indirectly in the pursuit of other worthwhile goals. Second, he realised that intellectual training is not enough; 'the internal culture of the individual' is also among the prime necessities of human wellbeing, and henceforth 'the cultivation of the feelings became one of the cardinal points in my ethical and philosophical creed'.[6]

The rest of Mill's life can be told more briefly. To the end, despite increasing responsibility at India House, he remained closely associated with the work of reform; among the causes which especially attracted his attention were the status of women and their admission to the suffrage, the enfranchisement of the working class and the reform of land tenure. For three years he was Member of Parliament for Westminster. Though never a socialist—he had a dread of state monopoly and a profound faith in competition—the tendency of his thought was towards greater public control in the interests of social wellbeing. In much of his work he was assisted by Harriet Taylor, the wife of a London merchant; their long and apparently innocent friendship came eventually to marriage in 1851 after the death of her husband. But their happiness was shortlived, for Harriet died only seven years later; during that time they wrote together the essay On Liberty, now perhaps the most widely known of all Mill's works; she also, he tells us, helped to keep him a radical and a democrat. During the middle years of his life Mill was much occupied with writing: the most important of his works, A System of Logic (1843), took the bulk of his spare time from 1830 to 1840; another major work, The Principles of Political Economy, appeared in 1848; On Liberty was published in 1859 and Considerations on Representative Government in 1861. The essay Utilitarianism (1863) expounds his ethical philosophy; and there were published posthumously Three Essays on Religion, which includes his mature reflections on this subject, and his Autobiography. In 1868 Mill retired to Avignon, where he had long had a cottage and where Harriet had died ten years earlier; here he lived with his stepdaughter, Helen Taylor, until his own death in 1873.

---

[5] *Autobiography*, p. 125.
[6] *Ibid.*, pp. 121, 122.

The problem of induction

Reference has already been made to a distinction between deductive and inductive inference: in very broad terms it can be said that the former proceeds from general premises to particular conclusions, the latter from particular facts to general conclusions. Until the seventeenth century the attention of philosophers had been concentrated on deduction; one reason for this was the authority of Aristotle, whose logical investigations were confined almost wholly to deductive and syllogistic reasoning; another was the prevalent presupposition about knowledge that identified it with certainty—and deduction does, of course, give certainty in its conclusions, though it is a certainty which (as we have seen) may be of little epistemological value. Inductive interference was not unknown even to Aristotle, who both practised it in his biological enquiries and theorised about its nature; moreover, recognised or not, induction is a commonplace of everyday practical reasoning, indispensable to mere survival as well as to life at more civilised levels. But it was close on two thousand years before philosophers resumed the exploration of inductive processes, which, tentatively begun by Aristotle, was submerged under the rationalist assumptions and logical preoccupations of later centuries.

The impulse to do so was an offshoot of the movement from rationalism to empiricism, from interest in ideas to interest in facts, which can be traced back to Roger Bacon and William of Ockham in the thirteenth and fourteenth centuries; these men not only emphasised the importance of experience and observation in the discovery of truth, but also attempted to formulate rules for inductive inference and to outline a scientific method. Ockham's 'razor', *entia non sunt multiplicanda praeter necessitatem* (p. 20), is now a well-established procedural rule; and in his tests for determining the cause of an event he strikingly anticipates both Hume and J. S. Mill. Francis Bacon also saw the need for inductive principles: the traditional syllogistic logic was 'not nearly subtle enough to deal with nature';[7] a new approach was needed based on close and careful observation, methodical appraisal of its results, and generalisations firmly based on induction, which, he says, 'is the true way, but as yet untried'.[8] He formulated rules for observation and experiment, for the accumulation and classification of data, for the elimination of incorrect hypotheses, and (as did Ockham) for determining causation. Though his account of induction was incomplete, and though he claimed more for it than it could perform, he nevertheless pointed to the urgent need for a theory of inductive

[7] *Magna Instauratio*, Preface; ed. M. T. McClure, in *Bacon: Selections* (London, Scribner's, 1928), p. 12.
[8] *Aphorisms*, I, 19; ed. McClure, p. 283.

inference which would be adequate to support the rapidly developing science of his time.

However, as further consideration was given to induction and to the methods of science, there came to be recognised a philosophical problem whose difficulty was first made conspicuous by the work of Hume. Very briefly the problem is this: how, if at all, can one justify logically the conclusions of inductive inference? And if one cannot, is not induction, and science with it, thereby invalidated as being indefensible by reason? By contrast let us look for a moment at the conclusions of deductive inference: these, if valid, are justifiable by logical rules—we know that, granted the premises, the conclusions must necessarily follow. That Socrates is mortal follows inevitably, *and can be shown to do so*, from the premises that all men are mortal and that Socrates is a man. This is equally true of other forms of deduction: that the sum of the internal angles of a triangle is 180° follows necessarily from the axioms of Euclidean geometry, *and can be shown to do so*. Deductive reasoning is demonstrative; it is capable of proof. This is not the case with induction, as can be shown from the following examples.

I find by observation that song-thrushes regularly lay eggs of a certain colour and markings—sky-blue with black spots; over a number of years and in different areas I find no variation from this; I conclude, therefore, that all song-thrushes, wherever their nests, lay eggs of this kind. Furthermore, I can use this generalisation predictively: whenever in the future I find song-thrushes nesting I shall expect their eggs to have the same colour and markings; and if ever I find a nest containing eggs of this kind, I shall assume, whether or not I have seen the birds, that they were laid by song-thrushes. Second, I find that in late spring and early summer I regularly suffer from nasal congestion and fits of sneezing; the attacks are especially frequent if I go out into the country and walk in the fields; I conclude, therefore, that there is some connection between hay-fever and the countryside. After further detailed observation I am able to pin this down to the inhaling of pollen and, more specifically, of pollen from a particular grass; hence my final generalisation that the pollen from, say, timothy grass 'causes' my hay-fever, from which I can predict that whenever in future I inhale pollen from it, I shall suffer from hay-fever (and this, of course, enables me to take appropriate avoiding action). Thus, the core of induction is generalisation based on observation of a number of (but not all the possible) particular items or events of a certain kind, and leading to the conclusion that *all* items or events of this kind have or will have the same characteristics.[9]

[9] It may be helpful at this point (but see also pp. 182–3) to distinguish between two kinds of induction—induction by complete enumeration and

Now there is clearly a logical gap in such inference. From the observation of *some* instances I cannot validly infer a conclusion which applies to *all*; nor can I validly infer from what I *have* observed to what I have *not* observed, nor from what *has* happened to what *will* happen. At least, I can do so only if one or the other of two logical premises is supplied: these are (*a*) that there is an intrinsic connection between items and between events in the natural world, such that song-thrushes *must* lay sky-blue eggs with black spots and grass pollen *must* cause the allergic condition known as hay-fever; or (*b*) that there is in nature a uniformity of operation which ensures that what happens in the future will resemble what has happened in the past. But both of these are thrown into doubt by David Hume, who argued that no such intrinsic connection is ever observed, and that mere repetition of an event in the past offers no logical (but only a psychological) justification for believing that it always will be repeated.

It seems, then, that there is something illogical, even irrational, in inductive inference; its conclusions appear to have no logical justification, but to be a kind of leap in the dark, hunches whose validity depends simply on the pragmatic test of whether or not they are successful. Nor is this the end of the matter, for there follow some disturbing epistemological considerations. Deductive inference can be valid without being true to fact; to be factually true its conclusions must derive from general premises which are themselves true to fact; but if general empirical premises of this kind can never be shown to be necessarily true, as appears to be the case, then deduction, too, is infected by the same weakness. Since it can do no more than explicate its own premises, if these are suspect, so too are the conclusions deduced from them. Lacking secure factual premises its efficacy is confined to a purely analytical explication of ideas without reference to fact. Furthermore, it is from inductive generalisations that the 'laws' of science are ultimately derived: repeated observation of falling objects suggests the need for an explanatory hypothesis; this is used predictively to show what *will* happen *if* the hypothesis is correct; the predic-

induction by simple enumeration. In the former *all* the possible examples of an item or event are observed; for instance, if there are six children in one family and all are observed to be blond, one can conclude that all the children in that family are blond and that if ever one meets one of them in the street, he or she will be blond; the conclusions here are necessary and certain because observation has covered all the possible instances. However, it is doubtful whether such inference is properly called inductive —at least as the word is normally understood; it is much closer to deduction and for our present purpose it can be ignored. The kind of induction which gives rise to the problem under discussion is the second—by simple enumeration—and is illustrated in the two examples where only a limited number of instances has been or can possibly be observed.

tions are verified experimentally, the hypothesis confirmed and the 'law' of gravity established. But if inductive generalisations lack logical justification, is not the whole fabric of science together with its picture of the world thereby rendered specious? What confidence can one have in methods and conclusions which are pervaded by a basic irrationality?

It is now time to turn to Mill. The full title of the book in which, among much else, he seeks to justify inductive inference is *A System of Logic —Ratiocinative and Inductive*; by 'ratiocinative' he means 'deductive'. In the preface he explains that the book 'makes no pretence of giving to the world a new theory of the intellectual operations'; rather it is an attempt 'to cement together the detached fragments of a subject never yet treated as a whole'. Mill's latter claim is substantially correct; he was indeed the first to bring together deductive and inductive inference into a single body of logic; it was his 'great achievement', so it has been written of him, 'to have found logic deductive and to have left it both inductive and deductive'.[10] Moreover, he established a pattern of logical studies— language, deduction, induction, methodology—which has been adopted in the majority of textbooks since his time; though his own book is not without errors, it is still of more than historical interest to the student of philosophy, and Book VI remains a useful introduction to the study of the social sciences.

As a philosopher Mill was not entirely disinterested; at heart he was a reformer, and he believed it necessary to support the practical work of reform by supplying it with a firm theoretical basis; at the same time he must attack the intellectual presuppositions of its opponents. Of these presuppositions the chief was the epistemological doctrine of 'intuitionism', namely, that there are truths which can be known *a priori* by direct intellectual apprehension; such truths, it was held, are synthetic, necessary and independent of experience. This is the rationalist position of Plato and Descartes; its contemporary exponent was William Whewell, whose *History of the Inductive Sciences* was published while Mill was writing his *Logic*. Intuitionism, Mill wrote in his *Autobiography*, was 'the great intellectual support of false doctrines and bad institutions'[11] and therefore a major obstacle to reform; it used the traditional deductive logic to argue from general *a priori* premises to particular conclusions about moral and social issues.

Mill on the other hand was an empiricist—though he did not use this word to describe his position:[12] knowledge comes only from experience

[10] Britton, p. 147.
[11] *Autobiography*, p. 191.
[12] For Mill, 'empiricism' signified a purely observational and experimental science without analysis or explanation.

and is established by inductive generalisation from the observation of particular facts. His aim in the *Logic* was to demonstrate the efficacy of inductive reasoning, its ability to supply proof as cogent as that of deduction, and to provide it with a system of rules similar to that long established for the traditional logic; in so doing he would also show that there is 'a larger logic which embraces all the general conditions of the ascertainment of truth', of which formal, i.e. deductive, logic, 'the smaller logic which only concerns itself with the conditions of consistency', is but a part.[13] His further purpose was to construct a scientific basis for the work of reform, to show that a science of human nature, of society, morals and politics was in fact possible, and that in these spheres, as Newton had already proved for the physical world, there could be discovered the operation of laws established by induction from experience.

Book I of the *Logic* is concerned with names and propositions, classification and definition; this is a necessary introduction, since an understanding of language is essential to clarity of thought. In the next Book he examines deductive reasoning and exposes what he believes to be its inadequacies. His attack centres on the syllogism which had been accepted since the time of Aristotle as the type or paradigm of deductive inference. Mill does not deny the value of syllogistic reasoning, nor is he an unsparing critic of the traditional deductive logic; his charge is that they do not of themselves give us truth, because they are not 'real' inference. The syllogism, he argues, is circular; it involves a *petitio principii*; it begs the question. Take, for instance, the familiar syllogistic pattern:

> All men are mortal;
> Socrates is a man;
> ∴ Socrates is mortal.

We cannot validly state that all men are mortal unless we have considered every particular human being and assured ourselves of his mortality; since this must include Socrates, we know in advance that Socrates is mortal; the conclusion therefore tells us nothing that was not already known: 'No reasoning from generals to particulars can, as such, prove anything, since from a general principle we cannot infer any particulars but those which the principle itself assumes as known.'[14]

All inference, Mill proceeds, is 'from particulars to particulars'. In order to reach the generalisation which constitutes the major premise of

---

[13] *An Examination of Sir William Hamilton's Philosophy* (London, 1867), p. 461; quoted in *J. S. Mill's Philosophy of Scientific Method*, ed. E. Nagel (New York, Hafner, 1950), pp. xxxi–ii. (Further page references to *A System of Logic* are to this edition.)

[14] *A System of Logic*, II, iii, 2; p. 121.

the syllogism, we examine a great number of particular cases; as a result of this examination we infer (inductively) a general principle, e.g., All men are mortal. 'Thus a general truth is but an aggregate of particular truths, a comprehensive expression by which an indefinite number of individual facts are affirmed or denied at once.' Once established it can be used predictively to include particular cases not previously examined or not yet known even to exist. 'The results of many observations and inferences, and instructions for making innumerable inferences in un-foreseen cases, are compressed into one short sentence.'[15] Hence the move-ment of inference involved in the syllogism is *from* the particular cases initially examined in order to form the generalisation, *through* the premise which states this generalisation, *to* the further particular cases which it enables us to infer:

All inference is from particulars to particulars; general propositions are merely registers of such inferences already made and short formulae for making more; the major premise of a syllogism, consequently, is a formula of this description, and the conclusion is not an inference drawn *from* the formula, but an inference drawn *according* to the formula, the real logical antecedent or premise being the particular facts from which the general proposition was collected by induction. Those facts and the individual instances which supplied them may have been forgotten; but a record remains, not indeed descriptive of the facts themselves, but showing how those cases may be distinguished respecting which the facts, when known, were considered to warrant a given inference. According to the indications of this record we draw our conclusion, which is, to all intents and pur-poses, a conclusion from the forgotten facts. For this it is essential that we should read the record correctly, and the rules of the syllogism are a set of precautions to ensure our doing so.[16]

Strictly speaking, 'the inference is finished when we have asserted that all men are mortal. What remains to be performed afterwards is merely deciphering our own notes.'[17] However, it is permissible to regard the deciphering as a form of inference and to distinguish it from the initial inductive ('real') inference by regarding it as only 'apparent'.

What now of Mill's contention that the syllogism involves a *petitio principii*? It may be objected that the induction which leads to the generalisation need not be, and usually is not, based on a *complete* enumeration of all the particular instances and that the conclusion of the syllogism cannot therefore be *known* to be true in advance. However, even where there is no complete enumeration, it is nevertheless assumed in the generalisation that if every case *were* examined the result would be the

[15] *Ibid.*, II, iii, 3; p. 124.
[16] *Ibid.*, II, iii, 4; p. 127.
[17] *Ibid.*, II, iii, 3; p. 124.

same; to that extent the conclusion is included in the general premise and tells us nothing new. It follows, if Mill is right, that the syllogism does not discover but merely mediates truth; it presupposes the discovery of truth by induction; it belongs to the 'logic of consistency', not to the 'logic of the ascertainment of truth'. Its value lies in its acting as a means to and a test of the application of truth to new instances. How far, in fact, he was right it would be beyond our purpose to consider; it is clear, however, that he exaggerates the role of the syllogism in deductive reasoning and of one form of syllogism to the neglect of others; that he pays too little attention to the place in inference of the minor premise ('Socrates is a man'); and that he is on doubtful ground in suggesting that the syllogism is not strictly inference. Nevertheless, he raised for the first time in the history of logic certain fundamental issues, some of which, for instance the nature of general factual propositions, are still undecided.

Mill's conclusion, then, is that deductive inference is only 'apparent'; the genuine inferential content of deduction is supplied by prior inductive reasoning. It follows that 'the main question of the science of logic' is to show 'what induction is and what conditions render it legitimate'. He defines it as 'the operation of discovering and proving general propositions',[18] and its central problem is how to justify the transition in inference from the particular instances observed to these general propositions which apply universally to all objects of the same class: 'Whoever can answer this question knows more of the philosophy of logic than the wisest of the ancients and has solved the problem of induction.'[19]

Mill's first task is to examine and reject what he believes to be erroneous accounts of induction. It is not the mere 'colligation of facts', as Whewell had maintained; this, Mill says, is no more than a 'descriptive operation which enables a number of details to be summed up in a single proposition'.[20] Nor does he allow what was known as 'perfect induction' or 'induction by complete enumeration'; that is to say, when it is possible to examine every member of a group (e.g. the people in a room) and to state that they are all of the same class (e.g. males, Englishmen). This, he argues, is not 'an inference from facts known to facts unknown', which is essential to his own conception of induction, 'but a mere shorthand registration of facts known'; the truly general proposition contains a reference to cases not actually experienced, whereas a statement based on complete enumeration is no more than concise expression of what is already known to us: it is an 'abridged notation', 'a verbal transformation'.[21]

[18] *A System of Logic*, III, i, 1, 2; p. 171.
[19] *Ibid.*, III, iii, 2; p. 186.
[20] *Ibid.*, III, ii, 3; p. 177.
[21] *Ibid.*, III, ii, 1; pp. 173-4.

Conventionally, 'perfect induction' was distinguished from 'imperfect induction' or 'induction by simple enumeration'; in the latter it is impossible to examine all the instances of a class, and the generalisation is inferred from a limited range; thus, every particular bird that I have ever seen has two legs, and from this I infer that all birds everywhere, now and in the future, are likewise two-legged. (The danger of this kind of inference is obvious: I might conclude from my observation that all birds fly, and this, of course, would be untrue.) Mill accepts 'imperfect induction' by simple enumeration as the basis of inductive reasoning; as it stands, however, it is a crude and fallible process which requires strengthening and refining in order to make it scientific. He seeks to do this in two ways, by assuming the principle of the uniformity of nature and by applying appropriate tests.

Now there are many kinds of inductive generalisation from experience; Mill recognises two main classes, 'causal laws' and 'empirical laws'. The former state uniformities in the sequence of events, such that whenever an event or set of conditions, A, occurs, then B invariably follows; thus, whenever heat is applied to an iron rod, the rod expands, and this can be expressed by saying that heat causes expansion.[22] The latter include statements of uniformity like 'All crows are black', which is clearly not causal. For the sake of simplicity only causal laws will be considered here. How, then, are they established? How is the induction which leads to them validated? Inductive proof, Mill declares, is impossible without assuming the uniformity of nature:

> There is a principle implied in the very statement of what induction is; an assumption with regard to the course of nature and the order of the universe, namely, that there are such things in nature as parallel cases; that what happens once will, under a sufficient degree of similarity of circumstances, happen again, and not only again, but as often as the same circumstances recur. . . . Whatever be the proper mode of expressing it, the proposition that the course of nature is uniform is the fundamental principle or general axiom of induction.[23]

The proof of causal laws assumes this uniformity in a particular form, namely, 'the law of universal causation' which asserts that 'invariability of succession' is found to obtain 'between every fact in nature and some other fact which has preceded it'; more simply, every event has a cause.[24] Mill cannot, of course, suggest that this is an *a priori* principle, given

---

[22] Mill defines cause as 'the antecedent or the concurrence of antecedents on which [a phenomenon] is invariably and *unconditionally* consequent'. Cf. Hume, pp. 149–50 above.
[23] *A System of Logic*, III, iii, 1; p. 182.
[24] *Ibid.*, III, v, 2; p. 195.

intuitively, like Kant's categories, which the mind brings to experience; it is part of his purpose to deny this. The law of universal causation is itself the result of induction: we infer from repeated observation that lightning is invariably followed by thunder, the application of heat to a metal by expansion, the eating of poison by illness, and so on; these and a vast number of other causal generalisations impress on us the conviction that *every* event has some cause; and since no exception has ever been found, it is safe to assume that the principle is universally valid.

Before showing how Mill uses the principle to validate induction, it is necessary to consider the tests which he applies to the separate causal laws.[25] He names four of these and later adds a fifth; they are the Method of Agreement, of Difference, of Residues, of Concomitant Variation, and the Joint Method of Agreement and Difference; we shall examine only the first, second and fourth. The Method of Agreement is stated thus:

If two or more instances of the phenomenon under investigation have only one circumstance in common, the circumstance in which alone all the instances agree is the cause (or effect) of the given phenomenon.[26]

Hence, if X_1 is preceded by ABC, X_2 is preceded by ADE, X_3 is preceded by AFG, it may be inferred that A is the cause of X. The Method of Difference states that:

If an instance in which the phenomenon under investigation occurs and an instance in which it does not occur have every circumstance in common save one, that one occurring only in the former, the circumstance in which alone the two instances differ is the effect, or the cause, or an indispensable part of the cause, of the phenomenon.[27]

That is to say, if X is preceded by ABCDEFG, and not-X by BCDEFG, it may be inferred that A is the cause of, or is causally linked with, X. Finally the Method of Concomitant Variation:

Whatever phenomenon varies in any manner whenever another phenomenon varies in some particular manner is either a cause or an effect of that phenonemon, or is connected with it through some fact of causation.[28]

More briefly, if two phenomena invariably fluctuate or vary together, there is some causal link between them.

In all five of the tests there are theoretical and practical weaknesses which can be ignored for the present purpose; suffice it to say that they are sometimes useful pointers, but they are by no means reliable criteria for causal inference. More important for Mill's theory of induction is the fact that

[25] Cf. Hume, *Treatise*, I, iii, 15, 'Rules by which to judge of causes and effects'.

[26] *A System of Logic*, III, viii, 1; p. 214.

[27] *Ibid.*, III, viii, 2; pp. 215–16.   [28] *Ibid.*, III, viii, 6; p. 227.

all of them operate by *elimination*. For instance, the Method of Agreement establishes the cause of X by excluding BC, DE, FG as possible causes and leaving only A; similarly the Method of Difference excludes BCD etc. as possible causes of X, since these belong equally to X and not-X, and leaves A as the cause since it is the only feature in which X and not-X differ. The Method of Concomitant Variation excludes as possible causes all those phenomena which, when a variation occurs in them, are not followed by a parallel variation in the phenomenon whose cause is being sought.

We are now in a position to see the importance of Mill's principle of universal causation. The argument supporting a particular causal law may be stated thus:

Every event has a cause;
Of the possible causes of X, namely ABCDE etc., all except A can be excluded;
∴ A must be the cause.

Has Mill proved his point? Has he shown that a causal law can be logically demonstrated? The answer must be 'no'. The above argument is valid only on two assumptions, first that the major premise (the law of universal causation) is true, second, that *all* the possible causes of X are known; if the former is untrue, the inference is clearly invalid; and if only some, not all, of the possible causes are known, A cannot be singled out as the actual cause. All that can be said is that in certain favourable instances where all the possible causes of X are known, the actual cause can be proved *granted the assumption* of the major premise. But this premise is itself suspect: Mill admits that it is reached inductively and that it is acceptable as valid because a vast number of causal generalisations point to it and no exception has yet been found; but this is not demonstrative proof. Further, it is doubtful if the law can be regarded as meaningful at all; to be such, it should be possible in principle to refute it by appealing to exceptions; but any appeal to apparently uncaused events could be dismissed by arguing that their causes are simply not yet known. A proposition which is thus unassailable by any contrary evidence is not so much a statement of fact as a procedural guide; as one critic has put it, the law is no more than 'a rule for investigators which happens to be couched in a rather misleading grammatical form'.[29] The fact seems to be that for Mill himself the law was an unacknowledged metaphysical belief, an intuitive assumption on a par with the categories of Kant; as such it was a relic of the rationalism from which he was trying to escape and which his *Logic* was intended to discredit.

[29] J. P. Day, 'John Stuart Mill'; ed. D. J. O'Connor in *A Critical History of Western Philosophy* (The Free Press of Glencoe, 1964), p. 349b.

These are not the only criticisms that can be made of Mill's 'proof' of induction. There is, for instance, a certain circularity in his argument: he uses causal generalisations (lightning/thunder etc.) as evidence for the universal law, but he also uses the universal law to support the generalisation. Again, after rejecting syllogistic deduction as only 'apparent' inference belonging to 'the logic of consistency', he uses it here to prove the validity of induction, 'the logic of truth';[30] this seems hardly congruous with his purpose. It may be said, too, that he exaggerated the importance of causation in induction by claiming that 'the notion of cause . . . [is] the root of the whole theory of induction';[31] by so doing he also complicated unnecessarily the issues involved.

A further criticism is that Mill's whole approach was misguided: induction and deduction are not opposed but complementary; each has a vital part to play in establishing knowledge, and it is pointless, therefore, to exalt one by discrediting the other. It is equally pointless to require for induction the logical cogency of deductive inference; inductive generalisations are incapable of the kind of proof that Mill was seeking; they are open-ended in the sense that, logically at least, refutation always remains a possibility; but this does not diminish their practical value in exploiting nature for human purposes or their theoretical use in hypothesis and prediction. It is probability, not proof, that gives validity to induction; but Mill has little to say about this and was unaware of its importance to his quest.

Finally, Mill's theory is weakened at its foundations by an inadequate analysis of concepts; 'cause' is an obvious example—had he explored it further on the lines of Hume, he might well have found it possible to abandon it altogether and thereby simplify his problem; 'law' is another— the concept of law in 'law of nature' is totally unlike that in 'civil law', but he makes clear neither the difference between them nor the metaphorical nature of the former.

What, then, did Mill achieve? The empiricism of Bacon, Locke and Hume had as yet no firm logical foundation nor any clear relationship with the logic of tradition; Mill sought to provide the former and clarify the latter, and, despite the obvious deficiencies of his work, he gave a new impetus to logical enquiry at a time when it was badly needed. Moreover, the sciences which were rapidly growing from the empirical approach to

---

[30] And cf. *Comte and Positivism* (University of Michigan Press, 1961), p. 58: 'A general proposition inductively obtained is only then proved to be true when the instances on which it rests are such that, if they have been correctly observed, the falsity of the generalisation would be *inconsistent* with the constancy of causation' (my italics).

[31] *A System of Logic*, III, v, 2; p. 194.

knowledge still lacked a coherent methodology—or any at all; this too Mill tried to provide by elaborating and justifying on the basis of his theory of induction what he believed to be the proper methods of science. The five tests of causal laws or 'methods of experimental enquiry', as Mill calls them, are an example of this. Here again, the deficiencies in his methodology, which would be apparent if there were space to examine it in detail, should not obscure the significance of his work; others were enabled to build more securely where he had shown the way.

Perhaps his most important contribution to methodology was his attempt to construct a scientific basis for sociological studies. The motivation for this arose, as was indicated above, from his involvement in the work of reform; for he was convinced that social improvement must spring from an understanding of the causes operative in social change and that this understanding must be securely based on scientifically established laws and principles. Yet it was clear to him that sociology could not be an exact science like physics, since the number and variety of factors operative in society would not allow a precise account of cause and effect; nor was it possible in sociology to conduct the kind of controlled experiment which is normal in the physical and biological sciences; moreover, though observation is possible without deliberate experiment, actual societies rarely present us with precisely the facts we wish to observe for the sake of a particular investigation. Now Mill believed that in observing society we are observing the actions of human beings and their consequences; ultimately, therefore, all social phenomena can be explained in terms of the psychology of individual men and women; the laws that operate in society are an extension of the laws of individual psychology. Hence the proper procedure in sociology is what he called the 'inverse-deductive' method: one must first observe society past and present, form generalisations on the basis of this observation and then test them by comparison with what can be deduced from the laws of psychology. Since direct deduction from basic sociological laws is impossible, we must employ an indirect or inverted process of validating sociological generalisations by referring to the laws of another science. Here too, as in his account of induction and of the methodology of science, Mill accomplishes valuable preparatory work; its significance is the greater because sociology has since become an academic discipline in its own right and has profoundly influenced social organisation and planning throughout the world.

The fact that Mill (nor anyone after him) did not provide demonstrative proof of the validity of inductive inference is no cause for undue alarm. Nor is the problem of induction as desperate in its implications for epistemology and science as has sometimes been supposed; there are even grounds for suggesting that it is really no problem at all. If one clings to the rationalist tradition of requiring for knowledge the certainty of deduction from proven *a priori* principles, then the situation is no doubt disturbing; but rationalism is not without alternatives. Induction is not rendered *irrational* by the failure to find for it a logical proof: to expect the future to resemble the past and to base prediction on this expectation, whether for scientific experiment or for purposes more mundane, is not necessarily to act unreasonably or even, in the extended sense, illogically. What matters is the amount and quality of the evidence by which prediction is supported. To argue from the observation of a few instances of *a* followed by *b* that the two are related by a causal link which will operate in future instances could well be hazardous; fifty observations might be regarded as reasonable evidence; ten thousand, together with the total absence of any contrary instance, would normally be regarded as overwhelming support for the assumption of a causal link. Thus, if there is no final proof for inductive procedures, there is certainly rational justification; probability—which mathematical techniques can now precisely calculate from the available evidence—is a valuable, and often the only, guide for generalisation and prediction.

Induction is also reasonable in the sense that it works. It has been shown to be a successful instrument for probing nature and discovering how things are; by means of hypotheses based on inductive generalisation we put questions to the world around us and bring to light those patterns and sequences which prompt us to speak of a 'universe', an orderly system of natural 'laws', instead of a haphazard conglomeration of things and events. It works too in its predictive efficacy; when we generalise from past experience—in life or in the laboratory—to forecast the future, we find with gratifying regularity that our predictions are substantiated. Here too induction is a successful practical instrument without which not only science but even life itself above a merely instinctive level would be impossible.

It matters little for these purposes that inductive inference lacks logical cogency; the pragmatic test of practical success is justification enough. Nor does it matter that inductive conclusions have no absolute finality—provided we are willing to accept them as tentative rather than definitive. Indeed the problem of induction is perhaps more psychological than logical, a question of viewpoint, of intellectual orientation, of adjusting mood and attitude to the reality of the situation instead of demanding that it be different from what it is. If we could be open-ended in our approach to knowledge, regarding it as provisional, as liable to refutation or modification by future experience, instead of requiring once and for all the finished map, we should be less inclined to worry about the apparent deficiencies of induction when judged by the criteria of deductive logic.

To adopt this view of induction is valuable in other respects. It points to the fact, too often overlooked, that science depends on *a priori* assumptions—or *one* at the very least—which are incapable of proof. Mill was entirely right in insisting that induction, and science with it, cannot operate without presupposing the uniformity of nature (though he was wrong in supposing that it could be proved); whether one regards it as a psychological disposition (as Hume), or a working hypothesis, or a procedural guide, or a means of logical justification, or a metaphysical principle of the universe, the assumption is essential to science; and it must be accepted without proof, on trust. This is a sobering and salutary thought for such an era of scientific achievement as the present. There is a further point: the forming of hypotheses is an essential part of inductive procedure within scientific method; these are the questions to be answered by observational or experimental test. But hypotheses spring, not so much from logic, as from imagination; to see in facts that which is common to them and which gives them pattern, and then to devise explanations which can be experimentally tested—this is an exercise involving the aesthetic and creative in human nature as well as the logical. To recognise this is to humanise science by acknowledging its affinity with the arts.

The criterion of moral choice

In considering Kant's ethic of duty we began with the question, 'What makes a person or an action morally good?' and we found his answer to be the good will 'estimable in itself and good apart from any further end'. The good will, he goes on to explain, is one which acts simply for duty's sake; but this leads to further crucial questions, 'How does one decide what *is* one's duty? What criteria determine moral obligation?' To this Kant replies that duty lies in obedience to the categorical imperative which requires that any principle of moral choice must be universalisable into a general law for all human beings. There is, as we saw, both strength and weakness in this answer: the former lies in its emphasis on such qualities as rational consistency, perseverance, self-discipline and loyalty to accepted ideals; its principal weakness lies in the failure of universalisability to provide a firm criterion of moral choice. We turn now to another and no less celebrated attempt to solve this problem, namely, 'the greatest happiness principle', of which mention has already been made (p. 165). This is commonly associated with the name of J. S. Mill under the title of utilitarianism, but in fact he was indebted to others, especially to Jeremy Bentham, for both the principle and its title.[32]

[32] 'Although Bentham had at least on one occasion used the word "utilitarian", it was Mill who introduced it into philosophy. He appropriated it, with some change of meaning, from a passage in the Scottish novelist John

Mill could not, like many of his contemporaries (but not his immediate associates) in the mid-nineteenth century, turn to Christian teaching for the justification of moral choice. His father's upbringing had excluded him from religion, and his own mature reflection convinced him that Christianity was untenable; he saw the Church as an area of social privilege, and he was impressed by the ruthlessness of nature and its disregard for human happiness—these, he argued, are wholly incompatible with the claim that God is both good and omnipotent. In Jesus himself he saw nothing 'so inherently impossible or absolutely incredible . . . as to preclude anyone from hoping that it may perhaps be true';[33] though permissive, he was unconvinced. For Mill orthodox religion was simply unnecessary, even morally; for morality, he believed, has independent foundations of its own in social tradition and human aspiration. What he could wholeheartedly commit himself to was the 'religion of humanity'—the belief in ideals which bettered human life, in the fight for good against evil:

The essence of religion is the strong and earnest direction of the emotions and desires towards an ideal object recognised as of the highest excellence and as rightfully paramount over all selfish objects of desire. This condition is fulfilled by the Religion of Humanity . . .[34]

—which in this respect is the equal, if not the superior, of any supernatural religion. But this still leaves open the questions what *is* good, what *is* excellent, what *are* the ideals worthy of commitment. It was to this fundamental problem that Mill addressed himself in the essay *Utilitarianism*.

'It is the business of ethics', Mill writes, 'to tell us what are our duties or by what test we may know them'[35]—that is, to show us what we ought to do and the criteria by which we may judge this. The main purpose of his *Utilitarianism* is to justify the principle of utility (or the greatest happiness principle) as the basis of obligation and to show how it can be applied as a criterion in ethical choice; in addition he hoped to rebut the intuitionists, like Whewell, who believed that moral principles were apprehended directly, and to prove that ethics can perfectly well be founded on inductive generalisation from experience. For the principle of utility itself he was mainly indebted to Bentham, who in turn declared his debt to Hume; but its ancestry reaches back to Epicurus and the Greek sophists. Briefly, it states that happiness is the only intrinsic good, the only thing desirable as

---

Galt's *Annals of the Parish* (Edinburgh, 1821)', J. J. C. Smart, in *The Encyclopedia of Philosophy*, vol. viii, p. 208.

[33] *Three Essays on Religion* (Longmans, 1874), p. 240.

[34] *Ibid.*, p. 109.

[35] *Utilitarianism*, ed. M. Warnock (Collins, 1962), p. 269.

an end in itself; therefore 'actions are right in proportion as they tend to promote happiness, wrong as they tend to produce the reverse of happiness. By happiness is intended pleasure and the absence of pain.'[36]

It does not necessarily follow—or at least Mill did not intend—that an action productive of unhappiness is always to be avoided; for if, as sometimes happens in actual life, the choice is between two actions either of whose consequences can only be painful (e.g. losing a leg or dying of gangrene), the criterion here will be, not the greatest happiness, but the least unhappiness.

Now, as stated so far, the principle could be interpreted as recommending a selfish pursuit of pleasure which ignored the happiness of others; but Mill insists that the proper criterion is not the happiness of the individual (or of him alone), but of all mankind or of as many as possible—hence the popular formulation of the principle, 'the greatest happiness of the greatest number'. He writes:

I must again repeat, what the assailants of utilitarianism seldom have the justice to acknowledge, that the happiness which forms the utilitarian standard of what is right in conduct is not the agent's own happiness, but that of all concerned. As between his own happiness and that of others, utilitarianism requires him to be as strictly impartial as a disinterested and benevolent spectator.[37]

As for the means by which men and women are to be acclimatised to such altruistic heights, Mill recommends that the utilitarian ideal must be embodied in 'laws and social arrangements' and established in individual character by the habituating power of education and public opinion.[38] (The implications of this recommendation seem to have escaped him; without effective safeguard it could lead to a totalitarian social ethic wholly incompatible with that freedom and variety of human experiencing which he so passionately upholds in *On Liberty* and elsewhere.)

However, that happiness is the proper criterion of moral choice is by no means obvious, still less that this implies the *general* rather than individual happiness. How, then, does Mill establish his case? He admits frankly that 'questions of ultimate ends are not amenable to direct proof', but there is, he asserts, 'a larger meaning of the word proof' which consists in rational justification, the adducing of good reasons, such as are 'capable of determining the intellect either to give or withhold its assent to the doctrine; and this is equivalent to proof'.[39] There are two lines of argument

---

[36] *Ibid.*, p. 257. [37] *Ibid.*, p. 268. [38] *Ibid.*, pp. 268–9.
[39] *Ibid.*, pp. 254–5. Cf. ch. iv, p. 288: 'To be incapable of proof by reasoning is common to all first principles, to the first premises of our knowledge as well as to those of our conduct.'

in Mill's 'proof' of the greatest happiness principle; both depend on what he takes to be an empirical fact demonstrable by observation, that every individual pursues happiness as the one thing desired for its own sake: 'to desire anything, except in proportion as the idea of it is pleasant, is a physical and metaphysical impossibility'.[40] From this he makes two deductions: first 'The only proof capable of being given that an object is visible, is that people actually see it. . . . In like manner . . . the sole evidence it is possible to produce that anything is desirable is that people do actually desire it.' Second, 'Each person's happiness is a good to that person, and the general happiness, therefore, a good to the aggregate of all persons.'[41] Now, both the premise and the conclusions inferred from it fall short of logical cogency and are acceptable only within the terms of reference that Mill himself sets forth, namely, that 'questions of ultimate ends are not amenable to direct proof'; judged by strict logical criteria they are invalid.

In the empirical premise there are two weaknesses: one is that, despite its claim, it does not match up to the facts of experience; for happiness (or pleasure) is not the only thing that individual men and women pursue for its own sake, indeed to pursue it *for its own sake* is to run the risk of never finding it—Aristotle was nearer the truth when he decided that pleasure is a byproduct of an activity rather than its goal; personal integrity, social and political ideals, aesthetic creation—these are not, in ordinary experience, *means* to happiness but *ends in themselves*, which we pursue because they are worth while in their own immediate having. A possible rejoinder is that, if 'happiness' is interpreted widely enough, it can include these apparent exceptions; for example, the preservation of personal integrity gives a sense of satisfaction which is akin to happiness, and the loss of it brings a feeling of unease which is a kind of pain—and similarly with ideals and works of art. But this does not answer the objection that such things are pursued, not to achieve happiness *through* them, but for their own intrinsic worthwhileness; moreover, it points to the second weakness, which is that, if 'happiness' is stretched in this way, it can be made to mean 'whatever men desire' and its content can be as varied as the predilections of human nature. In this way the concept loses all normative force, for the question what is most worth desiring is now wide open and we are forced to seek criteria for distinguishing more and less desirable happinesses. We shall return to this point later; meanwhile let us look at the two conclusions which Mill infers from this dubious premise.

He arrives at the first of them by arguing that, since it is an empirical fact that happiness is universally desir*ed*, it follows that it is also universally desir*able*; he seeks to strengthen the argument by drawing an analogy

[40] *Utilitarianism*, ed. M. Warnock, p. 293.
[41] *Ibid*., pp. 288–9.

with 'seen' and 'visible'—the fact that people actually see an object is the only proof that it is visible. Neither the main inference nor the supporting analogy is valid: a conclusion containing an assertion of obligation can be validly inferred only from premises which contain a similar assertion (above, p. 34); one cannot infer from 'is' to 'ought', from fact to value; to attempt it is to commit what the Cambridge philosopher, G. E. Moore, has called 'the naturalistic fallacy'.[42] As for the analogy, Mill is guilty here of linguistic confusion: 'visible' means 'able to be seen', *not* 'ought to be seen' or 'worth seeing'; both 'seen' and 'visible' are therefore factual terms and it is quite correct to infer from one to the other—if an object is seen it must be visible. This is not the case with 'desired' and 'desirable', for the latter (in normal usage) means not 'able to be desired', but 'desireworthy'; one is a fact-term, the other a value-term. Thus there is no analogy between the pairs of words and no support here for the main argument.

Mill's second conclusion is equally defective: it does not follow from 'each desires his own happiness' that 'all desire the happiness of all' and that the general happiness is therefore the ultimate good; the fact that A desires his own happiness, B his own, C his own, and so on, in no way implies that A, B, C, etc. desire the *general* happiness of A, B, C, etc.; there is no logical link from the one to the other, and to suppose that there is commits the logical fallacy of composition—combining in the conclusion what were not combined in the premises. The fact is that Mill nowhere succeeds in showing why there is any *obligation* to pursue the general happiness, why a man *ought* to make this his aim rather than seek his personal pleasures. Now it can be objected that Mill never claimed to provide strict logical proof for his greatest happiness principle; indeed he denies that any such proof is available. This is true, but he should not then have tried to present his argument in a form which has the appearance of logical validity without the reality.

Attention has been drawn to the vagueness of Mill's central term, 'happiness', which has to be broken down into the different happinesses which men actually pursue, thus losing its normative force and leaving us with the problem of assessing the comparative worth of the various kinds of happiness. Originally it had seemed that the utility principle provided a quantitative criterion by which the rightness or wrongness of actions could be accurately assessed; by estimating the amount of happiness resulting or likely to result from an action it would be possible to determine whether or not it ought to be done; in this way morality could be placed on the same level of objectivity as the sciences—indeed it became the *science* of human conduct. So far Mill had followed Bentham; he came to see,

[42] *Principia Ethica* (Cambridge University Press, 1903; paperback 1959), p. 10 (in later edition) and *passim*.

however, that, since there are different kinds of happiness, quantity cannot be the sole criterion but that considerations of quality also enter into the estimate:

It is quite compatible with the principle of utility to recognise the fact that some *kinds* of pleasure are more desirable and more valuable than others. It would be absurd that, while in estimating all other things quality is considered as well as quantity, the estimation of pleasure should be supposed to depend on quantity alone.[43]

Now it can be argued that the *quantity* of pleasure (happiness) is measurable—though many would disagree; but its quality surely is not; and though the number of persons agreeing or disagreeing with a judgment of quality can be measured, the judgment itself cannot—it is a choice, a matter of taste and personal preference which is distinct from quantitative assessment. By introducing into the utility principle the element of quality Mill undermines its supposed objectivity and radically alters its nature as a criterion of right and wrong; on the other hand he makes it more human and to that extent more acceptable.

In judgments of quality the final appeal is to the wisdom, competence and experience of the person or persons judging. There are different levels of judgment just as there are different levels of experiencing. 'It is an unquestionable fact', says Mill, 'that those who are equally acquainted with and equally capable of appreciating and enjoying both [of two levels] do give a most marked preference to the manner of existence which employs their higher faculties.' Human life, even with its many imperfections, is preferable to complete sensual satisfaction at a lower level—'better to be a human being dissatisfied than a pig satisfied'. To the question, therefore, 'What makes one pleasure more valuable than another?' apart from quantitative assessment where this may be possible, there can be only one answer: 'Of two pleasures, if there be one to which all or almost all who have experience of both give a decided preference . . . that is the more desirable pleasure.'[44]

Mill is on much firmer ground here than in any attempt to base moral choice on a purely quantitative reckoning. Admittedly, there are some occasions when happiness *can* be subjected to tests which approximate to the quantitative: 'I shall get more pleasure from eating two sweets or from two weeks abroad than from one'; 'More people will get pleasure if I share my box of chocolates than if I keep them to myself'; 'To appropriate this man's property to make a public park will produce an amount of happiness outweighing the personal loss and unhappiness of the individual'. But judgments of quality cannot be evaded (and they are implicit

[43] *Utilitarianism*, pp. 258-9.   [44] *Ibid.*, pp. 259, 260, 259.

even in these illustrations—one man's pleasure in freedom and the use of his property, perhaps for wholly altruistic purposes, as against the pleasure of the community in using the land for funfairs or football); in the end one is thrown back on the moral authority of informed and experienced personal judgment.

One consequence of this, which did not escape Mill, is the need for an educated populace capable of making such judgments; utilitarianism, he says, 'could only attain its end by the general cultivation of nobleness of character'.[45] Another, which is an integral part of the argument of *On Liberty* but does not appear in *Utilitarianism*, is that moral authority must be sufficiently flexible and open-ended to admit innovation. If the majority verdict of competent authority were always the criterion of moral (or aesthetic) judgment, it would be difficult to depart from the norm of accepted standards; authority could thus degenerate into encrusted authoritarianism and quell the initiative of individual judgment which has so often been fruitful of moral advance.

It must be admitted that Mill's ethical theory is muddled and inconsistent. A principal reason for this is that he outgrew the Benthamist utilitarianism with which his father's training had imbued him: his nervous crisis of 1826, his reading of Wordsworth and other romantics, his friendship with and later marriage to Harriet Taylor, as well as his own growth in experience, led him towards a view of morality based on personal development and individual worth rather than the pursuit of the general happiness. An obvious expression of this is the essay *On Liberty*, especially the third chapter, 'Of individuality as one of the elements of wellbeing', where he writes: 'In proportion to the development of his individuality each person becomes more valuable to himself and is therefore capable of being more valuable to others.'[46] Men and women are not models to be set in motion, but like trees which develop 'according to the tendency of the inward forces' which make them living things.[47] And in *Utilitarianism*, as we have seen, everything depends on 'the general cultivation of noble character'. Thus there underlies Mill's exposition of utilitarianism an appeal to value commitments implied but unexposed, to norms other than those carried by the doctrine itself.[48] It would seem, moreover, that in the absence of such further appeal utilitarianism has only limited value as a criterion of ethical choice, for it could then be used, on the pretext of the

[45] *Ibid.*, p. 262.
[46] *Ibid.*, p. 192.
[47] *Ibid.*, p. 188.
[48] Britton, p. 103: 'The doctrine of the full development of individuality is Mill's version of the Natural Right to Happiness; and this, in turn, is precisely the suppressed ethical premise of Utilitarianism.'

general happiness, even to justify the perversion of truth and justice—as might happen, for instance, if a man known by the police to be innocent but declared publicly to be guilty were convicted in order to deter genuine criminals and so preserve public security.

Much more could be said on Mill's version of the greatest happiness principle, and a very great deal more on utilitarianism in general; but we must be content with indicating a few lines of criticism other than those already directed specifically at Mill. When the utility principle is applied to particular decisions, difficulty arises in the calculation of consequences: in order to choose between two possible actions some assessment must be made of the likely contribution of each to the general happiness. Sometimes the assessment is easy—the benefit accruing to society from restraining a criminal clearly outweighs the man's own pleasure in indulging his propensity for violence or theft. But what of capital punishment? So great is the complexity of making a decision which does justice to the security of the public, the morale of the police and the statistical evidence of deterrence, that in Britain after years of controversy no firm conclusion has yet been reached. (Indeed one is inclined increasingly to the view that the final choice here is not between a greater and a lesser amount of happiness, but between different valuations of human life.) It could well be argued that the consequences of some actions for good or ill are quite beyond any calculation even of the most refined computer: who, for instance, could assess, either in advance or after the event, whether or not the atom-bombing of Hiroshima and Nagasaki was justified in terms of the general good? How could it ever be assessed until human history has reached its conclusion—and perhaps not even then?

Against utilitarianism as a general principle of moral choice the objection is made that it implies a coldly prudential view of conduct which leaves no room for spontaneous beneficence—it is a doctrine of expediency which excludes the unpremeditated outflow of generosity. If men and women acted always on calculation of the happiness likely to result from their actions, human relations would surely be impoverished and many a recorded deed of heroism and sacrificial self-giving would have been quelled at the first impulse. This is a criticism which Mill himself anticipated and partly answered: 'It is often affirmed that utilitarianism renders men cold and unsympathising; that it chills their moral feelings towards individuals.'[49] If this means that utilitarians sometimes exalt the letter of their doctrine above its spirit and give too little regard for 'the other beauties of character which go towards making a human being lovable or admirable',[50] then Mill admits it; but the fault lies not in the doctrine itself

[49] *Utilitarianism*, p. 271.
[50] *Ibid.*, p. 272.

so much as in the human frailty which misinterprets it. 'Utilitarians are quite aware that there are other desirable possessions and qualities besides virtue, and are perfectly willing to allow to all of them their full worth.'[51] It can be said, moreover, that morality cannot properly exclude all consideration of consequence: a thoughtless benevolence, though superficially attractive, may bring harm to both donor and recipient and to society at large by dispensing charity to the shiftless and indolent who may abuse or misapply it; it is not impossible to combine kindliness and generosity with a prudent calculation of the context and consequences of their application.

A deeper criticism, which can be directed equally against Kant's ethic of duty, is that utilitarianism cannot serve as the single, unitary moral principle that Mill wanted it to be. The attempt to bring all moral decision under one universally applicable rule fails to allow for the diversity and complexity of the relationships which are the context of human behaviour: the ethic of duty emphasises rational consistency but underrates motive, habit and circumstance; the ethic of the greatest happiness, while pointing to considerations of great importance, underrates the part of justice, which is concerned with the distribution rather than the quantity of happiness, and of charity (in the best sense), whose warm affection for the individual hazards the consequences for the sake of his immediate good. But if it cannot provide us with a single, overriding moral criterion, the greatest happiness principle can be a valuable guide, especially (but not only) in decisions affecting society as a whole or smaller communities like schools or clubs. Here the final appeal must often be to the good of the majority, the wellbeing of the greatest number; to this the legitimate interests of the individual or the minority may, however regrettably, be required to yield— though not, it is to be hoped, without circumspection and careful consideration of the issues and values at stake. Hence, in part, derives the justification for compulsory purchase, the breathalyser, school rules and similar restrictions on individual freedom. (The danger here, of which Mill was acutely aware, is the imposing of a common norm which stifles individual excellence and the eccentricities which enrich community life— and sometimes enlarge truth by their departure from convention.)

Finally, utilitarianism provides us with a necessary reminder that decisions have consequences beyond themselves, sometimes immediate, sometimes remote, but none the less inevitable; to calculate them with any precision may be impossible, but the prudent person who is concerned for human happiness will not ignore them. Such a person might well question, for instance, the lavish exploitation of irreplaceable resources for the sake of present pleasure or economic gain; or the pollution of the natural

[51] *Ibid.*, p. 271.

environment to a degree which may endanger the health and even the lives of our grandchildren. Consideration of consequences, it has already been remarked, is proper to moral decision; and where coupled with honest regard for the interests of others can save us from choices which are misguidedly or shortsightedly selfish.

Further study

J. S. Mill

K. BRITTON, *John Stuart Mill* (Penguin, 1953) is among the best introductory books on Mill; for a contemporary account of him see A. BAIN, *J. S. Mill: a Criticism with Personal Recollections* (Longmans, 1882; New York, Kelley, 1969). More recent books include: T. WOODS, *Poetry and Philosophy: a Study in the Thought of J. S. Mill* (Hutchinson, 1961); R. P. ANSCHUTZ, *The Philosophy of J. S. Mill* (Oxford, Clarendon Press, enlarged edn, 1963); E. ALEXANDER, *Matthew Arnold and J. S. Mill* (Routledge, 1965); J. M. ROBSON, *The Improvement of Mankind* (University of Toronto Press; London, Routledge, 1968); and, most recently, A. RYAN, *The Philosophy of John Stuart Mill* (Macmillan, 1970).

The fullest life of Mill is M. ST J. PACKE (Secker & Warburg, 1954); there is also R. BORCHARDT, *John Stuart Mill the Man* (Watts, 1957). On his relations with Harriet there are F. A. HAYEK, *John Stuart Mill and Harriet Taylor* (Routledge, 1951), and H. O. PAPPÉ, *John Stuart Mill and the Harriet Taylor Myth* (Cambridge University Press, 1960). Readers may also be interested in A. J. MILL, *John Mill's Boyhood Visit to France* (University of Toronto Press, 1960).

Most of what Mill wrote is readable, some of it eminently so; his *On Liberty* is a well-established classic; so too (within education at least) is his *Autobiography*; and his *Utilitarianism* and *Three Essays on Religion* certainly deserve to be more widely read, even if in disagreement. The *Inaugural Address*, which he delivered on the occasion of his installation as Rector of St Andrews University, is a well-known statement of liberal education. These and his other works can be obtained in various editions both British and American; Mill's complete works are gradually being published by the University of Toronto Press.

Science and logic

From Mill the reader may wish to turn to such books as: S. TOULMIN, *The Philosophy of Science* (Hutchinson, 1953); D. W. THEOBALD, *An Introduction to the Philosophy of Science* (Methuen, 1968); M. BLACK, *Critical Thinking* (2nd edn, Prentice-Hall, 1952); H. R. F. HARROD, *Foundations of Inductive Logic* (Macmillan, 1956); W. C. KNEALE, *Probability and Induction* (Oxford, Clarendon Press, 1949); R. B. BRAITHWAITE, *Scientific Explanation* (Cambridge University Press, 1953); K. R. POPPER, *The Logic of Scientific Discovery* (Hutchinson, 1959); and M. R. COHEN and E. NAGEL,

An Introduction to Logic and Scientific Method (Routledge, 1934); there are many others.

More general introductions to logic include: M. R. COHEN, *A Preface to Logic* (Routledge, 1946); A. A. LUCE, *Logic* (English Universities Press, 1958); S. STEBBING, *A modern Elementary Logic* (Methuen, 1943); there is also her more advanced *A Modern Introduction to Logic* (Methuen, 7th edn, 1950); and among more recent books: C. L. HAMBLIN, *Elementary Formal Logic: a Programmed Course* (Methuen, 1966); G. B. KEENE, *Language and Reasoning* (Van Nostrand, 1961); and D. MITCHELL, *An Introduction to Logic* (Hutchinson, 1962).

Utilitarianism

The third volume of L. STEPHEN, *The English Utilitarians* (Duckworth, 1900), is a valuable study of Mill; see also J. P. PLAMENATZ, *The English Utilitarians* (2nd edn, Blackwell, 1958), which is the title of his edition of *Utilitarianism*; and E. ALBEE, *A History of English Utilitarianism* (Sonnenschein, 1902). A study (by A. M. QUINTON) of utilitarianism as an ethical theory is due shortly in the Macmillan series, 'New Studies in Ethics'. There is a collection of Mill's ethical writings (under that title), ed. J. B. SCHNEEWIND (New York, Collier Books, 1965).

11 Logical positivism

Science and metaphysics

Historical note

*Logical positivism is an extreme form of empiricism which
was promulgated originally by a group of philosophers in Vienna, later by
their disciples and adherents in many other countries including Britain
and the U.S.A. 'Promulgated' is used advisedly, for the Vienna Circle, as
it was known, proclaimed its doctrines with a fervour reminiscent of
religious and political evangelism; not only were they convinced of the
rightness of their cause, but they were determined that the world should
know and share it. In 1922 Moritz Schlick was appointed Professor of the
Philosophy of the Inductive Sciences at Vienna; around him gathered a
number of men who had a common interest in certain problems within
the fields of science and mathematics and a common dislike of metaphysics.
Among the leading members of the group, apart from Schlick himself,
were Rudolph Carnap, Otto Neurath and Friedrich Waismann; the best
known British exponent of logical positivism, Professor A. J. Ayer, was
associated with the Vienna Circle during a period of postgraduate study,
but never strictly a member of it.*

*It has already been noted that philosophy, since it is a human activity,
is conditioned by the human context—social, cultural, historical—in which
it is practised. This is as true of Plato as it is of Aquinas, Locke and Mill;
the logical positivists are no exception. The growth of science over the past
hundred years and its spectacular success, both in advancing knowledge
and in contributing to the enrichment of life, have given it enormous
influence and prestige. The scientist, it is clear, produces results; there is
no apparent limit to his exploration and mastery of the world. By contrast,
religion and speculative philosophy seem feeble and impoverished, and
their results neither secure nor agreed. This contrast was heightened by
certain extreme forms of metaphysical theory which were developed from
or influenced by the work of the German philosopher Hegel and of which,
in this country, F. H. Bradley's* Appearance and Reality *is an eminent*

*example. Not only were these speculations remote in themselves from the
world of common sense and empirical fact, but they made apparently un-
founded claims, and in farfetched language, about the nature of the
universe and man's life within it. Such was the intellectual climate which
fostered the growth of logical positivism. Not that its doctrines are without precedent in the history of philosophy: there are hints of the positivist
viewpoint in the Greek sophists and Epicurus; obvious forerunners are
Hume, Comte, J. S. Mill and Ernst Mach, the last of whom was Schlick's
immediate predecessor in the chair at Vienna; in logic they were indebted,
among others, to Russell, Whitehead and Wittgenstein.*

*The principal aims of the Vienna Circle were, first, to demonstrate that
all knowledge is ultimately based on observation and sense experience,
and that science, assisted by mathematics, is sufficient to provide it; the
particular sciences, integrated and unified, could, so they thought, furnish
that total picture of the universe which metaphysical philosophers had for
so long tried, and conspicuously failed, to construct. Second, as a corollary
to this, they must show that metaphysics and speculative philosophy are
vacuous activities incapable of providing knowledge of any kind. To
achieve these aims they organised international congresses in Prague, Paris,
Cambridge and elsewhere, published a journal,* Erkenntnis *(Understanding, Insight), later renamed* The Journal of Unified Science, *and issued a
series of monographs under the title* Unified Science; *in addition members
of the Circle produced a number of books under the collective title* Schriften
zur Wissenschaftliche Weltauffassung *(Writings on the Scientific World-
conception), which included works on ethics, causality, sociology and
the logical syntax of language. During the 1930s the Circle gradually
disintegrated as a result of the death or dispersal of its members, the
hostility of the Nazis and, eventually, the onset of war. Individual philosophers in various countries continued to develop and disseminate its
doctrines, but logical positivism ceased to exist as a coherent movement
and few, if any, living philosophers would use this term to describe their
work.*

An attempt was made in chapter 1 to describe briefly the
branch of philosophy known as metaphysics, and illustrations of it have
appeared in Plato's examination of the problem of universals, Aristotle's
analysis of being and Descartes' quest for certainty; some would also
include within metaphysical philosophy Aquinas' arguments for the
existence of God; and Kant's enquiry into the *a priori conditions* of knowledge is also metaphysics as he himself conceived of it. Traditionally
metaphysics has been regarded as 'the science of being', as concerned with

reality or ultimate reality; closely linked with this is the view that it investigates 'ultimate problems'—problems of life's purpose, of human destiny, of freedom and determination, immortality and the like. A special feature of metaphysical philosophy has been its partiality for comprehensive systems of explanation which attempt to bring all experience and all knowledge, fact and value, 'is' and 'ought' within a single pattern of interpretation; Plato is an obvious example of this and Descartes another. A characteristic common to a great deal of metaphysics (but not all) has been transcendence, the impulse to overstep the bounds of sense and observation and to seek a knowledge which is supposedly secure and absolute in its independence of the vagaries and uncertainties of sense experience. Again this is clearly seen in Plato, for whom the man most likely to discover the Forms is the one who 'as far as possible rids himself of eyes and ears, indeed you might say of his whole body, since when he associates with it, it confuses him and prevents his mind from achieving truth and understanding'.[1] It is not, however, true of Kant and those who, following him, have taken metaphysics to be the exploration of the presuppositions of knowledge, of the assumptions of the various sciences, and of the concepts which are essential to our investigation of experience.

Metaphysics is as old as philosophy and almost as old as European civilisation; science, by contrast, is a comparative newcomer. True, there are hints of it in the researches of Aristotle, Archimedes and other Greek and Alexandrian investigators; but science as we know it was conceived in the Renaissance and born in the seventeenth and eighteenth centuries. So stupendous have been its achievements in the past three hundred years and so unlimited is its present horizon, that we forget how recent is its origin. Science implies a systematic exploration of experience which follows carefully devised procedures and aims at formulating theories which can be put to experimental test and thus be shown to correspond, or not, to the facts of observation. It employs inductive reasoning to arrive at general laws and by deduction it infers from laws and theories to consequences which can be checked by observation and experiment. Essentially it is tied to what can be perceived by sense or instrument and to the inferences which can be made therefrom; it is an activity firmly grounded on the data of observation, and though imagination and intellectual invention play a vital part in it, these are strictly controlled by reference to fact and established general laws.

In the past, metaphysical philosophers have often claimed to do what would now be regarded as the work of scientists. The earliest of the Greeks, for instance, devised numerous theories to explain the constitution and operation of the physical universe: one thought it was made of water,

[1] *Phaedo*, 66a.

another of air, yet another that its basic material was an undifferentiated primal substance which he called 'the unlimited' and supposed to separate off into the elements which compose the visible world; yet another of the Greeks proposed with uncanny prescience an atomic theory of matter which anticipated the discoveries of the twentieth century and gave us the word 'atom' itself. In later centuries, while allowing the scientist his proper sphere of activity, metaphysicians still claimed to see beyond the frontiers of science and to picture the world as it 'really' is; they claimed to weave into a coherent and intelligible pattern the theories of the separate sciences which in isolation gave only a fragmentary impression of the whole; or else they claimed to set forth, by a pure ratiocination transcending all observation and sense experience, the genuine reality of things as against the insecure appearance of the phenomenal world. Their motives were as various as the results they produced: in some it was a kind of religious fervour, in others a passion for the security of cognitive certainty; others again found aesthetic satisfaction in the construction of systems displaying the perfect coherence of rigorous logical entailment; in others it was that basic urge that spurs both scientist and philosopher—the struggle to dispel mystery, to make intellectual sense of the perplexities and paradoxes that confront us as we survey the world and our situation within it. Philosophy of this kind was often prejudiced against inductive reasoning and the mundane accumulation of factual data—reasoning deductively from intuitive premises was a surer road to truth, it seemed, than observation, experiment and inductive generalisation. Above all it was *transcendental*: it claimed access to a superior knowledge which eluded the grasp of the plodding, feet-on-the-ground scientist; bypassing empirical investigation as unnecessary or even obstructive it claimed right of passage via *a priori* truths of reason to what it believed to be the very heart of reality.

There have always been those, even from the earliest centuries of philosophy, who have dissented from such rationalist endeavour to disclose the truth. Empiricism has its roots among the ancient Greeks: the atomist Democritus allowed its own legitimacy to knowledge derived from sense perception; 'no one', wrote Aristotle, 'can ever learn or understand anything in the absence of sensation'.[2] But it was only from the fourteenth century onwards that effective protest began the process of destroying the long-established sovereignty of rationalist metaphysics, and it was not until much later still that systematic alternatives were devised to replace it. It was the optimism born of the successful application of science to technology and the consequent industrial revolution that produced, in the eighteenth and early nineteenth centuries, the first major attack on

[2] *De Anima*, ii, 8, 432a.

metaphysics and its pretensions. At the time of the French Revolution
the French writer and social reformer, Henri, comte de Saint-Simon,
recommended the creation of an industrial society whose material and
spiritual direction would be in the hands of scientists; to the viewpoint
and methods of science, which he hoped would supersede both religion
and philosophy, he gave the name 'positivism'. His ideas were adopted
by Auguste Comte, who developed positivism into a systematic doctrine
proclaiming the supremacy of science and wholly antagonistic to metaphysical philosophy or any form of investigation which turned its back
on facts—these alone are valid objects of knowledge and science is the
only means of ascertaining them. The heart of the matter is stated thus
by J. S. Mill in a passage from *Auguste Comte and Positivism* which
carries distinct echoes of Hume:

> We have no knowledge of anything but phenomena; and our knowledge
> of phenomena is relative, not absolute. We know not the essence nor the
> real mode of production of any fact, but only its relations to other facts
> in the way of succession or of similitude. These relations are constant, that
> is, always the same in the same circumstances. The constant resemblances
> which link phenomena together and the constant sequences which unite
> them as antecedent and consequent are termed their laws. The laws of
> phenomena are all we know respecting them. Their essential nature and
> their ultimate causes, either efficient or final, are unknown and inscrutable
> to us.[3]

(J. S. Mill was, of course, deeply influenced via his father, James Mill, and
Jeremy Bentham by the social applications of positivism.) Thus there can
be no transcendent causes, forces or substances; the function of philosophy,
which enjoys no superior insight and has no method distinct from those
of science, is to discover the principles common to all the sciences and
apply them to personal conduct and social organisation. Human society
has moved through two distinct historical stages and is now approaching
a third: the first was the theological, when men supposed that natural
phenomena were the result of direct action by supernatural agents; the
second was the metaphysical, when these supernatural agents were
replaced by abstract forces which were thought capable of producing the
same effects; finally comes the positive or scientific stage, now dawn-
ing, when men use observation and reasoning to discover the laws of
phenomena and utilise them in the betterment of their condition.

Later in the nineteenth century a similar protest against metaphysical-
ism appears in the American philosophy of pragmatism, initiated by
C. S. Peirce and developed by William James and John Dewey. Truth is

[3] *Auguste Comte and Positivism* (University of Michigan Press, 1961),
p. 6.

not disclosed in metaphysical abstractions and absolutes but in factual consequences; an idea is true if it works: 'Truth *happens* to an idea,' writes William James; 'it becomes true, is *made* true by events.'[4] And C. S. Peirce: 'The rational meaning of every proposition lies in the future.'[5] In his essay 'From Absolutism to Experimentalism' Dewey acknowledges his debt to Comte in suggesting the application of science to social life,[6] and in *Reconstruction in Philosophy* he contributes his own protest against the rationalist tradition.[7] In the past, philosophers have indulged in 'impersonal and purely speculative endeavours to contemplate as remote beholders the nature of absolute things-in-themselves'; the 'real' and the 'ideal' have been static concepts, readymade and final, 'a mere asylum from empirical deficiencies'. Now, under the influence of science, philosophy must be transformed from contemplative to operative and knowledge become 'a certain kind of intelligently conducted doing'; philosophers will find consolation for the loss of their 'dealings with Ultimate and Absolute Reality' in the task of 'enlightening the moral forces which move mankind and in contributing to the aspirations of men to attain to a more ordered and intelligent happiness'.

However, the most vocal and best organised assault on metaphysics has come during the present century from the philosophical movement known as logical positivism.[8] A brief statement of the origins of the movement in the so-called Vienna Circle and of its aims and progress has been given in the introduction to this chapter, and there is no need to repeat it. The following presentation of its teachings relies largely on A. J. Ayer's *Language, Truth and Logic*, first published by Gollancz in 1936 and in a revised edition in 1946. Despite the common viewpoint of the Vienna

---

[4] *Pragmatism* (Longmans, 1907), p. 201.

[5] *The Collected Papers of Charles Sanders Peirce*, ed. C. Hartshorne and P. Weiss (Harvard University Press, 1931–35), vol. v, 427.

[6] *John Dewey on Experience, Nature and Freedom*, ed. R. J. Bernstein (Liberal Arts Press, New York, 1960), pp. 3 ff.

[7] Boston, U.S.A., Beacon Press, paperback edn, 1957, pp. 26, 122, 121, 27.

[8] 'Logical positivism' was the name given in 1931 by A. E. Blumberg and Herbert Feigl to the ideas of the Vienna Circle; 'positivism' derives from Comte and Saint-Simon; 'logical' was added because it was wished to strengthen the positivist position by associating it with recent discoveries in logic. A number of alternative names have been suggested, such as 'logical empiricism', 'scientific empiricism', 'consistent empiricism' and 'scientific absolutism' (the last by J. K. Feibleman in *Inside the Great Mirror* (The Hague, Nijhoff, 1958, p. 133)). 'Logical positivism' is sometimes inaccurately used to include the analytical and 'ordinary language' philosophy developed at Oxford and Cambridge, the techniques of which the positivists did, however, borrow for their own purposes.

Circle and a degree of cohesion unusual among philosophers, it is difficult to present logical positivism as a tidy philosophical position: as its ideas were challenged, so they were modified to meet criticism; and because the members of the Circle were not always agreed on what the modifications should be, there resulted some notable divergences of view even about basic principles. Ayer's book, by contrast, gives an admirably clear and coherent picture of the essentials of logical positivism (albeit through one man's eyes and incorporating ideas from English philosophers like Russell and Moore); it is readily accessible—being among the few philosophical best-sellers—and is a bold, forthright proclamation (a word which matches its prophetic fervour) which has been described by one writer as 'a young man's book, lively, uncompromising, belligerent' and by another as written 'with almost hypnotic clarity and force'.[9]

The attack on metaphysics in the 1920s and 1930s came not only from the logical positivists—though they were the most clamorous—but also from English philosophers following the lead of Russell and Moore at Cambridge (chapter 12). This latter group believed that much philosophical perplexity could be dispelled, or at least clarified, by logical analysis of language, for instance, of sentences to reveal their logical form and of concepts to disclose their content and structure (see below, pp. 228 ff.). The Vienna Circle accepted the practice of analysis as proper to philosophy, but were not always careful to distinguish it from logical positivism as a separate assault on the pretensions of metaphysics. Both are found in *Language, Truth and Logic:* Ayer condemns metaphysics, partly because it claims as factually significant statements which fail the positivist criterion of verifiability (p. 208), partly because its language and concepts will not stand up to rigorous logical analysis (pp. 215-16).

The principal aim of the Vienna Circle was to vindicate science and mathematics and to discredit metaphysics; it was necessary to devise a means of doing this. They found it in an account of language foreshadowed by Hume and developed by Ludwig Wittgenstein (for the latter see the next chapter; see also Kant's distinction between analytic and synthetic statements, pp. 157-8). In the final paragraph of his first *Enquiry* Hume writes as follows:

If we take in our hand any volume, of divinity or school metaphysics for instance, let us ask, *Does it contain any abstract reasoning concerning quantity or number?* No. *Does it contain any experimental reasoning con-*

---

[9] Respectively, J. Passmore, *A Hundred Years of Philosophy* (Duckworth, 1957), p. 388, and G. J. Warnock, *English Philosophy since 1900* (Oxford University Press, 1958), p. 43. In fairness it should be added that Professor Ayer has considerably modified his views in later books without, of course, abandoning his fundamental empiricism.

cerning matter of fact and existence? No. Commit it then to the flames, for it can contain nothing but sophistry and illusion.[10]

What Hume is saying may be expressed thus: meaningful statements or propositions are of two kinds, those of mathematics and logic which are deduced from fixed premises, and statements of fact based on empirical investigation; propositions of any other kind are meaningless or, quite literally, non-sense.

Elaborating this the logical positivists held that, while empirical (factual) statements give us information about the world, those of logic and mathematics do not; these latter are tautologies, that is to say, they express the same idea in different ways, and their function is not to state fact but to explicate what is already contained in our words, ideas and concepts. To take some very simple examples, in the argument A = B, B = C, ∴ A = C, the conclusion offers no new facts about the world but merely indicates what is implied by the premises; A = C is another way of expressing part of the content of A = B, B = C, and is therefore tautologous. Similarly, 4 is another way of saying 2 + 2; it adds nothing to our knowledge of empirical fact, but expresses the same thought in a different way. However, 'tautologous' is not the same as 'meaningless'; the statements of logic and mathematics, though they tell us nothing about the world, are not uninformative, for, as Ayer says 'they do enlighten us by illustrating the way in which we use certain symbols'[11]—and, we might add, by clarifying their implications. There are, then, two and only two kinds of meaningful statement, factual statements about the world and the tautological statements of logic and mathematics; metaphysical statements belong to 'neither class—they are neither factual nor tautological and are therefore meaningless. Metaphysics is non-sense and as such beneath serious philosophical consideration. This, in brief, is the argument against metaphysics; it is fully developed in chapter 1 of Ayer's *Language, Truth and Logic* and in an article by Carnap, 'The elimination of metaphysics through logical analysis of language'.[12] (It is worth noting that the description '*logical* positivists' derives from their success in explaining the *a priori* character of logic (and mathematics) in such a way as to preclude the possibility of factual metaphysical statements; earlier positivists had not done this.)

Now it is easy to see that metaphysics does not claim to be logic or mathematics and is therefore excluded from this category of meaningfulness; it is not so clear that it is excluded from the category of factual

[10] Ed. Selby-Bigge, p. 165.

[11] *Language, Truth and Logic* (Gollancz, 2nd edn, 1946), p. 79.

[12] Included in *Logical Positivism*, ed. A. J. Ayer (Free Press of Glencoe, 1959), ch. 3.

statements, since it has always been the claim of the great metaphysicians, like Plato and Descartes, that they *were* describing the actual universe as it in fact is. How did the logical positivists rebut this claim? They did so by applying a rigid test of factual meaning expressed in what they called 'the principle of verification (or verifiability)'. In its original and uncompromising form the principle stated that the meaning of a statement is shown by the method of its verification and that a supposedly factual statement has meaning only if it can be conclusively shown by empirical observation to be true or false. Suppose, for example, I say to a friend: 'There is a table in the next room.' The meaning of this statement is shown by the various operations which he then undertakes to verify it: he goes into the next room; he looks and sees a shiny object, brown in colour, with four legs and a flat surface; he feels it and finds it hard and smooth, measures it and finds it three feet square, and so on. The meaning of the statement is revealed in the sum of the resulting perceptions—not in this room but through the door, square, shiny, hard, smooth, etc. And the statement has factual meaning *because* it can be verified in this way, equally it would have factual meaning—in this case false—if observation revealed no table.[13] This immediately rules out of court such metaphysical theories as Plato's Forms, for there is absolutely no empirical means of verifying them—if I said to my friend, 'There is a Form in heaven' (whether of table or anything else), he would not know where to look or what to look for and could not, therefore, verify my statement; it would have no meaning. Equally excluded from meaningful discourse are such metaphysical propositions as 'all is one', 'time is unreal', 'reality is spiritual' and 'all sense experience is illusory', for these too, while purporting to be factual, have no means of verification (as well as involving conceptual confusion). It also evacuates of meaning most of theology and all moral and aesthetic judgments, since these likewise seem not to be verifiable, or not *solely*, by empirical means.

In requiring conclusive verification as the test of meaning the logical positivists had evidently gone too far. Not only did they thus reduce to nonsense wide areas of human discourse outside metaphysics which had hitherto been regarded as beyond reproach, they also made it impossible to justify general statements based on experience—scientific 'laws' and similar generalisations—none of which can be shown conclusively to be valid or invalid (pp. 177-9 above). A distinction was made, therefore,

---

[13] Cf. Peirce, *ed. cit.*, vol. v, 9: 'In order to ascertain the meaning of an intellectual conception one should consider what practical consequences might conceivably result by necessity from the truth of that conception; and the sum of these consequences will constitute the entire meaning of the conception.'

originally by Moritz Schlick and accepted by Ayer, between a 'strong' form of verification, which was conclusive, and a 'weak' form which required only confirmation or relevant reference to experience:

A proposition is said to be verifiable, in the strong sense of the term, if, and only if, its truth could be conclusively established in experience. But it is verifiable, in the weak sense, if it is possible for experience to render it probable. . . . We say that the question that must be asked about any putative statement of fact is not, Would any observations make its truth or falsehood logically certain? but simply, Would any observations be relevant to the determination of its truth or falsehood? And it is only if a negative answer is given to this second question that we conclude that the statement under consideration is nonsensical.[14]

This is sufficient, Ayer thinks, to exclude metaphysics from the possibility of verification while avoiding the difficulty raised by general statements; at the same time the distinction allows him to assign *some* value to at least limited areas of metaphysics:

Although the greater part of metaphysics is merely the embodiment of humdrum errors, there remain a number of metaphysical passages which are the work of genuine mystical feeling; and they may more plausibly be held to have moral or aesthetic value.

Yet even these are literally senseless,

so that henceforth we may pursue our philosophical researches with as little regard for them as for the more inglorious kind of metaphysics which comes from a failure to understand the workings of our language.[15]

It may be as well to pause here and consider some of the criticisms that have been made of this attack on metaphysics and of the verification principle which is its main support. A serious difficulty which harassed the positivists from the start and was still troubling Ayer when he wrote the preface to the 1946 edition of *Language, Truth and Logic* was this: meaning is normally attributed to *sentences*; *propositions* are what sentences express, and it is propositions that are verifiable or non-verifiable, true or false; in identifying meaning and verifiability the positivists seemed, therefore, to be confusing the functions of sentences and propositions. This was a problem which they never satisfactorily resolved. Moreover, in confining meaningfulness to the pronouncements of mathematics, logic and science the logical positivists adopted too narrow a criterion of meaning; those of metaphysics, theology and ethics, even if they are admitted to be neither factual nor tautologous, are not necessarily vacuous or trivial; it seems perverse, therefore, to write them off as non-sense. 'God exists' and 'God is love' are neither mathematical nor, in the positivist sense, empirical; but they have meaning. Nor is meaning confined only to propositions; a picture

[14] Ayer, *Language, Truth and Logic*, pp. 37–8.   [15] *Ibid.*, p. 45.

or a poem or a national flag may have it too. The philosopher cannot simply disregard these, as one might infer from reading Ayer; for at the very least they pose problems in part philosophical about human nature and experience. A further criticism is that the logical positivists were attacking only a limited conception of metaphysics, that of the purely speculative or transcendental kind, while ignoring or even ignorant of the metaphysics of men like C. S. Peirce, the founder of American pragmatism, and A. N. Whitehead, which endeavoured to come to terms with empiricism. Transcendentalism is not the only kind of metaphysics; to prove their case they would have to show that no other kind is possible; but this they have not done.

Moreover, for all its protestations, logical positivism itself appears to involve metaphysical assertions. Such, surely, is the verification principle; for this cannot be shown to be true by its own criterion, namely, reference to empirical fact; nor, on the other hand, is it an analytical proposition or tautology; it seems rather to be an *a priori* assertion, an arbitrary rule prescribing how the word 'meaningful' is to be used. Indeed, Ayer himself writes: 'I wish the principle of verification itself to be regarded, not as an empirical hypothesis, but as a definition'—though he adds, somewhat unconvincingly, 'it is not supposed to be entirely arbitrary'.[16] This is tantamount to a position of personal commitment, a view of the world, a stand *vis-à-vis* experience, rather than obedience to observed fact. Evidently there is point in the harsh description of a logical positivist as 'one who does not know that he has a metaphysics and so supposes that no one else has one either, and hence concludes that there is no such thing as metaphysics'. In the words of the same critic, ' "Metaphysics is nonsense" *is* metaphysics',[17] and the logical positivists should have been aware of it.

[16] Ayer, *Language, Truth and Logic*, p. 16.
[17] Feibleman, pp. 154, 180. Cf. F. Waismann, 'How I see philosophy', in *Contemporary British Philosophy*, 3rd series, ed. H. D. Lewis (Allen & Unwin, 1956), p. 489: 'To say that metaphysics is nonsense *is* nonsense.' And J. Wisdom, 'Metaphysics and verification', *Mind*, 47 (1938), p. 454: 'When people bring out with a dashing air the words "The meaning of a statement is really simply the method of its verification", like one who says, "The value of a thing is really simply its power in exchange", in what sort of way are they using words? What is the general nature of their theory? The answer is "It is a metaphysical theory." ' And C. L. Stevenson, 'Persuasive definitions', *Mind*, 47 (1938), pp. 339–340: 'Shall we define "meaning" narrowly, so that science alone will receive this laudatory title, and metaphysics the correspondingly derogatory one of "nonsense"? Shall our terminology show science in a fine light, and metaphysics in a poor one? Shall we, in short, accept this *persuasive* definition of "meaning"? This is the question, though well concealed by the dictum that definitions are "merely arbitrary." '

One of the early criticisms of logical positivism was that it involved solipsism, that is to say, a situation in which each individual is immured in a self-contained world which is isolated from all possibility of communication with other individuals. In the final analysis, it was argued, fact for the extreme empiricism of the logical positivist consists of sense data, of what can be seen, heard, touched, etc. with the sensory organs or introspected with 'inner sense'. Every material object—tables, trees, human bodies—is known in the first instance as a collection of sense data (hard, soft, brown, green, pink, round, etc.); these are brought together to form a 'logical construction', for instance a table, in which numerous sense data are grouped together in a definite pattern or structure and so present the table as it is normally perceived. Thus, the basic constituents of knowledge, and therefore the ultimate grounds of verification, are primitive 'atomic' sensory experiences; but these, by their very nature, are private, for a man's sense data are neither observable nor open to inspection by anyone but himself; only he can have the immediate sensation which he calls green or hard. The same is true of inner sensations of pain, joy, etc. These too are private to the individual who experiences them and no one else can know them as he does. And since the material world consists of logical constructions from sense data, this too must be private, a separate universe for every individual. It follows, then, from the empiricist assumptions underlying logical positivism that each man's world is his own and that he can know no other nor even that other private worlds exist. It follows, too, that meaningfulness is also private and verification is valid only for the individual who makes it. Solipsism, however, is untenable in practice; for though much of a man's life is private and incommunicable, there is, nevertheless, a common world of shared experience; nor is it impossible to achieve some understanding of the private worlds of others.

In attempting to answer this criticism Schlick distinguished between the content of experience and its structure; the former is private, something that each man lives for himself; the latter is public, communicable. Thus my immediate experience of greenness can never be the same as yours, but the relation of green to other colours, its position in the spectrum, its belonging to different objects, its association with experiences we both remember—this we can each understand. So too with experience as a whole; its general pattern, the overall structure of the world, is intersubjective, communicable, but the primitive sensory items which compose its content are not. Yet it is difficult to see what meaning there can be in structure without content; the form of experience is so inextricably united with its substance, that neither is intelligible without the other. In fact, Schlick's answer found little acceptance and the logical positivists looked for other means of avoiding the charge of solipsism, though with little better success; indeed the task seems impossible for the extreme empiricist who regards atomic sense data as the sole fundamental constituents of experience.

Metaphysicians, it was noted earlier, have devoted much of their efforts to the construction of comprehensive systems of interpretation which bring all experience and all knowledge, fact and value alike, within a single embrace. Such systems have regularly embodied ethical norms—indeed it has been a part of their purpose to establish and justify such norms, 'to get morality transcendentally underwritten',[18] as it were, so that the values and principles to which we refer our decisions may be founded on something more secure than human predilections. A positivist attack on metaphysics could be expected, therefore, to offer from its own empirical resources an ethic which requires for its justification no heady flights into transcendentalism.

Within the Vienna Circle itself there were differences of view on ethical questions, but their general position is expressed in chapter 6 of *Language, Truth and Logic*. Here Ayer distinguishes three kinds of ethical theory. First, there is the 'subjectivist' view that the criterion of 'right' or 'good' is the feeling of approval which a person or group of persons has towards the action or object referred to; X is good in so far as, and to the degree that, I (or others) approve of it. Second, there is the utilitarian view which judges 'right' and 'good' by the standard of human happiness or satisfaction. These two theories are similar in that each attempts to judge value by reference to fact, approval in the first case, happiness in the second; and because they seek their criteria within the empirical sphere of natural science, they have sometimes been called 'naturalistic'.[19] These Ayer finds unsatisfactory: in ordinary use ethical terms have a normative element which is absent from statements of empirical fact; neither the subjectivist nor the utilitarian view does justice, therefore, to the way in which ethical concepts are actually used. The third type of theory is the 'intuitive': 'good' is simply *seen* to be good by some form of intellectual intuition; this means that value judgments are unverifiable (since there is no means of assessing one man's intuition against another's) and therefore, according to the verification principle, non-sensical.

All these theories Ayer rejects; instead he puts forward another which is best described in his own words:

The presence of an ethical symbol in a proposition adds nothing to its factual content. Thus if I say to someone, 'You acted wrongly in stealing

---

[18] D. F. Pears, ed., *The Nature of Metaphysics* (Macmillan, 1957), p. 15.
[19] Initially by G. E. Moore.

that money,' I am not stating anything more than if I had simply said, 'You stole that money.' . . . I am simply evincing my moral disapproval of it. It is as if I had said, 'You stole that money,' in a particular tone of horror, or written it with the addition of some special exclamation marks. The tone, or the exclamation marks, adds nothing to the literal meaning of the sentence. It merely serves to show that the expression of it is attended by certain feelings in the speaker.

Exactly the same is true of general statements of value like 'stealing money is wrong'. He continues:

In every case in which one would commonly be said to be making an ethical judgement, the function of the relevant ethical word is purely 'emotive'. It is used to express feeling about certain objects, but not to make any assertion about them.

At this point Ayer makes an important addition to the content of ethical terms and expressions of value: 'They are calculated also to arouse feeling, and so to stimulate action.'[20] That is, they have a persuasive or prescriptive element which aims at encouraging or commending the same value-attitudes in others. He concludes:

We can now see why it is impossible to find a criterion for determining the validity of ethical judgements. . . . [It is] because they have no objective validity whatsoever. If a sentence makes no statement at all, there is obviously no sense in asking whether what it says is true or false. And we have seen that sentences which simply express moral judgements do not say anything. They are pure expressions of feeling and as such do not come under the category of truth and falsehood. They are unverifiable for the same reason as a cry of pain or a word of command is unverifiable—because they do not express genuine propositions.[21]

All that Ayer says about ethical judgment holds equally for aesthetic judgments—'such aesthetic words as "beautiful" and "hideous" are employed as ethical words are employed, not to make statements of fact, but simply to express certain feelings and evoke a certain response'.[22]

Now if ethical terms and judgments are simply expressions of emotion; if, that is, they state nothing and are therefore neither empirical nor tautological propositions, they must, according to the principle of verification, be factually meaningless. Yet this is difficult to accept: emotional

[20] *Language, Truth and Logic*, 2nd edn, pp. 107–8. The use of 'emotive' which Ayer here adopts derives from *The Meaning of Meaning*, C. K. Ogden and I. A. Richards (Routledge, 1923). The emotive theory of ethics, briefly stated by Ayer, was fully developed by C. L. Stevenson in 'The emotive meaning of ethical terms' (*Mind*, vol. 46, 1937) and in *Ethics and Language* (Yale University Press, 1945).
[21] *Language, Truth and Logic*, 2nd edn, pp. 108–9.
[22] *Ibid.*, p. 113.

expressions at least give some information, even if indirectly, about a person's state of feelings; they are not strictly non-sensical or non-significant. But are they, in any case, *simply* emotive? Evidently not, for as Ayer himself suggests by way of afterthought, their purpose is also to arouse feeling, to persuade, commend, prescribe. This makes a further and very important addition to the content and meaningfulness of value terms, as well, incidentally, as showing up the inadequacy of his initial analysis. A further weakness is that he has nothing to say of moral obligation or of the 'oughtness' which is implicit in ethical judgments. Presumably Ayer would regard this as a problem not for philosophy but for the empirical sciences—'ethics, as a branch of knowledge, is nothing more than a department of psychology and sociology'.[23] Yet the experience of moral obligation raises problems of a non-empirical kind, such as the logical relation between 'is' and 'ought' (pp. 192–3 above) and the conflict between incompatible ethical systems.

The fact is that what Ayer is offering us is not an ethic or a morality justified on non-transcendental positivist premises, but a theory about ethical language. Now this in itself may be valuable; there is no doubt that recent analysis of the language of morals has both clarified our thinking in this field and greatly improved our understanding of moral judgment; but it does not show us how such judgment is justified—why one moral choice is preferable to another, by what criteria one should decide to commit oneself to, and use approving emotive language of, one value rather than another. Why commit oneself, for instance, to respect for persons instead of 'might is right'? Why praise self-sacrifice and blame the deceiver and the cheat? Even as an exercise in analysis Ayer's account of ethical language is inadequate: it is not the case 'that sentences which simply express moral judgments do not say anything' nor that 'they are pure expressions of feeling'. That they are not statements of fact (or not wholly so) and as such not verifiable by normal empirical means can be granted; but it does not follow that they say nothing or that they have no objective reference. On his own admission ethical terms are inter-personal—'they are calculated also to rouse feeling and so to stimulate action'—and as such they embody an objective reference, whether of acceptance or rejection, to the traditions and values of the society in which they are uttered. One must conclude, then, that from the resources of logical positivism Ayer offers no acceptable alternative to the ethical norms derived from metaphysics; transcendental morality may itself lack final justification, but no substitute is to be found in *Language, Truth and Logic*.

Now if metaphysics is non-sense and if ethical statements, so called, are

[23] *Language, Truth and Logic*, 2nd edn, p. 112.

no more than emotive and persuasive utterances, one may well ask what is left of philosophy. For in the past, metaphysics and ethics have together constituted a great part of philosophy, the one describing the universe as it 'really' is, the other showing how men and women ought to behave in relation to it. If these go, what remains? What is left for the philosopher to do? In answering these questions we come to the threshold of contemporary philosophy; for the principal, even the only, function which the logical positivists allowed the philosopher was that of analysis, and over the past fifty years it is the practice of analysis that has been philosophy's most obvious and characteristic task. This is not to say that the positivists invented analysis—like most things philosophical it is at least as old as Plato and can be seen in the work of all the major philosophers —but they found it an invaluable technique for their particular purpose of explicating meaning where meaning existed and of exposing non-sense where it did not; it was a major weapon in the attack on metaphysics.

They permitted, it will be remembered, only two kinds of meaningful statement, those which are tautologies in that they merely reveal the logical implications contained in words, concepts and premises, and statements of empirical fact. Analysis makes it possible to distinguish one from the other and thus avoid confusion. Very often statements are made and questions asked whose grammatical form suggests that they are concerned with facts, when they are really concerned with language and its logic. As an example Ayer cites the proposition, 'a material thing cannot be in two places at once', which, he says, is often quoted in evidence of the belief that an empirical proposition can be logically certain. But this is not a factual statement at all, he argues; if it is analysed carefully, it is seen to be a declaration of how we use language, in particular the concept of 'material object':

It simply records the fact that, as the result of certain verbal conventions, the proposition that two sense-contents occur in the same visual or tactual sense-field is incompatible with the proposition that they belong to the same material thing.

This, though logically necessary, is not an empirical fact; it is necessary 'only because we happen to use the relevant words in a particular way'.[24]

So, too, with 'truth'. The question is often asked, 'What is truth?' as if it were some actually existent thing or relation, or a mysterious metaphysical entity whose nature it is the peculiar task of the philosopher to reveal. Again, however, analysis shows that this is not so:

In all sentences of the type '*p* is true', the phrase 'is true' is logically superfluous. When, for example, one says that the proposition 'Queen Anne is

---

[24] *Ibid.*, p. 58.

dead' is true, all that one is saying is that Queen Anne is dead. And similarly, when one says that the proposition 'Oxford is the capital of England' is false, all that one is saying is that Oxford is not the capital of England. Thus, to say that a proposition is true is just to assert it, and to say that it is false is just to assert its contradictory. And this indicates that the terms 'true' and 'false' connote nothing, but function in the sentence simply as marks of assertion and denial. And in that case there can be no sense in asking us to analyse the concept of 'truth'. . . . We conclude, then, that there is no problem of truth as it is ordinarily conceived. The traditional conception of truth as a 'real quality' or a 'real relation' is due, like most philosophical mistakes, to the failure to analyse sentences correctly.[25]

Analysis is especially useful in exposing the factual vacuity and pretentiousness, as it seemed to the logical positivists, of metaphysics. Faced with concepts like 'substance' and 'transcendent reality' and propositions like 'God exists' and 'sense experience is unreal', they applied the principle of verification and demanded a translation of such concepts and propositions into terms of actual or possible experience. If no such translation was forthcoming (and if no meaning could be found for them within the category of tautologies), they were strictly non-sense. The assertion, 'There is a table in the next room', makes sense because it can be analysed into assertions about observations which could be made in order to verify it; for instance, if I were to go into the next room, I should see a brown object with four legs and a flat surface which would be hard to the touch etc. Similarly, the assertion that Julius Caesar died on the Ides of March, 44 B.C., though it is not accessible to immediate observation, can be translated into statements about historical evidence and the reliability of ancient authors. So too with the concept of gravitational force; this can be analysed in terms of the attraction of bodies, the movement of the planets and the weightlessness of astronauts. By contrast, the concept of transcendent reality cannot be analysed by reference to actual or possible experience. If something *transcends* experience, how can it *be* experienced? By reference to what sensory data or acts of perception can it be described? The answer is that it cannot and is therefore empty of factual content; it has no literal significance—'from which it must follow that the labours of those who have striven to describe such a reality have all been devoted to the production of nonsense'.[26]

Evidently logical positivism requires a conception of philosophy which is distinctive even within the empirical tradition. Obviously there is no place in it for metaphysical speculation or for normative ethical pronouncements derived from transcendent values; nor is it its function to discover fact—this is the scientist's business. What it can do, however, is

[25] *Language, Truth and Logic*, 2nd edn, pp. 88–9.
[26] *Ibid.*, p. 34.

bring us to a clearer understanding of our ideas and language, questions and perplexities, saving us at the same time from intellectual muddle and the fabrication of non-existent problems. This, it is claimed, is what philosophers have always been principally engaged in, save when they have been diverted into the extravagancies of metaphysics.

We are now in a position to see [says Ayer] that the function of philosophy is wholly critical. . . . If the philosopher is to uphold his claim to make a special contribution to the stock of our knowledge, he must not attempt to formulate speculative truths, or to look for first principles, or to make *a priori* judgements about the validity of our empirical beliefs. He must, in fact, confine himself to works of clarification and analysis. . . .[27]

Elsewhere he writes:'The result of philosophising is not to establish a set of philosophical propositions, but to make other propositions clear.'[28] Similar views are expressed by Hans Reichenbach, a Berlin associate of the Vienna Circle; philosophy, he says, 'is the clarification of meanings through logical analysis'; and 'Philosophy is no longer the story of men who attempted in vain to "say the unsayable" in pictures or verbose constructions of pseudological form. Philosophy is logical analysis of all forms of human thought.'[29] This is a wider view than Ayer's, who goes on to say: 'The propositions of philosophy are not factual but linguistic in character . . .; they express definitions or the formal consequences of definitions. Accordingly, we may say that philosophy is a department of logic.'[30] In the final paragraph of *Language, Truth and Logic* he further specifies the nature of philosophy by asserting that it 'must develop into the logic of science'.

This narrow conception of philosophy represents an extreme position which was not shared by all the logical positivists and was in any case modified under criticism to include a broader view. Friedrich Waismann, an original member of the Vienna Circle and later Reader in the Philosophy of Mathematics at Oxford, has been quoted above as describing philosophy in terms of vision and 'the breaking through to a deeper insight' (p. 10). Professor Ayer himself has moved to a less restricted position which, though still giving to philosophy a function dominantly linguistic and analytical, allows it a concern with language beyond the field of science and with 'the appraisal of conceptual systems'.[31]

It is sometimes claimed that logical positivism was a genuine innovatory

[27] *Ibid.*, pp. 48, 51.
[28] *The Revolution in Philosophy,* ed. G. Ryle (Macmillan, 1956), p. 79.
[29] *The Rise of Scientific Philosophy* (University of California Press, 1956), pp. 145, 308.
[30] *Language, Truth and Logic,* 2nd edn, p. 57.
[31] *Philosophy and Language* (Oxford, Clarendon Press, 1960), p. 22.

force, the main ingredient of the so-called 'revolution' which is said to characterise twentieth-century philosophy. In the main, however, its doctrines are a development of ideas already expressed by Hume and later empiricists; and the peculiar fervour of the movement was largely a reaction, justifiable no doubt, but still a product of historical circumstances, against the absurdities of recent metaphysical idealism. Even its claim that analysis of language is the *sole* business of philosophy and that there is nothing else for it to do was anticipated by Russell and Moore. As a coherent movement it has ceased to exist, but evidence remains of its impact. It has, indeed, contributed much of value to the practice of philosophy: it set high standards of detachment, logical rigour and intellectual responsibility, and insisted on care in the use of language; its criterion of factual significance, though far too limited as a test of meaning, did at least give a salutary jolt to the more metaphysically inclined philosophers and induce them to reconsider the 'vivid, violent and lofty imprecision'[32] of which some of them were guilty. In addition it renewed attention to problems associated with empiricism which were urgently in need of re-examination—the nature of sensation and perception, the relation between language and experience, solipsism and the nature and justification of value judgments. Finally, it raised in an acute and challenging form the deeper question of the sufficiency of empiricism to account for human experience. To this, in conclusion, we now turn.

The opposition between science and metaphysics thus sharply displayed in logical positivism takes us to the heart of epistemology; it presents us once again with the crucial problems of what we understand by knowledge, of what and how we know; it highlights the conflict between the contrasting claims of rationalism and empiricism, between truth of idea and truth of fact. Logical positivism is an extreme position, a protest against the contrary extreme of extravagant transcendentalism displayed in certain metaphysical philosophers of the late nineteenth and early twentieth centuries. Unfortunately it is a fault of such protest to overstep the limits of credibility by ignoring both its own weaknesses and the strength of its adversary.

Metaphysical rationalism has often been guilty of disdaining the empirical and of giving rein to fancy unchecked by reference to fact; its pronouncements have been derived from 'truths of reason', mere postulates without rational justification; its motives have sometimes been suspect, prompted more by the need for psychological security than by disinterested philosophical perplexity.[33] Nevertheless, metaphysicians have made their

[32] G. J. Warnock, *English Philosophy since 1900* (Oxford University Press, 1958), p. 53.
[33] Hume, *Enquiries*, p. 11: 'Here indeed lies the justest and most

contribution—and no insignificant one—to advancing man's knowledge of the world. They have devised new concepts, new ways of viewing and investigating experience: it was they, not the scientists, who first conceived of the atom; Aristotle's concept of potentiality sprang from metaphysical reflection on nature rather than from empirical investigation; Descartes' duality of mind and matter, for all its philosophical difficulties, facilitated the mathematical exploration of the physical universe; it is not impossible that Hegel's concept of history progressing by the merging of extremes into a synthesis which supersedes them was among the influences contributing to the theory of evolution—and it was acknowledged by Dewey to be among the sources of his own empirical philosophy of instrumentalism. Indeed it could be argued that we are indebted as much to the conceptual inventiveness of the metaphysician as to the experiments of the scientist for our understanding of the world. Nor is metaphysics necessarily transcendental in the speculative sense: there has been a task for it—and some would say still is—in bringing into intelligible pattern the discoveries of the separate sciences each of which alone gives us but a partial glimpse of the totality of experience; a task, too, in examining the concepts which we use to interpret experience—cause, freedom, person, will, purpose and a host of others—exploring their meaning, their content, their implications, their interrelationships. Certainly, the metaphysician does not give us facts—not, at least, as the scientist does; but what the greatest of them have done is give us a way of looking at facts, arranging them, interpreting them, so that we view them with a deeper insight into their significance. Their pronouncements are not propositions as the logician or the empiricist thinks of these, but rather interpretative suggestions—this is how I see things, this is how they make sense to me; they are thus neither true nor false, but they can be more or less adequate, satisfying, appropriate, illuminating in their mapping of our factual and conceptual experience.

The strength of empiricism lies in its obvious practical success. It works; it produces the goods; it cures disease; it gets men to the moon. It has opened up vast areas of knowledge—of ourselves, of society, of organic life, of the physics and chemistry of matter, of the immense cosmos of stars and galaxies; it has given us a more accurate picture of man and his

---

plausible objection against a considerable part of metaphysics, that they are not properly a science, but arise either from the fruitless efforts of human vanity, which would penetrate into subjects utterly inaccessible to the understanding, or from the craft of popular superstitions, which, being unable to defend themselves on fair ground, raise these entangling brambles to cover and protect their weakness. Chased from open country these robbers fly into the forest and lie in wait to break in upon every unguarded avenue of the mind and overwhelm it with religious fears and prejudices.'

environment than was accessible even to our parents, let alone our forebears in earlier centuries. It has given us sufficient understanding of the world to enable us to live in it with greater security, greater efficiency and greater happiness than ever was possible in the pre-empirical, pre-scientific era of human history. Surely this is justification enough? Yes and no: as means of investigating the phenomenal world and achieving technological mastery over its empiricism and the sciences it has fathered have proved their worth; but it does not follow that they are self-sufficient, epistemologically or otherwise, that they can answer all our questions and release us from the burden of philosophical puzzlement.

There are four principal reasons for disputing the self-sufficiency of empirical science: it depends on presuppositions whose validity it cannot demonstrate; its success derives in part from non-empirical sources; it is inadequate to describe the fullness of human experience; and it throws up problems which it cannot solve from its own resources.

It is a mistake to suppose that science is wholly 'objective' (indeed it is doubtful whether anything human is or can be) and that its activities involve no *a priori* assumptions. Fundamental to all scientific enquiry is the tacit belief that the universe is intelligible, that it is open to rational explanation, that the objects and events observed in it are interrelated or patterned in ways discoverable by the human mind. Without this initial faith in the order and constancy of nature, writes A. N. Whitehead, 'the incredible labours of scientists would be without hope. It is this instinctive conviction, vividly poised before the imagination, which is the motive power of research.'[34] And it *is* an act of faith; true, there exists a growing accumulation of evidence to support it, but initially it was a brave venture into the unknown and even now is incapable of final proof. A further assumption (also now strongly supported by results, though initially an act of faith) is that natural phenomena are amenable to the methods of mathematics, that measurement, quantification and calculation are means to factual knowledge. Yet another is the persistent belief in the simplicity and economy of nature expressed in such common sayings as *entia non multiplicanda praeter necessitatem* (attributed to William of Ockham, p. 20 above) and *natura nihil facit frustra* (nature does nothing in vain), and in Einstein's claim, said to have been made at a public lecture in Oxford, that 'in nature is actualised the idea of mathematical simplicity'.[35] Finally, the assertion that science is epistemologically self-sufficient and provides the only valid form of knowledge involves assumptions about

[34] *Science and the Modern World* (Cambridge University Press, 1926, repr. 1946), p. 15.
[35] C. A. Coulson, *Science and Christian Belief* (Oxford University Press, 1955; Collins, Fontana Books, 1958), p. 79 in the latter.

the nature of knowledge and the means of attaining it which are not demonstrable by empirical methods; not only the verification principle of the extreme empiricist but even more moderate claims for empiricism derive in the last analysis from commitments grounded on faith.

Next, the achievements of science are by no means wholly due to such empirical procedures as observation, generalisation and experiment: essential to all scientific advance are imagination, aesthetic sensitivity, intuitive vision and what can only be called inspired guessing. This can be abundantly illustrated from the pronouncements of scientists themselves. Here, for instance, is Michael Polanyi writing on the process of scientific discovery:

There exist . . . no explicit rules by which a scientific proposition can be obtained from observational data. . . . The part of observation is to supply clues for the apprehension of reality: that is the process underlying scientific discovery. The apprehension of reality thus gained forms in its turn a clue to further observations: that is the process underlying verification. In both processes there is involved an intuition of the relation between observation and reality: a faculty which can range over all grades of sagacity, from the highest level present in the inspired guesses of scientific genius, down to a minimum required for ordinary perception. . . . In the course of any single experimental enquiry the mutual stimulus between intuition and observation goes on all the time and takes on the most varied forms. Most of the time is spent in fruitless efforts, sustained by a fascination which will take beating after beating for months on end, and produce ever new outbursts of hope, each as fresh as the last so bitterly crushed the week or month before. Vague shapes of the surmised truth suddenly take on the sharp outlines of certainty, only to dissolve again in the light of second thoughts or of further experimental observations. Yet from time to time certain visions of the truth, having made their appearance, continue to gain strength both by further reflection and additional evidence. These are the claims which may be accepted as final by the investigator. . . . This is how scientific propositions normally come into existence.[36]

Professor A. M. Taylor, rejecting the popular view that scientific conclusions enjoy a proven certainty which scientists themselves pursue with passionless objectivity, writes thus:

The history of science shows us, again and again, great discoveries made by passionate adherence to ideas forged in the white heat of imagination. It shows us slow construction, brick by patient brick, of a scientific edifice, often in complete disregard of apparently conflicting evidence. It shows us bold imaginative leaps made in the dark, in unjustified anticipation of success, only later to receive astonishing experimental confirmation. The three attributes of commitment, imagination and tenacity seem to be the distinguishing marks of greatness in a scientist.[37]

---

[36] *Science, Faith and Society* (Oxford University Press, 1946), pp. 15–16.
[37] *Imagination and the Growth of Science* (Murray, 1966), pp. 4–5.

To which one might add that he also needs honesty, integrity, humility and cooperation—qualities which characterise the scientist even in those societies where ideological pressures are most likely to make them un-attractive. Observation and verification are not enough.

The third weakness of empiricism, at least as represented in logical positivism, is its failure to embrace the fullness and variety of human experience; the positivists, it can be justly said, were not empirical enough; they were precluded by their own presuppositions from a careful examination of phenomena which can legitimately be placed within the concept of experience—as can be seen in Ayer's abrupt analytical dismissal of the validity of religious experience.[38] But the criticism applies also to any empiricism which restricts itself to the categories and methods of science. For experience is not coextensive with sense experience; nor is it wholly, and least of all in its most important aspects, amenable to quantification and measurement. Religious and moral experience, aesthetic aware-ness, and the mutuality of knowing which springs from personal intimacy—the content of these is not exhausted by empirical investigation.

Fourth and finally, empiricism generates, or at least discloses, problems which it is not itself competent to resolve. There remains, for instance, the mystery of being, that there *is* anything at all: empirical science takes as given the existence of the objects and events it observes, measures and correlates; but *that* they are and *why* are problems which exceed its scope. Nor has it yet explained how the mind proceeds from *experience of* the world—the data provided by sense perception—to *knowledge about* the world, which is linguistic and propositional; the two belong to categories which are apparently distinct and the passage from the one to the other is fraught with obscurity. Again, we might consider what the empiricist means by 'facts': if he implies thereby the possibility of propositions about the world which are, as it were, aseptic, value-free, devoid of personal commitment, he is chasing a shadow; for facts incorporate inevitably a measure of interpretation, a judgment, a point of view (pp. 7-8 above). What then becomes of the ideal of objective knowledge? May it not be that knowledge is always to some extent *personal*—infused, that is, with elements peculiar to the person who has it? And if this be granted, are we not then faced with the equally intractable problem of solipsism—each of us immured in his own incommunicable private world?

There is a place, then, so it would seem, for a kind of enquiry which might be called 'metempirical', an enquiry whose purposes would be to examine the presuppositions of empiricism, to explore those areas of experience which are not obviously amenable to empirical techniques, and to investigate the philosophical problems which these techniques reveal

[38] *Language, Truth and Logic*, 2nd edn, pp. 114 ff.

without resolving—in fact very much the sort of task which metaphysicians have long claimed as part of their province. If such an enquiry should venture into the transcendental, this need be no cause for complaint; for we have seen how, in imaginative insight and inspired guess, scientists do and necessarily must overstep the bounds of sense and observation; every hypothesis, though initially suggested by the data of observation, is in itself a transcendental experiment. Empiricism and metaphysics need not be mutually exclusive, as positivists would have us believe. There is evidence in the history of philosophy of a rhythmic movement in human thought from the speculative to the critically sceptical and back again to speculation. Though lately we have been passing through a period of criticism, there are signs now of a tentative movement in the other direction; from the resulting synthesis we can reasonably hope for a further extension of our intellectual horizons.

Further study

Logical positivism

There is a good introduction to logical positivism in a series of articles by JOHN PASSMORE in the *Australasian Journal of Psychology and Philosophy*, vols 21 (1943), 22 (1944) and 26 (1948), and in ch. 16 of his *A Hundred Years of Philosophy*. Perhaps the best single book to start with is A. J. AYER, ed., *Logical Positivism* (Free Press of Glencoe, 1959) or his *Language, Truth and Logic* (Gollancz, 2nd edn, 1946). Also helpful is F. C. COPLESTON, *Contemporary Philosophy* (Burns & Oates, 1956). H. REICHENBACH, *The Rise of Scientific Philosophy* (University of California Press, 1956) is more easily read than Ayer's *Language, Truth and Logic*, and less finely argued; in other respects it is a comparable attack on metaphysics. Other books on logical positivism and its themes include: A. PAP, trans., *The Vienna Circle* (Philosophical Library, New York, 1953); J. JØRGENSEN, *The Development of Logical Positivism* (University of Chicago Press, 1951); G. BERGMANN, *The Metaphysics of Logical Positivism* (Longmans, 1954); and E. NAGEL, *Logic Without Metaphysics* (Free Press of Glencoe, 1956).

For metaphysics see the bibliography on p. 68.

12 Wittgenstein

Philosophy and language

Biographical note

Not only was Wittgenstein responsible, to a greater extent than any other philosopher, for the 'revolution' which has transformed English philosophy in the present century, but the man himself, by his originality of intellect, his impassioned pursuit of philosophy and the simple integrity of his powerful, restless spirit, made a vivid and unforgettable impression on those who knew him. In this he has been likened to Socrates, and the comparison is by no means ill-founded.

The youngest of eight children, he was born in Vienna[1] in 1889 into a family which was both rich and cultured; his father was an engineer, his mother had a passion for music. Wittgenstein reflects both sides of his parentage; during childhood he developed an interest in machines which he retained throughout his life and which was a regular source of imagery for his philosophical writings; lifelong too was an interest in music—he had thought at one time of becoming a conductor. His early studies were in engineering, first at a technical school in Germany, later, from 1908 to 1911, at the University of Manchester; here his interest began to shift to pure mathematics, and for this reason he left for Cambridge to study under Bertrand Russell. Both Russell and Moore recorded their impressions of him at this time: 'Getting to know Wittgenstein', wrote the former, 'was one of the most exciting intellectual adventures of my life';[2] and Moore:

I soon came to feel that he was much cleverer at philosophy than I was, and not only cleverer, but also much more profound, and with a much better

---

[1] He became a British subject when Hitler occupied Austria in 1938.

[2] 'Ludwig Wittgenstein', *Mind*, 60 (1951), p. 298. Russell also tells how Wittgenstein came to him at the end of his first term at Cambridge and asked: ' "Will you please tell me whether I am an idiot or not." I replied, "My dear fellow, I don't know. Why are you asking me?" He said, "Because if I am a complete idiot, I shall become an aeronaut; if not, I shall become a philosopher." I told him to write me something

insight into the sort of inquiry which was really important and best worth pursuing, and into the best method of pursuing such inquiries.[3]

Most of the time between the summer of 1913 and the outbreak of war in 1914 he spent in Norway; here, in an isolated place north-east of Bergen, he built himself a hut to which he could retire in complete seclusion. When war came, though exempt from service for reasons of health, he enlisted in the Austrian army, trained as an officer and was eventually captured and imprisoned in 1918. After his release there followed a period of uncertainty; his Tractatus Logico-Philosophicus, *finished in 1918, was now ready for publication; for the time being he felt that his philosophical work was completed. In 1912 he had inherited a considerable fortune from his father; he now gave it all away, and henceforth his personal life was one of austere simplicity; among the few possessions he kept for himself was the hut he had built in Norway. About this time he was deeply influenced by his reading of a book of Tolstoy on the Gospels; this may partly explain his somewhat surprising decision to become a teacher. For five years he taught in a number of village schools in Lower Austria; in this work he showed himself kind, painstaking, original, but overexacting; he resigned from the profession in 1926. For a time he now thought of entering a monastery and during the summer of 1926 he worked as a gardener in a monastery near Vienna; however, he abandoned this idea and spent the next two years helping to design and build a mansion for one of his sisters. Finally, in 1929, he was persuaded to return to Cambridge; in the same year he was awarded a Ph.D. for his* Tractatus *and in 1930 was made a Fellow of Trinity.*

His life in college was one of almost monastic simplicity: his room had no easy chair or reading-lamp; its walls were bare, and a few flowers were the only decoration. Here, in a manner that most would regard as highly unconventional, he lectured to his students; one of them has described the occasions thus:

His lectures were given without preparation and without notes. He told me that once he had tried to lecture from notes but was disgusted with the result; the thoughts that came out were 'stale', or, as he put it to another friend, the words looked like 'corpses' when he began to read them. . . . Wittgenstein sat in a plain wooden chair in the centre of the room. Here he carried on a visible struggle with his thoughts. He often felt that he was

during the vacation on some philosophical subject and I would tell him whether he was a complete idiot or not. At the beginning of the following term he brought me the fulfilment of this suggestion. After reading only one sentence I said to him, "No, you must not become an aeronaut." '
Portraits from Memory (Allen & Unwin, 1956), pp. 26–7.
[3] 'An Autobiography'; ed. P. A. Schilpp, *The Philosophy of G. E. Moore* (Evanston and Chicago, Northwestern University, 1942), p. 33.

confused, and said so. Frequently he said things like 'I'm a fool!', 'You have a dreadful teacher!' 'I'm just too stupid today'.[4]

When his Fellowship expired in 1936, Wittgenstein went to Norway for a year and began writing his Philosophical Investigations; *he returned to Cambridge in 1937 and two years later succeeded Moore in the Chair of Philosophy. Then came war again; abandoning philosophy he first served as a porter at Guy's Hospital and later worked in a medical laboratory at Newcastle. He went back to Cambridge after the war but resigned his Chair in 1947 and retired to a lonely farm on the coast of Connemara in western Ireland; thence he moved to Dublin, where he finished writing the* Philosophical Investigations. *Although he was now suffering from cancer, he was able to visit a friend, Norman Malcolm, in the U.S.A. and his family in Vienna and to spend a few weeks again in Norway. He died in Cambridge at the house of his physician in 1951:*

On Friday, April 27th, he took a walk in the afternoon. That night he fell violently ill. He remained conscious and when informed by the doctor that he could live only a few days, he exclaimed 'Good!' Before losing consciousness he said to Mrs Bevan [the doctor's wife] ... 'Tell them I've had a wonderful life.'[5]

The most important of Wittgenstein's philosophical writings are the Tractatus Logico-Philosophicus, *published in German in 1921*[6] *and in a parallel German–English edition in 1922, and the* Philosophical Investigations, *published posthumously in 1953. In addition there are* Notebooks 1914-16 (1961) *and* Blue and Brown Books (1958); *the latter consists of notes dictated to students during the years 1933-35 and has the editor's subtitle 'Preliminary studies for the* Philosophical Investigations'.

Interest in language has been an outstanding feature of British and American philosophy in the twentieth century; so much so, that language has sometimes seemed to be the philosopher's only concern, as if he had no other business than to unravel the confusions into which it misleads the unwary. Here, certainly, is where the emphasis has been for the past fifty years, and there is little sign as yet of any change. Nevertheless, an interest in language and a recognition of the philosophical problems which it generates is far from novel; indeed, it dates back to the ancient Greeks, and of the major philosophers since that time there are few in

[4] N. Malcolm, *Ludwig Wittgenstein: A Memoir* (Oxford University Press, 1958), pp. 24, 26.

[5] *Ibid.*, p. 100.

[6] Under the title *Logische-philosophische Abhandlung*; the Latin title is said to have been suggested by G. E. Moore.

whom it cannot be found. This needs to be said, for it is often wrongly supposed that such interest belongs uniquely to the contemporary world as a result of a revolution in the content and techniques of philosophy. This is not so.

It has already been shown how Parmenides constructed a metaphysical system on a misunderstanding of the function of the verb 'to be', and how Plato put him right (p. 57); this is a notable instance of philosophical error derived from linguistic confusion and of the means of correcting it. Plato himself, in his dialogue *Cratylus*, examines the origin and nature of language and the extent of its correspondence with reality—a problem which has exercised some of the keenest minds of the present century; and many of his other dialogues are concerned, wholly or in part, with the meaning and use of concepts like 'justice', 'courage' and 'temperance'. Aristotle's doctrine of 'substance' is clearly indebted to the grammatical distinction between subject and predicate: 'substance' is that which is always the subject to which predicates are assigned and is not itself a predicate of anything else. St Thomas Aquinas was well aware of the deceptions inherent in language: he complains against Plato that he 'teaches all things figuratively and by symbols, meaning by the words something else than the words themselves mean'.[7] He distinguishes between grammatical and logical form; for instance, he sees that 'creation out of nothing' does not mean that God made the world from a strange material called 'nothing', but that He made it 'not out of anything'; nor does he suppose that the statements 'John is a man' and 'Peter is a man' imply the existence of a universal essence of man outside the mind. Locke devotes Book III of his *Essay* to a study of language, for he too understands 'the inconveniences of obscurity or uncertainty in the signification of words' which make it difficult 'to discourse with any clearness or order concerning knowledge'.[8] Berkeley distinguishes different functions within language—'the raising of some passion, the exciting to or deterring from an action, the putting the mind in some particular disposition'—and he is no less aware than his predecessors of the need for philosophers to abandon 'received prejudices and modes of speech and retire into themselves and attentively consider their own meaning'.[9] Hume's analysis of the causal concept is to an important extent an examination of how we should and should not use language in describing the relations between natural objects and events. These examples are sufficient to dispel the misconception that an interest in language is a prerogative of twentieth-century philosophy.

[7] In *De Anima*, 3 c 1, *lectio* 8; quoted by F. C. Copleston, in *Aquinas* (Penguin, 1955), p. 68.

[8] III, i, 6.

[9] *The Principles of Human Knowledge*, introd., § 20; § 144.

The contemporary emphasis on language as the focus of the philosopher's interest and the source of his problems is due in the main to the work of three men, G. E. Moore, Bertrand Russell and Ludwig Wittgenstein. Moore and Russell were at Cambridge together in the 1890s and it was largely the latter's influence that persuaded Moore, who was a year younger, to switch his studies from classics, in which he had already distinguished himself, to philosophy. Both men shared a common revulsion from the abstruse idealism of F. H. Bradley: 'He took the lead in rebellion,' Russell wrote of Moore, 'and I followed, with a sense of emancipation.'[10] Yet the development of their thought was different. Russell was a mathematician whose thinking was deeply penetrated by science; Moore, on the other hand, wrote of himself: 'I do not think that the world or the sciences would ever have suggested to me any philosophical problems. What has suggested philosophical problems to me is things which other philosophers have said about the world or the natural sciences.'[11] Thus, while Russell investigated the relationship of mathematics and logic, Moore devoted himself to the elucidation of the puzzles which, so it seemed to him, philosophers had manufactured for themselves as a result of linguistic and conceptual confusion.

The philosophy in vogue when Moore and Russell went to Cambridge was the idealism of F. H. Bradley and his followers. Bradley's *Appearance and Reality*, first published in 1893, had sought to prove that ordinary experience is illusory, a tissue of appearances which obscures from us the real, the Absolute. Moore was a man of very different temperament from Bradley; he had, as G. J. Warnock puts it, 'no particular religious or cosmic anxieties',[12] no discontent with the common world, no special propensity for metaphysics. He was perplexed and troubled, therefore, by the paradoxical pronouncements of idealist philosophy such as 'time is unreal', 'reality is spiritual', 'there are no material objects', 'there are no other minds—or at least we cannot know that there are', 'all statements of fact are hypothetical'. For him the commonsense world was real, objective, meaningful; not that he was unsympathetic to metaphysics as such; nor was he inclined to the positivism of the Vienna Circle; he was content simply to accept experience as straightforward and unpuzzling.

A principal reason, so Moore believed, for the paradoxical assertions of idealist philosophers in defiance of common sense was their insensitivity to and misuse of ordinary language; as a result they contradicted not only the way in which people normally speak, write and understand one another

[10] 'My Mental Development'; ed. P. A. Schilpp, *The Philosophy of Bertrand Russell* (Northwestern University, 1944), p. 12.

[11] Moore, 'An Autobiography', ed. Schilpp, p. 14.

[12] *English Philosophy since 1900* (Oxford University Press, 1958), p. 12.

but also their own conclusions. More specifically, the contradictions arose from the use of vague generalities instead of reference to actual cases and situations, and from tampering with the ways in which language is ordinarily used. For instance, Bradley and others used 'time', 'real', 'material object' in ways quite out of keeping with common usage: time thus became a strange, shapeless entity which denied the experience of having breakfast *before* lunch and going for a walk *after* it; 'real' referred no longer to the things we see, hear and handle in daily life, but to an obscure property possessed by different things in different degrees and by the Absolute completely; 'material objects' like chairs, tables and mountains, which '*seem* to be very different from us', are strangely assimilated to human beings by the assertion that they are somehow spiritual.[13] It was not that he objected to the invention by philosophers of new words to express novel ideas; rather, they took familiar words, like those just instanced, and put them to unfamiliar uses or used them in different senses in the same argument. Much of Moore's practice of philosophy, therefore, consisted in the analysis of meaning in order to uncover these various senses and the confusion which resulted from failure to distinguish them. Examples of this, which are worth careful study, can be found in the chapters 'Is Time Real?' and 'The Meaning of "Real" ' in his book *Some Main Problems of Philosophy.*

Moore was not unaware of the deficiencies of ordinary language; he knew that it was sometimes ambiguous, sometimes loose—though he was willing to admit that on occasion these qualities might well be virtues. Nor again did he wish to make it a criterion of correct verbal expression or to regard it as unalterable; he did claim, however, that if we came to know it more intimately and to use it more sensitively, we should find it nearly always adequate for our purposes and not wish to change it; in particular, we should be saved from being deceived by the pretentious but vacuous claims of idealist philosophy and prevented from making them ourselves.

Russell's interest in language came from a different source and was of a very different kind from that of Moore. Like many earlier philosophers, Russell was impressed by the vagueness, ambiguity and unclarity of the natural languages: 'The influence of language on philosophy has, I believe, been profound and almost unrecognised. If we are not to be misled by this influence, it is necessary to become conscious of it, and to ask ourselves deliberately how far it is legitimate.'[14] Now Russell was primarily a mathematician and logician, and his work in these fields affected his view of language in two important ways. First, it sharpened for him the contrast

[13] *Philosophical Studies* (Routledge, 1922; paperback 1960), ch. 1.
[14] 'Logical atomism'; *Logical Positivism*, ed. A. J. Ayer (Free Press of Glencoe, 1959), p. 38.

between the *grammar* of a language and the *logic* of what it says. An obvious example of this is the distinction between subject and predicate. In grammar this distinction is clear, but it often masks logical relationships which are crucial to correct understanding: grammatically, the sentences 'this table is wooden' and 'this cake is nice' are of the same type—subject–copula–predicate—but whereas 'wooden' directly qualifies 'table', 'nice' does not similarly qualify 'cake' but refers rather to the person eating it— *his* pleasure and satisfaction, not a quality in the cake; thus it carries logical implications of comparison with other cakes and other persons' feelings, as well as elements of value judgment combined with empirical assessment, all of which are absent from 'wooden'. The logical pattern of the two sentences is quite different, despite their grammatical similarity. Second, Russell's work in mathematics and logic led him to the concept of an ideal language, one which was, as it were, 'context-free' or 'disinfected'; such a language would not be contaminated by the vagaries of grammar, which differs from language to language, but would display the basic logical structure common to all languages.

When this structure has been revealed, what does it express, what represent? At this point Russell abandons the empirical tradition to which he claims allegiance and expounds what amounts to a metaphysical view of the world, for which he invented the name 'logical atomism'.[15] There is a parallelism, he asserts, between the logical skeleton of language and the structure of the world. There are, on the one side, 'atomic facts', the simplest of which consist of a 'particular' associated with a quality or relation; these 'particulars' are not the objects of everyday experience, like trees and bodies which are structured out of atomic facts and are vastly more complex; indeed, it is difficult to say exactly what Russell does intend by them, for he gives different accounts in different places and excuses this imprecision on the grounds that 'the whole question of what particulars you actually find in the real world is a purely empirical one which does not interest the logician as such'.[16] The simplest atomic fact, then, consists of 'particular' plus quality or relation ('this is white', 'this is to the left of that'); there are, however, more complicated ones consisting of three, four, or any number of 'particulars', but still 'atomic' in the sense that, according to Russell, they appear to be the 'last residue' in the process of logical analysis. They can also be negative as well as affirmative, general ('all men are mortal') as well as particular ('this is white').

[15] 'The reason that I call my doctrine *logical* atomism is because the atoms that I wish to arrive at as the sort of last residue in analysis are logical atoms and not physical atoms.' *Logic and Knowledge*, ed. R. C. Marsh (Allen & Unwin, 1956), 'The philosophy of logical atomism', p. 179.
[16] *Ibid.*, p. 199.

Corresponding to atomic facts are atomic propositions which express
them; there are also molecular propositions which are composed of atomic
propositions and are dependent on them for their truth or falsity. Thus,
'this is white', 'A is to the left of B', 'A is between C and D' are all atomic
propositions representing atomic facts; from these it is possible, by means
of logical connectives like 'and', 'if . . . then' 'or', to compose molecular
propositions: 'this is white and this is round', 'if A is to the left of B, then
B is to the right of A'. It is clear that the truth of the latter propositions
depends on the truth of their components.

There is a good deal in logical atomism that is unsatisfactory. It is not
based, as it surely should have been, on a careful, empirical examination
of language and its function; instead it is an expression of the logician's
ideal—an aseptic instrument of discourse which communicates precise
packages of meaning with unambiguous exactitude. And Russell's picture
of the world is forced—again without deference to empirical investigation
—to fit this tidy picture of language. His purpose was, as he puts it,
'to prevent inferences from the nature of language to the nature of the
world, which are fallacious because they depend upon the logical defects of
language'.[17] Yet he is himself guilty of fallacious inference to the nature
of the world from the requirements of logic. Moreover, language as it is
used in human intercourse is far more subtle, more elusive than Russell
allows; later he came to see this and repudiated some, but not all, of his
atomism; Wittgenstein after first accepting, then modifying and developing it, finally rejected it completely for a very different conception
of language. The fact is that language *in use* can never be context-free;
atomism goes astray 'through the pervasive error of neglecting *the circumstances in which* things are said—of supposing that *the words alone* can
be discussed, in a quite general way'.[18]

Exposition of Wittgenstein's philosophy is difficult for a number of
reasons. There is the obvious one that he was pioneering new areas of
thought and new philosophical techniques. The difficulty is increased by
the form of his writings, for these are not set out chapter by chapter but
in numbered paragraphs of different lengths; in the *Tractatus* the numbering is decimal-wise to indicate the main propositions, the comments
on these, the comments on the comments and so on; in *Philosophical
Investigations* the numbering is in simple sequence without indication
of connection or change of topic. Again, in the earlier work the thought
is compressed and the style concise, aphoristic, prophetic (in the Old
Testament sense); it has indeed been likened to a sacred text which must

[17] *Ibid.*, p. 338.
[18] J. L. Austin, *Sense and Sensibilia* (Oxford University Press, 1962),
p. 118.

be interpreted rather than read.[19] The later work reads like an argument within the writer's mind; it consists of 'thoughts . . . the precipitate of philosophical investigations which have occupied me for the last sixteen years . . . philosophical remarks';[20] here too there is compression and subtlety of argument enlivened occasionally by homely imagery and touches of wit. Perhaps the greatest obstacle to understanding Wittgenstein, however, is the fact that his thought divides clearly into an earlier and a later period, represented by the *Tractatus* and *Philosophical Investigations* respectively, in the latter of which he drastically revised the conclusions of the former.

In the earlier period Wittgenstein developed a form of logical atomism which was akin to Russell's but more elaborate and refined; nor was it merely an account of language and its relation to the world, but also—and despite what he himself says about metaphysics—a metaphysical theory. Like Russell he approached language through logic and mathematics; but although he too was impressed by the unclarity of language as normally used, he did not assert, as Russell did, the need for a *new* language of logical precision and purity. Instead he maintained that there was a logic already embedded in language, in *all* language, and that the need was to disclose this and make it explicit.

Language contains elementary propositions which cannot be analysed into simpler propositions; they are composed of 'names', by which he means terms that can be neither analysed nor verbally defined—they are 'primitive signs' which refer to items in the world (these he calls 'objects') which too are incapable of analysis. Only if a 'name' denotes something observable can it be defined, and then only ostensively, by pointing to the corresponding 'object'. Elementary propositions are combined to form the complex propositions which are used in normal communication; these latter are 'truth-functions' of elementary propositions, that is, their truth or falsity depends entirely on the 'truth-value' of the elementary propositions which compose them.

The structure of language is paralleled by that of the world; here too there are simple, unanalysable elements—'objects'; these are combined to form 'facts'; some 'facts' are elementary or atomic; these are the simplest things that can exist by themselves in isolation ('objects' can be said to exist only in combination with other 'objects'); they are, as it were, the building-blocks of which the world is made. From elementary 'facts' are built all the other 'facts' which, in their varying degrees of complexity,

[19] G. Pitcher, *The Philosophy of Wittgenstein* (Prentice-Hall, 1964), p. 17.
[20] *Philosophical Investigations*, trans. G. E. M. Anscombe (2nd edn, Oxford, Blackwell, 1963), p. vii.

constitute the material of ordinary human experience. Wittgenstein also writes of 'states of affairs', the interpretation of which is not entirely clear; it seems, however, that a 'state of affairs' is the same as a 'fact'; an actually existing 'state of affairs' is a positive elementary 'fact'. But there are also, he maintains, negative 'facts' which correspond, presumably, to non-existent but possible 'states of affairs'. The conclusion to be drawn from this is that reality is larger than existent 'states of affairs' and includes also a shadowy realm of non-existent 'states of affairs', an area of potential but unrealised existence. If this interpretation is correct, the metaphysical tendency of Wittgenstein's thought is obvious.

If the perplexed reader asks for examples of what Wittgenstein means by 'object', 'state of affairs', 'fact' and their counterparts in language—'names' and 'elementary propositions'—the answer is that the *Tractatus* does not supply them. Wittgenstein was concerned with the logical structure of language and of the reality which language depicts; his approach was theoretical and *a priori*, not empirical; he therefore left to others the task of giving substance to the logical forms which he enumerated.

There is, then, a correspondence between language and the world—the logical structure of the former reflects that of the latter; the word that Wittgenstein uses to describe this correspondence is 'picture', both as noun and verb. Strictly speaking it is only elementary propositions that picture, and they picture 'facts' or 'states of affairs'; picturing implies not only a one-to-one correspondence between the constituents of propositions and of 'facts' (i.e. between 'names' and 'objects') but also an identity of the structure or internal arrangement of the constituents. The truth or falsity of a picture is determined by comparing it with the reality it purports to represent, and language makes sense only when it pictures 'fact'. From this it follows that only factual propositions, statements about the world, the propositions of natural science, make sense; the rest are non-sense.

What, then, of logic and mathematics, of metaphysics and philosophy? Are these all non-sensical? The propositions of logic and mathematics are indeed non-sense, but they are not meaningless; those of logic are *tautologies*—they repeat the same thing in different ways; those of mathematics are *equations*—they state identities, either of one thing with another or of a thing with itself; they are meaningful each within its own system of symbols, but they tell us nothing about the world and are therefore without sense. With metaphysics the case is very different; metaphysical propositions are indeed nonsense in the normal meaning of the word. This is partly because they arise from a misunderstanding of language, partly because they attempt to say what Wittgenstein asserts to be unsayable, namely to express the nature of the relationship between language (and therefore human thought and experience) and the world which language pictures; they seek by means of language to transcend the capabilities of language. For the essential function of language is picturing —the picturing of 'facts' by elementary propositions; but the actual picturing is something no proposition can express; it cannot be *said*, for language is not such as to be able to say it. Similarly, although in a sense the grooves of a gramophone record picture a piece of music, they cannot express the fact or the manner of that picturing, since their 'language' is not designed for such a purpose: 'What expresses *itself* in language, *we* cannot express by means of language' (4.121).[21] Metaphysics, therefore, in trying to describe *by* language a reality which is reflected *in* language exceeds the bounds of what is linguistically possible.

As for philosophy in general, this would seem at first sight to be entirely redundant:

The correct method in philosophy would really be the following: to say nothing except what can be said, i.e. propositions of natural science—i.e. something that has nothing to do with philosophy—and then, whenever someone else wanted to say something metaphysical, to demonstrate to him that he had failed to give a meaning to certain signs in his propositions (6.53).

Yet there *is* still a task for it to perform, as even this passage suggests. Language as ordinarily used conceals the underlying logic whereby it pictures reality; it thus gives rise to puzzlement and confusion, which in turn raise problems which in fact are non-existent: 'Language disguises thought. So much so, that from the outward form of the clothing it is impossible to infer the form of the thought beneath it' (4.002). The function of philosophy is to dissolve problems (not to *solve* them, for they are not real problems) by revealing the logic concealed within language—'All philosophy is a critique of language' (4.0031). He continues:

Philosophy aims at the logical clarification of thoughts.
Philosophy is not a body of doctrine but an activity.
A philosophical work consists essentially of elucidations.
Philosophy does not result in 'philosophical propositions', but rather in the clarification of propositions.
Without philosophy thoughts are, as it were, cloudy and indistinct: its task is to make them clear and to give them sharp boundaries (4.112).

The task of philosophy, therefore, though in a sense destructive and negative, is not unimportant; it is propaedeutic, preparatory to a proper understanding of language and what can meaningfully be said by it. Philosophy aims to make itself superfluous by exposing the sources of

[21] This and the following quotations from the *Tractatus* are taken from the edition of D. F. Pears and R. F. McGuinness (Routledge, 1961).

pseudo-problems—we throw away the ladder when we have climbed it (6.54).

The importance of the *Tractatus* waned as it was overtaken by Wittgenstein's later thought. Nevertheless, its influence remained powerful for many years, particularly as it affected the development of logical positivism; though never officially a member of the Vienna Circle, Wittgenstein contributed something to the formation of its central tenets—the primacy of sense experience and scientific knowledge, the rejection of metaphysics, and verification as the criterion of meaning. On the other hand the Vienna Circle had no place for the strain of mysticism which appears repeatedly in the *Tractatus* and is a part of its fascination. Behind its crisp and emphatic aphorisms one senses the desire of an imprisoned spirit to escape from bonds it cannot loosen:

> The sense of the world must lie outside the world. . . .
> If there is any value that does have value, it must lie outside the whole sphere of what happens and is the case (6.41).
> It is not *how* things are in the world that is mystical, but *that* it exists (6.44).
> There are indeed things that cannot be put into words. They *make themselves manifest*. They are what is mystical (6.522).

The *Tractatus* is indeed, as one writer has put it, 'a haunting work'.[22]

Wittgenstein began to write *Philosophical Investigations* in 1936; in the period between this date and the publication of the *Tractatus* in 1921 his thought had undergone a profound change. In the preface to the earlier work he had written: 'The *truth* of the thoughts that are here set forth seems to me unassailable and definitive. I therefore believe myself to have found, on all essential points, the final solution of the problems.'[23] In the preface to *Investigations* (dated 1945) he writes: 'Since beginning to occupy myself with philosophy again, sixteen years ago, I have been forced to recognise grave mistakes in what I wrote in that first book.'[24] He attributes the change to the criticism of two men, Frank Ramsey and Piero Sraffa, lecturers in philosophy and economics respectively at Cambridge; no doubt his experience in the postwar years, especially as a teacher, also played some part in it.

Philosophical Investigations repudiates with great candour and searching self-criticism the basic assumptions about language which characterise the *Tractatus*; it will be helpful to recall what these were. First, language

[22] Pitcher, p. 17.   [23] *Tractatus*, p. 53.
[24] This and the following quotations from *Philosophical Investigations* are taken from Anscombe's edition (English text, Blackwell, 1963); the numbers refer to the paragraphs in Part I; references to Part II are given by page.

has a clear logical structure which, however much it may be obscured in ordinary daily use, can nevertheless be uncovered by careful analysis. Second, the essence of language is 'picturing'—the reflecting in its own logical structure that of the world about us; from which it follows that the prime function of language is the stating of facts. Third, since the simplest elements in language (excluding the logical constants 'and', 'or', 'not' etc.) are 'names', each referring to an 'object', the meaning of a word consists essentially in what it refers to.

All these assumptions, Wittgenstein now asserts, are false. There is no precise logical structure concealed within ordinary language; this is a logician's dream, an ideal foisted on the facts. Believing that this order, this ideal, must be found in actual language, 'we become dissatisfied with what are ordinarily called "propositions", "words", "signs" ' and look for 'something pure and clear-cut'. However, 'the more narrowly we examine actual language, the sharper becomes the conflict between it and our requirement. (For the crystalline purity of logic was, of course, not a *result of investigation*: it was a requirement)' (107). Language is more like 'an ancient city: a maze of little streets and squares, of old and new houses, and of houses with additions from various periods; and this surrounded by a multitude of new boroughs with straight regular streets and uniform houses' (18). Nor is there any final, definitive analysis of language, no ultimate residuum of elementary propositions and 'names' to which it can be reduced, no '*single* completely resolved form of every expression' (91); what is 'simple' depends, not on the nature of language or of the 'objects' and 'facts' which language is supposed to reflect, but on one's point of view. There is more than one way of analysing words and sentences, and 'simplicity' depends on how it is done:

But what are the simple constituent parts of which reality is composed?— What are the simple constituent parts of a chair?—The bits of wood of which it is made? Or the molecules, or the atoms?—'Simple' means: not composite. And here the point is: in what sense 'composite?' It makes no sense at all to speak absolutely of the 'simple parts of a chair'. . . . We use the word 'composite' (and therefore the word 'simple') in an enormous number of different and differently related ways. (Is the colour of a square on a chessboard simple, or does it consist of pure white and pure yellow? And is white simple, or does it consist of the colours of the rainbow?—Is this length of 2 cm simple, or does it consist of two parts, each 1 cm long?) (47).

We imagine that there is some essence of language, 'something that lies within, which we see when we look *into* the thing, and which an analysis digs out' (92). This too is an illusion; the search for 'essence' imposes on language preconceptions which distort our view of it; 'it is like a pair of glasses on our nose through which we see whatever we look at. It never occurs to us to take them off' (103).

Nor is 'picturing' an adequate account of what language is and does; it misrepresents language by limiting it to a single function, the portrayal of fact, and by imposing on it a rigidity which is quite alien to its actual nature:

How many kinds of sentence are there? Say assertion, question and command?—There are *countless* kinds: countless different kinds of use of what we call 'symbols', 'words', 'sentences'. And this multiplicity is not something fixed, given once for all; but new types of language, new language-games, as we may say, come into existence, and others become obsolete and get forgotten (23).

Words, too, have numerous uses: 'Think of the tools in a tool-box: there is a hammer, pliers, a saw, a screw-driver, a rule, a glue-pot, glues, nails and screws.—The functions of words are as diverse as the functions of these objects . . .' (11). Their use is not confined to 'naming', as though 'learning language consists in giving names to objects' (26): there are very many words which cannot be said to be names of anything; and those that are have no single, essential meaning, no exactly determinable sense fixed for all time. Moreover, the *Tractatus* assumes that 'naming', the relation of 'names' to 'objects' by which the former denote the latter, is a simple process of indication or pointing. This is not so, however: 'naming' *may* consist in pointing to an object, but equally it may take other forms, such as recalling an object to mind when it is mentioned or writing the 'name' on the 'object': '. . . It is clear that there is no one relation of name to object, but as many as there are uses of sounds or scribbles which we call names.'[25] The relationship between language and the world is more complex, more diverse than the *Tractatus* allows. From these criticisms of 'picturing' and 'naming' it follows that meaning can no longer be regarded as consisting in simple reference of 'name' to 'object', A to B; rather it consists in how a word is used in the actual context of its use. Wittgenstein imagines a builder working with an assistant and using a language composed of the words 'block', 'pillar', 'slab', 'beam'; if the former calls out 'Slab', what does he mean?—he is not pointing and saying, 'This is a slab,' but giving an order ('Bring me a slab'), uttering an exclamation ('A slab again!—I wanted a block') or even asking a question ('Any more slabs there?'). It is the *use* of a word that is significant, not its reference to an object.

How has this misunderstanding of language arisen? It has not been due to failure of intelligence or simple error but to something more akin to a bewitchment which 'can only be removed by turning our whole examination round' (108). The source of the bewitchment lies partly in the human

[25] *Blue and Brown Books* (Oxford, Blackwell, 1958), p. 173.

propensity for seeking a unity, a simplicity, an essence, whether of language or of meaning, which is non-existent: thus by imposing on language a *'preconceived idea* of crystalline purity' (108), by trying to grasp its 'incomparable essence' (97), we arrive at the totally false conclusions of logical atomism. It lies also in our looking at language out of context, when it is 'on holiday' (38) or 'like an engine idling' (132); thus we isolate it from the life to which it belongs, in which it is used, in which alone it has meaning. As will be seen later, it is the function of philosophy to release us from this enchantment, to liberate us from these false preconceptions about language and the philosophical errors to which they give rise. Meanwhile we must examine Wittgenstein's positive account of language and its operation as he now presents it in *Philosophical Investigations*.

Language has neither the unitary structure nor the simplicity of function assumed in the *Tractatus*; it is multiform, flexible, subject to modification, and adaptable to an indefinite number of purposes. These include:

Giving orders and obeying them—
Describing the appearance of an object, or giving its measurements—
Constructing an object from a description (a drawing)—
Reporting an event—
Speculating about an event—
Forming and testing a hypothesis—
Presenting the results of an experiment in tables and diagrams—
Making up a story; and reading it—
Play-acting—
Asking, thanking, cursing, greeting, praying— (23).

These various functions Wittgenstein calls 'language-games', a phrase that has already appeared in a quotation on p. 237.[26] The builder and his assistant are also playing a language game with their 'slab', 'beam', etc.; so is the atomic physicist with his 'electrons', 'protons' and 'neutrons', the theologian who talks about 'love' and 'grace', and the mother who prattles to her child in the language of the nursery. There is no single pattern governing the whole of language, no single set of rules, but an infinite number of activities or 'games', each of which has its own rules, its own mode of activity and behaviour; yet the rules are not fixed—they can be changed, and we may even 'alter them—as we go along' (83). Nor are the rules learnt explicitly, as the rules of chess are learnt from a book or teacher; rather they are learnt by actually playing the game, by involvement in the activity itself. Moreover, there is no *essence* of language game, any more than there is an essence of game in the ordinary sense; we must not say: 'There *must* be something common, or they would not be called "games" ';

[26] The analogy between language and games apparently occurred to Wittgenstein when he was watching a football match. See Malcolm, p. 65.

instead we must *'look and see'*, and we shall find 'similarities, relationships . . . in a complicated network of similarities overlapping and crisscrossing' (66).

Further, a language game is not a mere matter of words and how they are used; it includes also gestures, feelings, attitudes, skills—a whole complex of related elements which together compose the particular 'form of life'. For that is what a language game is: 'To imagine a language means to imagine a form of life' (19; cf. *Phil. Inv.*, p. 226). Language has as many rules as there are forms of life; it is infinitely fluid and variable, a complicated texture of overlapping language games which often share the same words yet give them different meanings (like 'ball' in billiards, rugby and dancing). The meaning of a word, therefore, is to be found, not in some hidden essence to be exposed by logical analysis, but in the part it plays in the language game to which it belongs:

When philosophers use a word—'knowledge', 'being', 'object', 'I', 'proposition', 'name'—and try to grasp the *essence* of the thing, one must always ask oneself: is the word ever actually used in this way in the language-game which is its original home? (116).

Meaning, as was observed earlier (p. 237), is contextual—'an expression has meaning only in the stream of life'.[27] To understand the meaning of a word, therefore, does not consist in attaching a name or label to an object; it is not a mental act at all, but a process of coming to know how the word is used within its language game.

What is the bearing of this on philosophy? In *Philosophical Investigations*, as in the *Tractatus*, philosophical problems arise from language and the task of philosophy is clarification; but the origin of the problems and the techniques of exposing them are different. It is not a question of analysing propositions in order to reveal a logically correct form concealed beneath the outward vesture of language; there is no logically correct form —'every sentence in our language "is in order as it is" ' (98). The philosopher must understand what a proposition *does*, its purpose, its function within the language game where it operates; and he must also be aware of the sources within language of the problems that confront him. A philosophical problem is an indication that language has misled us; its solution or resolution—for the problem is not solved but disappears—lies in unmasking the deception—'philosophy is a battle against the bewitchment of our intelligence by means of language' (109).[28]

[27] Malcolm, p. 93; a remark made by Wittgenstein during a conversation with Malcolm.
[28] Cf. *Blue and Brown Books*, p. 27: 'Philosophy . . . is a fight against the fascination which forms of expression exert upon us.'

Whence does this bewitchment arise? The causes are numerous. Underlying them all, as generic sources of confusion, are the human propensity, already noted, for unity and simplicity, and the misunderstanding of the nature of language. Among the specific causes is the fact that grammar is less flexible, less subtle, than the uses for which language is required: 'A main source of our failure to understand is that we do not *command a clear view* of the use of our words.—Our grammar is lacking in this sort of perspicuity' (122). For instance, the adjective 'real' is used in a number of ways—'real butter', 'real elephants', 'real enjoyment', 'real life'; and because the function of common adjectives like 'big', 'white', 'heavy', is to ascribe a property to an object, it is assumed, as by G. E. Moore in his lecture 'The Meaning of "Real" ', that 'real' does the same; that there is some property, 'being real', 'reality', that anything must have which we describe as 'real'.[29] But there is no such property; we have been misled by a grammatical classification which is simpler than actual usage. Similarly, it is easy to assume that 'good', because it is an adjective, ascribes a property to the noun it qualifies and to conclude, again as did Moore, that 'good' refers to a property in things which is so elusive that it must be regarded as indefinable.[30] Moore is also misled here, Wittgenstein would argue, by his desire to find a single, identifiable item to which 'good' refers —an *essential* meaning—and by equating meaning with 'naming' or reference to an object.

Grammar has misled philosophers in other important ways: in ordinary language names are often used to refer to objects, and these objects are assumed to exist; from this assumption it is easy to pass to another, that *all* nouns refer to existing objects, and so to be involved in a tangle of philosophical problems. It was partly thus that Plato was led to affirm the existence of 'Forms' of goodness, beauty, being, etc., which exist independently of the empirical world and which, though alone fully 'real', yet share their nature with particular objects. Hence arose the further problems of where and how these universals exist and how they share their nature; hence too the metaphysical distinction between 'reality' and 'appearance' and the problems of 'being' and 'absolute values'.

Another fertile source of confusion is that there lies embedded in our use of language certain ways of viewing the world, 'pictures' (not in the *Tractatus* sense) or perspectives which give a slant to our thought and limit it by exluding other 'pictures'. For instance, we speak of the 'stream of time' with its implication of beginning and end and flow; we speak of 'empty space' (in the cosmological sense), as though space were a kind of

[29] *Some Main Problems of Philosophy* (Allen & Unwin, 1953), ch. 12; see also p. 229 above.

[30] *Principia Ethica* (Cambridge University Press, 1903), ch. 1.

container with an inside and outside like a box; hence arise difficulties concerning the nature of time and space which a clearer understanding of language would help us to avoid. So too with 'truth': by assuming that truth is correspondence of a proposition with a fact we blind ourselves to other possibilities—truth as coherence and truth as pragmatic success. Two such 'pictures' which have caused great trouble in the history of philosophy are 'proof' and 'mind': obsessed with a picture of proof taken from mathematics and logic—deductive proof which *must* be so—philosophers have required the same degree of rigour in empirical enquiries; but empirical generalisations reached by induction are not logically necessary, and hence the problem of induction *versus* deduction and the various attempts to 'justify' the former because it falls short of what proof is thought to demand. So too with 'mind': this we regard as analogous to body—a self-contained entity, separate from other minds, a receptacle which can take in, assimilate and store as the body does its food; yet mind is both crucially different from body—by memory and imagination it can move back and forth at will in space and time—and at the same time 'contained' in the body. Thus we arrive at the concept of 'the ghost in the machine' (p. 98 above), a 'picture' which gives rise to philosophical problems like solipsism and the dualism of mind and matter, and to unsatisfactory epistemologies like those of Locke and Hume which are based on 'ideas' etc. accepted from outside and stored in a kind of mental library for future reference.

Here and in the other examples 'a *picture* held us captive. And we could not get outside it, for it lay in our language and language seemed to repeat it to us inexorably' (115). We were misled by imagery 'absorbed into the forms of our language' (112), 'by certain analogies between the forms of expression in different regions of language' (90) which 'are hidden because of their simplicity and familiarity' (129). We have not understood that the meaning of words and propositions is determined by their appropriate language game; in consequence we have sometimes confused one game with another (e.g. the 'mind' game with the 'body' game), sometimes regarded a single language game as the only one (e.g. logical atomism), sometimes supposed that different games were the same (e.g. the different uses of 'real').

An important source of these misleading 'pictures' lies in the various theories put forward by philosophers themselves—metaphysical constructions which assume or propose a certain view of the world; among these are Plato's Forms, Descartes' dualism of mind and matter, Hume's 'impressions' as separate existences, the verification principle of the logical positivists, Wittgenstein's own logical atomism. These are both the result and the further cause of problems whose roots lie in linguistic misunderstanding.

'What *we* do', Wittgenstein claims, 'is to bring words back from their metaphysical to their everyday use' (116). And to the criticism that his work 'seems only to destroy everything interesting' he replies: 'What we are destroying is nothing but houses of cards and we are clearing up the ground of language on which they stand' (118). What, precisely, then, is the function of philosophy as Wittgenstein now understands and practises it? Some indication of this has already been given, but its importance requires a closer examination.

As a result of the misunderstanding and misuse of language perplexities arise which baffle and confuse us; the sources of this 'bewitchment', some of which have just been mentioned, are so deeply structured into our habits of thought and speech that they go unnoticed. Hence we are left with problems whose solution is obscured from us, not so much through simple ignorance of fact, but through failure of insight; we are lost, disorientated, as if in a forest where we can identify every plant and tree but have no idea which direction to move in, which path to follow; we know the facts but we still cannot see our way: 'A philosophical problem has the form: "I don't know my way about"' (123). The philosopher's task is to help us to see our way clearly; it is, Wittgenstein insists, *descriptive*—not in the primary sense of imparting straightforward factual information, but in a deeper sense of revealing the hidden sources of our confusion, of showing how we are misled and how we can reorientate ourselves. 'What is your aim in philosophy?—To show the fly the way out of the fly-bottle' (309).[31] Philosophical problems are solved

by looking into the workings of our language, and that in such a way as to make us recognise those workings: *in despite of* our urge to misunderstand them. The problems are solved, not by giving new information, but by arranging what we have always known (109).

Philosophy 'leaves everything as it is' (124); it 'simply puts everything before us, and neither explains nor deduces anything' (126).

What the philosopher aims at is 'the uncovering of one or another piece of plain nonsense and of bumps that the understanding has got by running its head up against the limits of language' (119). He thus enables us 'to pass from a piece of disguised nonsense to something that is patent nonsense' (464). The result should be clarity, *'complete* clarity. But this simply means that philosophical problems should *completely* disappear'

[31] Cf. Malcolm, p. 51, who quotes Wittgenstein: 'A person caught in a philosophical confusion is like a man in a room who wants to get out but doesn't know how. He tries the window, but it is too high. He tries the chimney but it is too narrow. And if he would only *turn around*, he would see that the door has been open all the time.'

(133). Philosophy is a kind of therapy (133, 255): philosophical problems are symptomatic of something wrong; treatment consists in exposure of the roots of intellectual dis-ease which lie in language, in revealing language as a texture of interwoven language games which correspond to 'forms of life' (p. 226), and in helping us both to accept these 'forms' as given and to understand the language games in which they find expression.[32] It may be asked what need there is of the philosopher when he merely shows us what is already before our eyes. The answer is that language deceives by its very familiarity; language games are so much a part of everyday life, that we look right through them; their very obviousness disguises them. To see the obvious, to recognise its importance and to display the subtlety of the deceptions it imposes on us requires a degree of intellectual skill which is granted only to a few.

The techniques of this therapeutic process are numerous and there is space only for a brief reference to a few of them. Basic to them all is the description of the uses of words in order to clarify their meaning and to correct misrepresentation; this involves the careful examination of usage, the collection of instances, 'assembling reminders' (127), so that a picture may be formed of the language game or games to which words belong. This is not, of course, a haphazard activity; it demands selection and arrangement; it is guided by the particular problem in hand; the reminders are assembled 'for a particular purpose' (127). Sometimes usage is clarified by finding or inventing 'intermediate cases' (122): in order to disclose the working of a word or phrase within the total area of a given language game, it is not enough to provide only two or three instances of its use which may not be obviously related; it is necessary also to show the connection between them, how one shades into or grows from another; intermediate uses are required as links to bridge the gaps. Thus when we are considering what it means to be guided, we must not only cite the obvious instances of guidance but imagine others:

You are in a playing-field with your eyes bandaged, and someone leads you by the hand, sometimes left, sometimes right; you have constantly to be ready for the tug of his hand, and must also take care not to stumble when he gives an unexpected tug.

Or again: someone leads you by the hand where you are unwilling to go, by force.

---

[32] In regarding philosophy as a therapy Wittgenstein has been compared with Socrates, whose critical questioning (*elenchus*) was aimed at exposing confusion and clarifying thought, and with Freud, whose method of psychoanalysis reveals the roots of neuroses in contradictory beliefs which are held unconsciously. See J. K. Feibleman, *Inside the Great Mirror* (The Hague, Nijhoff, 1958), pp. 206–7.

Or: you are guided by a partner in a dance; you make yourself as recep-
tive as possible, in order to guess his intention and obey the slightest
pressure.

Or: someone takes you for a walk; you are having a conversation; you
go wherever he does.

Or: you walk along a field-track, simply following it (172).

Another technique is the deliberate invention of language games in order
to reveal the difficulties involved in a particular point of view or to throw
up by contrast the correctness of another. For instance, philosophers have
sometimes thought that, in our present world, 'I have a pain' is just like
'I see something red'; by imagining a world in which these statements
were in fact alike Wittgenstein shows how different it would be from the
the world we know and how untenable therefore the view in question:

Let us imagine the following: The surfaces of the things around us (stones,
plants, etc.) have patches and regions which produce pain in our skin
when we touch them. . . . In this case we should speak of pain-patches on
the leaf of a particular plant just as at present we speak of red patches (312).

Or again, it may be illuminating to invent primitive language games
like that of the builder with his 'slab', 'beam', etc., in order to distinguish
more clearly important features within the far more complicated language
games of actual life. They are set up 'as *objects of comparison* which are
meant to throw light on the facts of our language by way not only of
similarities, but also of dissimilarities' (130). Further examples of the
techniques of linguistic clarification can be found in *Philosophical Investigations* and in the work of philosophers like J. L. Austin who have followed
Wittgenstein along the same road.

No one man has exercised a more powerful influence on twentieth-
century philosophy than Ludwig Wittgenstein. His work has been the
stimulus to a vast amount of careful, critical exploration of philosophical
issues; not only has he opened up a whole new area of activity in linguistic
analysis, but he has also compelled the reconsideration of longstanding
problems by means of the new techniques which he himself had shaped.
From this there has come a deeper insight into the origination of philosophical problems, into the logical implications of linguistic forms, and
into the influence of language in determining thought. The techniques he
devised have been developed and refined into instruments of great subtlety
for the clarification of thought in all areas of human discourse—religion,
science, morals, education and, of course, philosophy itself. Outside the
circle of academic philosophy his influence is apparent among educated
people generally in a greater sensitivity to language and a greater care in
the use of words.

Yet to many his account of philosophy is disappointing: he restricts unduly its scope and role by overemphasising the importance of language; he makes it appear destructive, negative or at best neutral. The criticism is not without justice; undoubtedly language is a fertile source of puzzlement, not to say deception; yet there are other sources, for example in the sheer limitations of human experience and intellectual capacity, in faulty logic, in the nature of the cosmic environment (time, space, growth, individuality), in moral conflict; and the problems arising thence are neither entirely the product of linguistic confusion nor soluble simply by linguistic analysis. It must be admitted, too, that much of Wittgenstein's work is destructive, as he himself was well aware: 'Where does our investigation get its importance from, since it seems only to destroy everything interesting, that is, all that is great and important? (As it were all the buildings, leaving behind only bits of stone and rubble)' (118). But, he goes on, it is only 'houses of cards' that he is destroying. The grandiose systems of the metaphysical philosophers and the imaginary entities with which they are peopled are no more than dreams fabricated out of linguistic muddle; as such they are baseless, fraudulent, dangerous, and it is an essential part of the philosopher's task to dispose of them; philosophy is therapeutic, and therapy involves the destruction of disease. But, the critic may well reply, must it stop there? Must philosophy disappear when the cure is complete? Wittgenstein's own practice suggests that it need not, for many of his discussions have a positive interest of their own which does not obviously arise from initial puzzlement.

A major clue to the understanding of Wittgenstein's position—and it is a link, too, between the *Tractatus* and *Philosophical Investigations*—is that he was impelled, like Plato, by a passion for the ideal. In Plato this is seen in the doctrine of the Forms, the absolute essences of qualities like goodness and beauty which in human life are experienced only partially and imperfectly; it is seen in the ideal city of the *Republic*, in the soul's pursuit of the knowledge which raises it to the highest levels of being and endows it with immortality. In Wittgenstein it appears first in the quest of the *Tractatus* for the pure logical structure which he supposed to underlie the language of everyday; in *Philosophical Investigations* the ideal is the plain, undistorted reality of language in its actual use. Both books, despite their contrasted views of language, exhibit the function of philosophy as instrumental to this quest; it is a technique of purification which enables us to reach the unsullied immaculacy of the ideal. Viewed in this light, Wittgenstein's account of philosophy has a positive content which makes it more than a simple agent of demolition.

Further Study

Wittgenstein

There is a short life of Wittgenstein which is well worth reading, by N. MALCOLM, *Ludwig Wittgenstein: A Memoir* (Oxford University Press, 1958); and there are two brief and very helpful introductions in K. T. FANN, *Wittgenstein's Conception of Philosophy* (Blackwell, 1969) and W. D. HUDSON, *Ludwig Wittgenstein* (Lutterworth Press, 1968)—the former with an extensive bibliography. Other useful introductory books are J. HARTNACK, *Wittgenstein and Modern Philosophy* (trans. M. Cranston, Methuen, 1965) and D. F. PEARS, *Wittgenstein* (Collins, 1970); a longer and more detailed treatment can be found in G. PITCHER, *The Philosophy of Wittgenstein* (Prentice-Hall, 1964). More specifically for the *Tractatus* there are: G. E. M. ANSCOMBE, *An Introduction to Wittgenstein's 'Tractatus'* (Hutchinson, 1959), M. BLACK, *A Companion to Wittgenstein's 'Tractatus'* (Cambridge University Press, 1964), and J. GRIFFIN, *Wittgenstein's Logical Atomism* (Oxford, Clarendon Press, 1964); and for *Philosophical Investigations* there is D. POLE, *The Later Philosophy of Wittgenstein* (Athlone Press, 1958).

There is a translation of the *Tractatus* by D. F. PEARS and B. M. MCGUINNESS (Routledge, 1961), and of *Philosophical Investigations* by G. E. M. ANSCOMBE (Blackwell, 1953). Other published writings include *The Blue and Brown Books: Preliminary Studies for the Philosophical Investigations* (ed. with preface by R. RHEES (Blackwell, 1958), and *Notebooks 1914–1916*, trans. G. E. M. ANSCOMBE and edited with G. H. VON WRIGHT (Blackwell, 1961).

Philosophy and language

A great deal has been written about and in illustration of linguistic philosophy during the past fifty years. Among useful introductory books are: G. B. KEENE, *Language and Reasoning* (Van Nostrand, 1961); W. P. ALSTON, *Philosophy of Language* (Prentice-Hall, 1964); and J. O. URMSON, *Philosophical Analysis* (Oxford, Clarendon Press, 1956); ch. 1 of HOSPERS' *Philosophical Analysis* is helpful, and so too are many of the chapters in WARNOCK's *English Philosophy since 1900*, and some in G. RYLE, ed., *The Revolution in Philosophy* (Macmillan, 1956). A much more extensive book is F. WAISMANN, *The Principles of Linguistic Philosophy* (Macmillan, 1965). The two books edited by A. G. N. FLEW, *Logic and Language* (1st and 2nd series, Blackwell, 1951, 1953) have many examples of this kind of philosophising; a particular aspect of it is shown in V. C. CHAPPELL, ed., *Ordinary Language* (Prentice-Hall, 1964). Further illustration can be found in the writings of G. E. MOORE and J. L. AUSTIN, and in Professor IAN RAMSEY's exploration of religious language in, for instance, *Religious Language* (S.C.M., 1957) and *Christian Discourse* (Oxford University Press, 1965).

As a kind of antidote to such books the student might turn to some of the essays in H. D. LEWIS, ed., *Clarity is not Enough* (Allen & Unwin, 1963).

Index

Index

Index

philosophy—*continued*
    methods of, 10–11, 243–4
    political, 27, 28
    subject matter of, 15 ff.
    value of, 19 ff., 215–17, 242–3
Plato, 2, 9, 10, 11, 14, 18, 22, 23, 25,
        26, 31, 36, ch. 2, 55, 56, 57, 58,
        59, 60, 61, 62, 64, 66, 71, 73, 76,
        79, 98, 102, 103, 105, 138, 179, 201,
        202, 208, 227, 240, 245
    Form of Good, 25, 47, 48, 50, 58,
        64, 138
    Theory of Forms, 18, 20, 40, 43 ff.,
        58, 76, 86, 98, 102, 138, 202, 208,
        240, 241, 245
pleasure, see 'happiness'
Polanyi, Michael, 221
potentiality, 60 ff., 75, 77, 219
prediction, 134, 139, 145–7, 150, 156–7,
        162, 177, 178, 181, 186, 188
probability, 97, 109, 148, 186, 188
proof, 30–1, 176 ff., 191–2 and note,
        241
psychology, 51, 115, 150
puzzlement, 6, 9, 10, 15, 32, 66, 220,
        234, 237–8, 239 ff., 245
Pythagoras, 1, 22, 39, 42, 45, 49, 71

rationalism, 10, 22 ff., 56, 86, 103–4,
        111, 115, 117, 133, 140, 141, 144,
        155, 156, 164, 176, 185, 188, 203,
        205, 218–19
realism, 51–2 and note, 134–5
reality, 2, 3, 12, 15, 21, 22, 25, 35 ff.,
        42, 46, 48–9, 56 ff., 67, 121, 163,
        164, 201–2, 203, 205, 216, 232–3
    and appearance, 57, 121, 203, 240
reason, 3, 7, 9–11, 12, 22 ff., 31–2, 56,
        71–2, 75, 82, 86 ff., 93, 103, 115,
        141, 158, 167, 168, 169
    truths of, 24 ff., 111, 203, 218
reasoning, 28–30
refutation, 90
Reichenbach, Hans, 17, 36, 217
relatedness, 14, 16
religion, 2, 7, 9, 71–2, 96, 124, 132,
        190, 200, 222
representationalism, 99, 110–11
Republic (of Plato), 2, 40, 48, 50, 76,
        245

revelation, 31, 71–2, 73, 75, 103
right, 32 ff.; and see 'ethics'
Rousseau, J. J., 138, 155
Russell, Bertrand, 3, 51, 201, 206, 218,
        224, 228–31
Ryle, Gilbert, 98, 113–14

Saint-Simon, Comte de, 204
scepticism, 2–3, 18, 20, 22, 23, 32, 90 ff.,
        97–8, 103, 108, 123, 125, 155–7;
        and see 'doubt'
Schlick, Moritz, 200, 209, 211–12
science, 2, 3, 12, 15, 18, 61, 72, 80, 86,
        90, 101, 103, 104, 109 and note,
        122, 132, 139, 150, 157, 159, 162–3,
        176–7, 178–9, 186–7, 189, ch. 11
scientist, 10, 12, 13, 15, 16, 17, 18, 20,
        31, 58, 97, 109, 123, 139, 140, 156,
        200, 219, 221–2
self, 92–3, 94, 95–6, 111–12, 115; and
        see 'individual'
sense-perception, senses, 10, 22 ff., 31–
        32, 44, 49, 59, 72–3, 73–4, 75, 86,
        95, 96, 105–6, 108–9, 115, 121–2,
        127–8, 133–4, 141 ff., 159, 160 ff.,
        203, 211–12
sociology, 187
Socrates, 11, 18, 19, 32, 39, 40, 42, 45,
        47, 49, 80, 224, 243 note
solipsism, 211–12, 222, 241
sophists, 39, 50 and note, 190, 201
soul, 46 and note, 49, 111, 169
Spinoza, B., 14, 60, 67
Stevenson, C. L., 210 note, 213 note
Stoicism, 2, 71, 80
substance, 20, 59–60 and note, 61–2,
        93, 94–5, 112–13 and note, 125,
        227
syllogism, 29, 89, 176, 180–2, 186
synthetic statements, 78–9, 97 note,
        157–8, 206–7

Taylor, A. M., 221
Tertullian, 71, 72
Thales, 6, 56, 86
theologian, 12, 15, 21, 64, 74, 97, 111
theology, 15, 59, 64, 71–2, 73, 74, 208
thought, 91–3, 161–2
transcendental philosophy, 158 and
        note

250